To Ann
with my warm
best wishes
Aline Dobbie

INDIA
The Tiger's Roar

By

ALINE DOBBIE

Published by

**MELROSE
BOOKS**
ESTABLISHED 1969

An Imprint of Melrose Press
St Thomas Place, Ely
Cambridgeshire
CB7 4GG, UK
www.melrosebooks.co.uk

FIRST EDITION

Copyright © Aline Dobbie 2004

The Author asserts her moral right to
be identified as the author of this work

Jacket Photography by kind permission of Chris Brunskill
© Copyright Chris Brunskill 2004
Jacket Design by Ross Hilton
Interior Photography by kind permission of Harshad Patel
© Copyright Harshad Patel 2004
All other photography © Copyright Aline Dobbie 2004

ISBN 0 9548480 2 0

All rights reserved. No Part of this publication may be reproduced,
stored in a retrieval system, or transmitted, in any form or by any means
electronic, mechanical, photocopying, recording or otherwise,
without the prior permission of the publishers.
This book is sold subject to the condition that it shall not,
by way of trade or otherwise, be lent, re-sold, hired out or
otherwise circulated without the publisher's prior consent
in any form of binding or cover other than that in which
it is published and without a similar condition including
this condition being imposed on the subsequent purchaser.

Printed and bound in Great Britain by:
Bath Press Limited
Lower Bristol Road
Bath BA2 3BL
United Kingdom

DEDICATION

This book is dedicated to the Tigers of India, together with all the other great cats of the Indian subcontinent such as the Asiatic Lion, the Leopard and the Snow Leopard.

The Tiger, the king of the jungle is both beautiful and powerful; he walks alone with stealth and grandeur. Since my infancy tigers have continued to fascinate me; I want to encourage an awareness of their magnificence and their vulnerability, and help ensure their continued existence in the wild.

All creatures have an equal right to live on this Earth

Mahatma Gandhi

BY THE SAME AUTHOR

India: The Peacock's Call

For more information please visit:
www.thepeacockscall.co.uk

ACKNOWLEDGEMENTS

My deep gratitude for my husband Graham's great support and encouragement; he has been a constant source of strength throughout my research and writing. I would also like to say a big thank you to Harshad Patel for the use of his wonderful black and white wildlife photography which I have been so generously allowed to use. Chris Brunskill too has with such enthusiasm and warmth allowed me the use of his beautiful colour photography of tigers for the cover from his own book Tiger Forest.

There are other friends like Shreela Flather, Viola Hallman, Hemant Patel, Mala Sen, Krishan Ralleigh, Premen Addy, Divyabhanusingh, Tony de Souza, and Tim Scollary who have all helped me with their encouragement and support. To them all I say thank you for your belief in me.

Finally to all who helped me within India be they Travel Personnel, Guides, Forest and Park Personnel, Naturalists, Military Personnel and my Drivers, plus naturally my Indian friends, both old and new – Thank You.

Aline Dobbie

Sketch Map of India

INDIA
The Tiger's Roar

★ National Parks and Wildlife Sanctuaries
• Places of Interest
• Major Towns and Cities
◎ CAPITAL CITY

—— Major Rivers

········ STATE BOUNDARIES

CONTENTS

CHAPTER ONE
A Happy Return

As I stand in the six inch deep snow in our garden here at Rosewood, distributing pheasant food and bird seed, I look up into the vivid blue sky with the weak winter sunshine touching the hilltops and think of three months ago, when I was in Delhi on Diwali day.

After an interval of a couple of years, Graham and I had given ourselves a much longed for return to India. My first book had been published in Britain in the summer of 2002 and that autumn presented an excellent opportunity to go to India to research and enjoy some of the great wildlife parks as well as to visit an area of India to which I had previously been only fleetingly, Madhya Pradesh; the very heart of India.

The garden is covered in a blanket of snow and most of Scotland is having a challenging time weather wise but, here in my beloved Peeblesshire, conditions are not at all bad, in fact rather beautiful. The eight pheasants who think that they belong to us and thus arrive at least once daily to be fed are a source of pleasure. On a *maidan* in a jungle clearing in India one would inevitably see peacocks, here in the gentle Scottish Borders however, it is more likely to be pheasants. Raju accompanies me to feed them. He was a kitten whilst I wrote my first book, *India: The Peacock's Call* but now he is a mature, sleek black cat with wonderful green eyes like two peridots. He knows that the pheasants are forbidden to him and they all co-exist very happily, sometimes it has to be said with the occasional rabbit also on the scene. Graham is not at all happy about the rabbits!

India had been wonderful, as usual. Of course, it is the land of my birth and therefore there probably exists for me a sort of natural love of the place and a feeling of belonging but Graham also has a great affection for the country and we have a sort of ritual that we indulge ourselves in when we first arrive.

On this last occasion, we had chosen BA as the carrier and were not disappointed. It was the first long haul flight that we had encountered after the appalling incidents of 9/11 in 2001. We decided to choose the national carrier and were impressed by the thorough security checks and standard of service. The flight, though all ready to roll, was held up at the last minute (because of the careless behaviour of a passenger) until every single passenger and their baggage was reconciled with the passenger list. Frustrating and boring though this was, it impressed us and the pilot made up the time lost.

Sadly, Indira Gandhi airport, Delhi's international airport, had improved very little in the intervening years since my last visit in 1998. Immigration took one hour for us mere mortals before we were out on the concourse looking for the welcoming faces of Naveen Kumar and the driver from Travel House. Driving through the suburbs of Delhi at three in the morning is always so interesting. Now it was the run up to Diwali so there were one or two extra sights to behold. The famous sweet makers around Bengali Market were working frenetically through the night to provide their customers with mounds of sweetmeats, like *jalebis, burfi, laddoos, rusgullahs, gulab jamuns* and so forth. As we passed through the centre of Bengali Market one could almost smell the sugar and fragrance of rose water as well as see the feverish activity under huge electric lights that made it possible for the *mitthai wallahs* to continue to work right through the night. Graham and I grinned at each other, and just wished the rest of the family could be with us. Having been fed sweetmeats since a toddler by my father who won *jalebi* eating contestants with his men in the army, I have a great love for them and Graham found no difficulty whatsoever in sharing this particular pleasure. The heaven of a crisp fried *jalebi* golden and curled which drips glorious golden juice when bitten into is a family pleasure with us. We resolved that later in the day we would return to buy some sweetmeats and experience the whole human chaos and confusion that is obligatory in any build up to a religious festival the world over.

Naveen dropped us at the gate to Martin and Annie's delightful home and we made our way to their comfortable spare bedroom and crept into bed. It was four in the morning, and already I could hear the muffled sounds of the start of another day in the back streets around us. The warmth of welcome, peace and comfort of Martin and Annie's Delhi pied-à-terre is a haven for so many of their friends. At eight, we roused ourselves and went and said hello. The ever efficient Anjoli brought us a much needed tray of tea and Martin and Annie were full of their usual welcome and interest. This is a friendly household and one was aware gently that various members of Anjoli's family were discreetly inspecting us. There is nothing discreet about Yashodi, Anjoli's little granddaughter however. She comes along to give one a vigorous inspection and is such fun. Yashodi is four and speaks Hindi and Nepali, and is learning English at her English medium school. She is a poppet and very bright and not at all inhibited in what she says, though sometimes Anjoli scolds her if she goes beyond the bounds of respect. 'Yash' as she is normally called loves Martin 'Jai papa' and Annie 'Jai mama' and they adore having her as an on the spot honorary grandchild. Breakfast was a lively affair which had all the ingredients I could want, namely, papaya (paw paw to some) followed by a tomato omelette and tea.

Four hours sleep after a long haul is fine if one jumps in a shower and dons lovely summer clothes and has the anticipation of a very full day ahead. The sky was blue, the birds were full of their raucous morning chatter, fireworks were exploding – this was after all Diwali! And the music and razzamatazz of a festival could be heard. Eternal India, so energising and promising. We decided on an auto rickshaw ride to the Imperial Hotel. This grand old hotel had had a complete renovation and was looking wonderfully majestic and elegant. You cannot drive up to the Imperial in an auto rickshaw; the driver drops one off across the street. It seems that the Imperial's management feel that anything less than a taxi would diminish its splendour – no matter, we just crossed the road and walked up the drive. For those not familiar with an auto rickshaw, it is a funny little motorised, three-wheeled, canopied scooter in which two or three passengers can sit, that is European style. Indian style there appears to be no limit to the numbers squeezed in. Now auto rickshaws have been required by law to convert to eco friendly fuel, CNG (compressed natural gas), which is a very positive way of helping Delhi with its huge environmental challenges. Most auto rickshaw drivers speak with pride about the conversion of their respective vehicles. We were impatient to accomplish our money changing at the vastly improved and positively elegant Thomas Cook offices and then begin exploring the beautiful renovated great rooms and lobbies of the hotel. The high quality of all the work in the marble flooring and intricate carvings plus timeless elegance of the fusion of east and west in the décor made it all very pleasing. It only required us to go and sit on the veranda and order a *nimbu pani* and fresh *gulab jamun!* The waiter was amused and explained that we might have to be patient as the cook was only just making the sweetmeats. We did not mind, the anticipation was even greater and amply rewarded when the hot fresh *gulab jamuns* arrived in their fragrant warm rose flavoured syrup. For our return, we took a taxi and enjoyed some of Anjoli's vegetarian cooking.

But now I am going too fast. First, there was a smiling Naveen waiting to go over our itinerary with us and confirm certain arrangements. We liked him and appreciated his attention to detail. Together we walked up to Nathu's to purchase the sweetmeats. That was truly an experience. There were masses of men, crammed into a smallish shop all gesticulating and ordering and waiting for boxes of the sweets they had requested. The pace was manic and the expertise with which the staff fulfilled orders was amazing. Their judgement was so fine – a kilo of sweets to the last morsel. Graham and I were the subject of some interest as of course the mass of people were Indian, Naveen quietly watched and was amused by our glee. In case it should be thought we were going to make gluttons of ourselves I should explain that the sweets would be our Diwali gift when we visited Butterflies later in the afternoon.

Butterflies is the charity that supports and helps the street children of Delhi, and has been reaching out to the children in Delhi since January 1988. We have a personal commitment to them and, before we embarked on a round of dazzling Diwali socialising, Graham and I wanted to go and say hello and talk and meet with the organisers. Again, because of a shortage of taxis we jumped into an auto rickshaw and embarked on a mad dash to the southern suburbs. Initially, we wanted to do a quick bit of shopping for some soft furnishings but time was running on and travelling anywhere in Delhi takes a long time because of the sheer congestion, never mind the fact that on this Saturday afternoon it was the equivalent of the pre Christmas rush back in the West. The auto rickshaw was exchanged for a taxi and the driver given the address details. He looked a bit funny to me and I whispered to Graham that I though he was perhaps a bit 'hung out' on dope. Graham looked alarmed and hoped I was not correct – I think I was judging by his head and arm gestures – but, after lots of false stops, we arrived finally at the Butterflies address. All the false stops had put my rusty Hindi to the test and, by and large, people tried to be very helpful.

Mary Pearson, who was helping organise Butterflies, is a mature British woman, whose children have flown the nest and Mary wanted to do something really worthwhile whilst she has the energy and determination. She chose to help Butterflies and I am quite sure they are very grateful for her decision. We had only corresponded by email previously but we got along famously. Several of the children had been brought along for us to meet. What a lively lovely bunch they are. So agile minded, articulate and eager for affection. I talked in halting Hindi and they replied and tried out their English. It was explained to them why we had come and they understood immediately that I had mentioned the charity in my first book. One young fellow said shyly but firmly in Hindi 'Look Ma'am, you are wearing the same outfit as in this picture in your book'. I replied yes that this was so that they might find it easier to identify me – I needn't have worried! These are alert youngsters, sadly their lives require them to be, but they miss nothing and have such a simple appreciation of things. I was amazed at some of their drawings that encapsulated ideas of preserving the environment. Sweets were gorged on and photographs taken and lots of *namastes* (the Indian form of greeting) and some hugs. They wanted to be tactile and that was fine by me.

The author with children at the Butterflies Charity

Butterflies is accredited by the National Institute of Open Schooling, but it encourages children to attend formal schools wherever possible. It offers an alternative education scheme of daily non-formal classes on the streets including training in life skills, theatre, radio and print journalism as well as vocational training in carpentry, plumbing and electrical maintenance and repair. Butterflies believes that children are born as children, neither as destitutes nor as delinquents. To quote from their own newsletter "Apart from love, the two most valuable gifts we can bestow on our children are roots and wings. Butterflies aim is to provide both; a stable basis of listening and caring and the motivation and confidence to fly when the time is right."

We left, after having had a happy encounter, with a promise that Graham and I would return whenever possible. The surly taxi driver was looking even more exhausted or relaxed, depending on whether one is of an optimistic viewpoint or not! I cajoled him into taking us back to the Howard residence and we paid him very fairly and wished him happy Diwali. Four hours sleep in 34 was beginning to take its toll, never mind the change in climate and the endless activity. We entered the house and little Yash came running up to say hello. Martin then appeared and said jovially that he had just had a relaxing massage from the visiting masseuse and would I like one – you bet! Oh! Was that sublime. Elizabeth was a strong woman with a competent technique. Yash came to supervise. Subsequently, I heard from Annie and Martin that Yash is apt to inspect their female guests who, like me, are not over modest. She then fills Martin in with a running commentary on their various attributes. I remarked dryly that then I would surely be considered a 'real girl' since there is nothing stick like whatsoever about me – Yash doesn't approve of women who look like men, i.e., have flat chests and small bottoms. In Yash's eyes what is the point of being a girl if you end up looking like a boy – sort of.

A jump in the shower and then into party attire and we were off to a glittering party. Nayana and Prafull Goradia, our hosts, are distinguished each in their own right. Nayana wrote a very well thought of book on Lord Curzon, the Viceroy, and Prafull sits in the Rajya Sabha, the upper house of the Indian parliament. They had originally come from Gujarat and like to hold a pre-Diwali party to bring all their friends and any guests that they may have visiting together in an informal friendly way. For us, just arrived in the early hours, it was a superb way of ending our first day back in India. People are so friendly and willing to communicate and in no time at all we had found mutual friends and acquaintances all over India, and exchanged business cards for future reference. I was, however, very glad to hit the pillow late that night, and even the Diwali crackers did not keep me awake.

CHAPTER TWO

Tikli Bottom

We were up very early the next morning feeling refreshed and ready for the day. The whole household was bustling with young Yash dashing everywhere and insinuating herself into all the activity. Martin and Annie own the most beautiful house a little out of town called Tikli Bottom. Four years ago, they completed the building of a gracious new Lutyens's style bungalow, which has now matured into a most elegant and comfortable home. Tikli Bottom is a fusion of east and west with large well proportioned public rooms and four bedroom suites all opening on to a veranda and courtyard. The entrance portico stands exactly opposite the big archway in the far side of the house so one is able to see the temptation of an elegant pool in green lawns and the vista spreading beyond. Every bit of the house has been designed and built with great attention to detail. Martin has a perfectionist's eye for detail and Annie has a wonderful way with décor. Martin wanted the house to be like the old colonial bungalows that, of course, I grew up in and know to be cool in the great heat of the summer months. The ceilings are high and there are usually at least four skylights right at the top of the walls where they meet the flat roof, so that the hot air as it rises can be dispelled. There is no air conditioning deliberately but in the colossal heat of the Haryana summer one is able to ascend to the roof by a wide staircase and sleep on the roof on *charpoys*, a simple but comfortable Indian style bed, which, instead of springs or wooden slats, has an interwoven rope base on wooden legs, that makes for a very comfortable bed underneath the stars in the cool of the night – realistically under a mosquito net for obvious protection!

Tikli Bottom – A most gracious home

The courtyard has a charming fountain and pool adding that luxurious and practical touch of tinkling water that also helps to challenge the heat. Annie compliments Martin with all her little touches and thoughtful detail. Each bedroom suite has everything one could wish for in a five star establishment, except air conditioning and television. There are four gracious large bedrooms each with their dressing room and en suite full bathroom. Every room has a lovely view and of course being built in a large square no two have the same view. Weary travellers who have arrived to stay chez Howard at the beginning of a trip to India, or indeed at the end would find complete relaxation. There is a full household of servants, who are mainly Nepalese, and the management of the house is excellent with lovely food. People sit round the dining table or on the terrace and eat with Martin and Annie. Martin collects and delivers people to the international and domestic airports which are not far away.

Graham and I were enchanted. Tikli Bottom was not complete when we were last in Delhi but now sitting on the terrace of this serene country house, with its immense style, is sublime. The silence and tranquillity of the garden with its acacia trees, bougainvilleas, hibiscus, bauhinia, oleanders and other glories, and the charming half moon pool forming a serene focus with a backdrop of the Aravalli hills, all to the gentle sound of birdsong, immediately set my memory into action recalling similar beauty spots of my past. Again, one is reminded that India can appear frenetic to the newcomer but, given an opportunity to visit in the country, one can soon lose the sounds and cacophony of the multitudes and choking traffic.

Inside the house there was a great deal of activity preparing for a luncheon party under the capable direction of the housekeeper and cook, Muna and Gokal. One is again reminded how in India by maintaining such a property one can also sustain several retainers who all have their allotted responsibilities and work. The Howards have a small farm with buffalo, crops, and fruit trees including mangoes, papayas, and oranges. There is an ambition to branch out into keeping geese, but they are very vulnerable to the local jackal population however careful one is – realistically all the jackals may not have four legs!

They have also planted about 1000 teak trees all over the place. Martin reckons that, at least, he will rest in a better coffin as a result of his efforts! Hopefully, the land may soon be considered a plantation, which has wider implications for the future benefit of the local villagers.

Graham was taken on a tour of the whole place by Mahendra, who helps Martin administer the farm. Mahendra is charming and friendly and communicated in soft, slightly halting, or possibly carefully considered, English. Bolaram, an ex *mali* who had worked for Martin previously, joined them. Bolaram is so typical of a straightforward hardworking Indian who takes pride in his occupation – being a gardener. He was very proud of having worked for the British High Commission in his time, and now his ambition is to purchase some property which he will be able to leave to his family. He and I had talked in the jeep driving from Delhi. Our conversation ranged through my broken Hindi and his halting English, but we soon understood and appreciated each other. Fundamentally, we are both mature parents and have a great desire to see our various offspring happy and secure – the aspirations of parents the world over. Gardening was the second topic of conversation and then a careful polite exploration of my background and Indian credentials.

Martin is justifiably very proud of what he has achieved at Tikli. There are five buffalo, one of which was a recently acquired bull, which resulted in a even more recently born calf, and then all the females were pregnant. Buffalo apparently do not show the season of their breeding cycle easily and previous attempts at artificial insemination had not been successful. All the beasts were in excellent condition being fed on a mix of chopped wheat straw and alfalfa type lucerne sweetened by the croppings from the sugar cane.

Segregated from the buffalo were the cow and her two calves. This is no ordinary cow, being a cross between a buffalo and a Holstein. Thus, they all had the typical Holstein black and white markings and looked very familiar but with short tiny buffalo horns. Both the offspring were themselves pregnant. Typical of thoughtful Martin he had introduced a new feeding and management regime for the calves, which ensured they were allowed to suckle from day one after birth in the morning, but in the evening the milk is taken for human consumption in the household or sold. The results are larger and healthier calves which matched in size at one year those of two years of age but reared under the traditional harsh methods.

The papaya trees are planted in a two/three year rotation and in between were lime – *nimbu* – guava and mango. There was also an acre or so of sugar cane and several acres of gladioli. These bulbs cost one rupee each and, as several thousand are required, Martin grows on the little bulbs produced by the parent plant after flowering and, a year later, he has thousands of bulbs at a cost effective price. Gladioli are a supreme favourite of Indians and you will see bunches of them for sale at street vendors let alone in the established flower markets. He thinks everything out most carefully to see if his theories translate into practical farming or horticulture before he passes on his ideas to the local villagers where everything must be totally cost effective.

The beautiful and peaceful pool at Tikli Bottom

Martin is full of ideas and the local villagers of Tikli are so fortunate in having this pair living in their midst with their genuine and unpatronising determination to contribute to rural life not just for their own benefit but for all. Interestingly, in discussions, we heard how inevitably there are those locals who would attempt to exploit or feed on what they see as a benevolent outsider, but the local *sarpanch* – the village head man has great authority and is not wet behind the ears about some of his countrymen's less attractive attempts to make a 'quick buck'.

There is an ancient saying from the Parayana Vathugatha, "Wisdom makes light of the darkness of ignorance". No-one is claiming, least of all me, that Indian villagers are ignorant, but all of us know that a pooling of knowledge contributes to a communal richness. Previous generations of my own family made their own contributions to their communities in India, now here is a satisfying example of coexistence between races in an ancient land in the twenty first century.

The luncheon party was excellent with a skilful mix of interesting people: ambassadors, high commissioners, authors and media personalities plus a number of charming guests who all had their respective talents when one talked and communicated. Many of the guests had brought their little children, who were immediately taken off by Yash to play and be amused in different ways. Annie had arranged for the *jadu wallah,* the local magician, to come and give us all a show of his excellent slight of hand. He brought with him the obligatory cobras with a mongoose. He seemed to be slightly amazed at our western anxiety for the mongoose and did not have a perception of the fact that generally we do not find animal exploitation attractive these days. Certainly the mongoose was a healthy agile little beast and the two cobras were what cobras always are – elegant serpents who performed their habitual 'party piece' and then slid noiselessly, and I suspect thankfully, back into their hessian sack! Anne Wright, Martin and Annie's charming neighbour, who owns a wonderful stud, bought the mongoose to let it free.

As ever, there was a wonderfully eclectic mix of people eating delicious food in elegant surroundings. I was struck again at the way Indian society discusses a broad spectrum of subjects vigorously which makes for very worthwhile conversations, such as I had with a remarkable and charming clairvoyant, whom I found amazing. Shuba has a serious day job but has this interesting and accurate talent which she can put into effect at her own wish. She kindly chose to focus on me and was astonishingly accurate about my life, yet we had never met previously and she could not have known anything about me. I hope we meet again some day. She yearns to visit Scotland and I have urged her to be our guest. Barbara and Rob Hepworth, who have worked with the World Bank in various developing countries, are another interesting couple with whom one had an immediate rapport. Then, there was Raju, who is a talented yoga teacher, and so many others. I always find something very special about meeting strangers in a convivial atmosphere in a different land. Somehow one dispenses with all the superficial nonsense and finds topics of mutual interest and value. Occasionally, one meets someone silly and shallow, but that is the beauty of a large function – one can, with grace, just move on.

In the late afternoon sunshine, Graham and Annie and Yash and Raju swam. The rest of us, remaining quietly on the terrace, drank some tea and chatted and just absorbed the tranquillity. I asked where Bolaram had gone as I knew he would like to see the photographs I had brought of our developed garden. Everyone was interested, Bolaram wondering how we managed the whole thing by ourselves, to which the response was we work hard and are passionate about what we have created – an oasis of Scottish tranquillity.

The Indian dusk arrived suddenly and we all piled back into the jeeps for the return journey to Delhi. Mahendra was coming with us to help him on his way to his own village to celebrate Diwali the following day. He and I talked quietly in the back of the vehicle. He had first learnt English at the age of eleven, but, as no-one else in the family spoke it, he found it difficult to practise the language, nevertheless he spoke well once he relaxed, and our conversation roamed over India's strengths and challenges as a food producer – he was trained in agriculture. He has a gentle humour and made the point that British people say thank you 10,000 times a day but Indians do not. They only actually say thank you for really important things – so, in his opinion, an Indian thank you is heartfelt. I had never really thought of it that way. In our society, we have a culture of acknowledging someone or something by saying thank you but India has other ways of being respectful that are not catered for in our language. It made me more aware of the whole business of courtesy for the following month of my travels, but I still consider it a good thing to show gratitude by saying thank you in either English or Hindi. However, thereafter, I watched more carefully for the response and realised sometimes how surprised some were, i.e., people who serve and are taken for granted by the large majority.

Back in Delhi, Yash could not wait to put on her Diwali attire; she looked adorable in a sort of burgundy outfit of chiffon salwar chameeze with sparkling shoes. We adults duly changed and set off for yet another sparkling party, this time at the gracious home of Kamal and Anita Meattle. They have a son called Saumya who is charming and the same age as our youngest son Stewart. Both our sons Hamish and Stewart work in information technology at a specialised level as does Saumya, so he and I found all sorts of topics of mutual interest. Their huge garden was festooned with twinkling lights, streamers of marigolds hanging down from the branches of trees, and candles; the mellow background music was a contrast to the ever rising noise of animated party chatter. Bearers, with trays of drinks, pressed amazing cocktail eats on the guests and this was followed by a delicious buffet dinner. This was Delhi en fete, truly as I remembered Diwali just exactly forty years ago! It seemed that the whole diplomatic community had been invited and had come – but with the obvious absence of the American ambassador. Our own British High Commissioner,

Sir Rob Young, and his talented wife Catherine, who was also launching a book, were there. I spotted the Belgians, the Mexicans, the Austrians, who had been at Tikli, and the Finnish and Irish who we had seen earlier as well. It was an excellent evening rounded off with some delicious *masala chai,* which was welcome as the dew was falling quite heavily towards the end of the evening.

Martin decided to do a quick *chukka*, i.e., tour, round the gracious monuments and buildings of Delhi which are well lit. India Gate looks particularly fine these days with some sensible improvements to its lighting arrangements. Everywhere we drove however I noticed pretty heavy security. The tragedy of terrorism has left its mark widely in India but of course the increased security is reassuring to the visitor. It was interesting, however, to be peremptorily stopped on a main road and required to wait, for what? Yes, as ever, a politician making his way, presumably from a Diwali party, to his home. I counted the number of vehicles in his entourage; there were five. It was not someone important like the President of India or the Prime Minister, just one of the many ministers, but India has this curious capacity to puff up even the most insignificant of her politicians, which to western eyes seems foolish and so shallow and unworthy of this great democracy.

Martin was becoming impatient and Annie chided him to be careful – none of us wanted an officious policeman interfering with our return home.

Again, bed was a most welcome retreat after such a full day of pleasurable activity.

CHAPTER THREE

Happy Diwali

Hinduism someone once said is 'a museum of religions'. No other religious tradition is so eclectic, so diversified in its theoretical premises as well as its practical expressions. It is the only major religion that has not been traced to a specific founder.

In India, mythology has always been very close to the actual life of the people. There are hundreds of myths about gods, goddesses, heroes, sages, demons, and natural phenomena like the sun and the moon, lakes, rivers, mountains, trees, flowers and animals. These myths are absorbed and remembered by the people even if they have no formal education. They are kept alive by fairs and festivals, and the daily round of religious ritual, during which myths are celebrated in folk songs, folk plays and dances. In classical Indian music too, mythology provides the main subjects.

Vishnu is, in the belief of his particular followers, the highest of the gods. When he is asleep, the universe is in a state of dissolution. When he wakes up, the universe evolves. The cycle continues. Periodically, however, Vishnu descends to earth to protect truth and virtue and to destroy evil. His earlier *avatars* (descents) were in animal forms. In his seventh, eighth and ninth incarnations or descents, Vishnu appeared as Rama, Krishna and the Buddha, respectively. Vishnu's wife is Lakshmi, the goddess of prosperity.

It is important to note that the personality and teachings of the Buddha have illuminated the lives of millions in Asia, but it was in India that the light was first kindled. The Buddha was born in India, and he lived and died there. His philosophy and teachings should be seen in the light of his Indian heritage. A thousand years after his death he was accepted as another incarnation of Vishnu, one of the three highest gods in the Hindu pantheon.

Diwali or Dipawali (literally a row of lights) is celebrated 20 days after the Dussera festival. Dussera is, essentially, the commemoration of the victory of the warrior-goddess Durga who has other names confusingly such as Sati, Parvati and Kali; she is also thought of as Devi, or Mahadevi – great goddess – the consort of Shiva, who is himself one of the three great principal gods, together with Vishnu and Brahma, the *trimurthi* or supreme trio in the Hindu belief. She had won a huge victory after a 10 day battle against the buffalo-demon Mahishasura and she is worshipped together with Rama – a god king – an incarnation of Vishnu, who had won an epic battle over Ravana, the ten-headed king of Lanka, who had abducted Rama's wife, Sita. Rama and Sita are in popular terms the ideal heavenly couple, to which ordinary mortals may aspire. Dussera lasts for ten days, culminating in an evening spectacle commemorating Rama's victory symbolising the triumph of good over evil in his ten-day battle against Ravana. On the nine previous evenings, the epic story the *Ramalila* has been narrated or presented in some form of drama, and the climax is on the tenth night when colourful effigies of Ravana, complete with curling moustaches, and princely ornaments, his son and his brother are burnt, setting off a fusillade of fireworks and, thus, goodwill again prevails for another year!

Continuing the story of Rama (Vishnu in an incarnation you may remember!), Diwali commemorates the hero-king's return from voluntary exile. Twinkling oil lamps, *divas*, replaced latterly by candles, or even electric bulbs, light up every home, symbolising the lifting of spiritual darkness. Fireworks explode, there is great rejoicing and the ritual focuses on the worship of Lakshmi (wife of Vishnu, who is the goddess of wealth and prosperity) of whom Sita (who was rescued) was an incarnation! Diwali is the beginning of the new financial year and is particularly significant for traders and businessmen. Old books are closed, new accounts opened, and there is a general emphasis on a fresh beginning. Lakshmi also symbolises purity and cleanliness and homes are cleaned and freshened to ensure her favour. Women, be they in the North or the South are renowned for their artistic skills in decorating the walls and doors and entrances of their homes. Diwali is the most important festival at which they paint the ground in front of the entrances. These drawings are meant to draw Lakshmi's attention and she, being the goddess of wealth, likes drawings of certain themes in certain colours that praise her. Very often, there is a simple and a quick mixing of white paste made from ground rice and water which is used to draw elephants and other designs on the walls and *rangolis* on the ground. The *rangolis* can be done with coloured powders or with flowers. It is a time of family gathering and fellowship with a warm welcome to visitors. Good food, particularly sweets, *mitthai*, are consumed in large quantities and the whole of India settles down to celebrate and enjoy the festivity. Indeed, on our flight, which was fully booked, it was obvious that a great many of our fellow passengers, from the evidence of their hand luggage, were returning to spend Diwali with their respective families. For us it was so special to be with Martin and Annie, and to participate in the rituals in their household, plus of course be warmly welcomed at the various parties.

I have given the most cursory of explanations because it would take a huge book to truly explain the festivals and rituals of the Hindu faith, and I am not best placed to do that despite my respect and recognition of that ancient system of belief and values.

Waking up on Diwali morning everyone is wishing everyone else 'Happy Diwali' with affection and good humour. It is so like our Christmas ritual and absolutely essential to greet everyone you meet that day and wish them well.

Martin drove off to Tikli accompanied by the faithful little Yash, who had made sure she had been greeted and had greeted everyone. Yash says 'Happee Diwalee' in a lovely singsong way and Graham and I grinned and adopted her way of saying it to just about everyone we met that morning. We decided that we had some important shopping to accomplish and, as Annie was very busy, we walked out on to the street and flagged down an auto rickshaw. Naturally, we greeted the driver, but he responded with a great diffidence. I asked in Hindi if all was well in his house and wished him good fortune and he smiled shyly and thanked me. I instructed him to take us to The Imperial Hotel, or just outside it, and we chugged along and then suddenly alongside came a much more vigorous auto rickshaw driven by a smart confident man, beautifully dressed. We became aware that we were sitting in a rather shabby CNG-converted vehicle that seemed to be held together by an elastic band! The other driver and I conversed whilst driving along at approximately 30 km an hour, until he finally commanded our own driver to stop and suggested that he could take us to an alternative shopping centre. He really was a cheeky but likeable fellow! Interestingly, our original driver seemed totally submissive and did not demur. I wondered if he was of a much lower caste, or perhaps a man of tribal origin because he just accepted the other's rather arrogant behaviour. We decided that perhaps the other vehicle was a better proposition so we paid off our chap the agreed amount and moved over to the smart one.

We arrived at the Cottage Industries Emporium and were effusively greeted. We were the first customers of the day and, after all, this was Diwali. The jewellery was disappointing so we withdrew from that and went with Mr Butt to look at carpets. After a long dilemma when we had viewed a number of beautiful carpets we came to a financial agreement, once the boss intervened and made the price right for all parties! There was huge rejoicing, drinking of *masala chai* and hugging and handshaking. It was very propitious to do a good deal that early in the day and our various documents were marked with red swastika like marks to demonstrate that it was a Diwali deal. We jumped back into the auto rickshaw and went as fast as possible to the house, where a patient Naveen was waiting to finalise our travel arrangements.

Naveen's careful scrutiny flagged up a discrepancy in our plans and we had to resort to plan B. This happens so much in travel throughout India that one has to be philosophical about it. When an airline suddenly decides to change the departure time of an internal flight, this can have a huge impact on the follow on arrangements. This had happened to us and had he not looked carefully at all our prearranged tickets we would have been sadly inconvenienced in two weeks time. I valued the fact that Naveen had taken the time to come on Diwali day. It was one of the last times that we met on this occasion because he was to be married in two weeks time, and was taking leave to help organise the wedding celebrations. He invited us to his wedding and we would have loved to attend, but we had to be hundreds of miles away for something equally important to us.

We ate a hurried simple lunch and departed with Annie for Tikli. On our arrival it was lovely and simple and peaceful. All the families of the retainers assembled to have Coke, crisps and sweets and receive a *razai*, an Indian form of quilt that is both colourful and warm, for each family. I took photographs of the children in the afternoon sunshine against the vivid colours of the bougainvilleas. The women and children were all dressed in their beautiful best – a myriad of bright colours in saris and salwar chameeze. Yash being small had started out in her best burgundy outfit but must have had a water fight or something and was now in tomboy dress.

Martin and Graham went on to the roof to start lighting the little oil lamps with which the roof would be outlined. This proved more difficult than anticipated and I think Martin has decided that next year he will adopt a more foolproof method. It was lovely. Gradually the sun set, the neighbouring peacocks called, and the horses in the next door stud could be seen quietly grazing. There was the gentle buzz of chatter and happy laughter from the servants' houses and I just kept an eye on Yash and another small child who were larking around on the roof.

As dusk approached, Martin and Annie put candles and lamps at the entrance to their home and we opened the wide gracious doors and quietly stood there, each of us silently welcoming the goddess Lakshmi into the house. It was a timeless moment, with a gentle breeze moving the trees and no other noise – even the two dogs had fallen silent. The children were awed by the moment and quiet and well behaved. It was very special.

**Martin and Graham lighting
Diwali lights**

We said farewell to the servants who were anxious to return to their festivities. Sometimes, it must seem to the traveller that India is in a permanent state of festival or ritual. The day before Diwali had been the day for *puja*, that is prayer and supplication, for the dogs. Both house dogs had been garlanded with flowers round their necks. This is a particularly Nepalese custom and they ensure that on that day the dogs are fed and garlanded before any of the human family eats. The day before the dogs was the special day of the crows. The day after Diwali is for the cows and so it goes on.

We drove off in the two jeeps to yet another Diwali party. This time we were to be the guests of the Thapars. Of course, I knew this well known name, and indeed had already met Karen Thapar, who is a media personality, but my memory was nagging me and I asked a few questions. Bimla Thapar is the widow of General Thapar who had been the army chief and a friend of my late father's. Bimla is a most gracious beautiful old lady with enormous charm and warmth. Bimla and Martin are brother/sister bonded with rakhi, which is an amulet, usually a thread tied round the wrist. There is, quite obviously, a mutual admiration between these two wise and friendly people. I asked if there was anyone in the family called Premala and, indeed, there was; Bimla's daughter, who was named after her own young sister. That was the connection for me. 'Aunty Prem' as she had been known to me was a dear friend of my own mother's. When this was told to them a 'phone call was made to Aunty Prem and I spoke and told her who it was. 'Little Aline!' she said, Hmm, not so little these days but awfully glad to hear her youthful voice and indulge in some shared memories. It was over 40 years since I had spoken to Aunty Prem. She has promised to come and visit us in Scotland and I very much hope she finds the opportunity to do that.

The party was in full swing with an endless barrage of fireworks being set alight on the lawn. One landed on fire at my feet whilst I stood on the terrace – that was a bit alarming! I retreated inside to hear what a fellow guest was saying, because the noise on the terrace was so loud, and also because I am fond of my eyebrows. Bimla and her late husband had been Ambassador to Afghanistan in the 1960s. Again, we found people we knew: my school friends had been daughters of the then British ambassador – it truly is a small world. There were some lovely photographs of HM The Queen on her last visit to Delhi taken speaking to Bimla; there is still a huge respect for the Queen in India.

Among the guests were the Belgian Ambassador his wife and daughter, the British High Commissioner, Sir Rob, and his wife Lady Young, Catherine as I shall call her. Her book 'Letters from India' is an absolute delight. She has the artist's eye for observing all sorts of little things and a warm appreciation of all her experiences in this country. ' Letters' represents the alphabet so naturally there are 26 chapters each on a subject the name of which starts with a respective letter, i.e., a is for ayah, b is for buffalo, etc. It is such a good read illustrated by Catherine's whimsical little drawings. She was kind enough to inscribe a book to me and I had done so with one of mine for them. This couple are hugely admired and liked in Delhi and people will be sad to see them leave later on this year.

The third diplomat was the Acting High Commissioner for Pakistan and his charming wife. They are a handsome and intelligent couple and I warmed to them very quickly. Rather diffidently in a discussion on the probable Iraq war I put forward some theories and the High Commissioner was immediately interested. As a student of history, I was easily able to recall my studies on imperialism in the generic form, going back to the first 'imperialists'. Ironically, this was probably the land we now know as Iraq, but was then the ancient kingdoms in Mesopotamia. In India, it became obvious through archaeological excavations that great cities such as Mohenjo Daro and Harappa (now in present day Pakistan) and Kalibangan in India had risen above a purely agricultural economy and conducted trade overseas with places as far afield as Mesopotamia in the third millennium BC. The Dravidian peoples, who spread into almost every part of India and Sri Lanka, were a mixture of native populations of India and Proto-Dravidians, who appear to have entered India in large masses from approximately 4000 to 2500 BC.

The so-called Indus Valley civilisation developed from a Neolithic village culture based on agriculture or hunting in Baluchistan and Sind. This incorporated elements of the Mesolithic culture as depicted in the earliest known paintings in rock shelters of bison, elephant and buffalo – as indeed Graham and I were to see in our travels in Madhya Pradesh. This influence stretched from Afghanistan to beyond present day Delhi and down into Gujarat, and we cannot tell whether some of the remarkable visual similarities indicate beliefs derived from Mesopotamia or are the results of iconography borrowed from that ancient civilisation.

Imperialism, to quote the dictionary 'is the policy or practice of extending a country's influence over other territories by conquest, colonisation, or economic domination.' Throughout history, the strong have sought to conquer and aggrandize their own countries, it is a human instinct sadly to prey upon the weak be it nationally, internationally or individually. In the Middle East, there are states who wish to subjugate their own people and there are those who forget their own tragic recent past and appear to have no empathy for the aspirations of other neighbouring people.

It is worth reflecting that, exactly 400 years ago, the Scottish king James VI succeeded to the English throne in 1603. The Tudor dynasty ended in the death of a raddled old woman whom history has variously called 'the Virgin Queen', 'Gloriana', and 'the woman with the heart of a man'. Yes, Elizabeth I of England brought stability and pride to a little nation, but with a despotic rule that tolerated no threats to her position, or the form of religion in which she believed. Her cousin, the Scottish queen was executed on her orders for the threat she posed to Elizabeth, and ordinary men were hanged, drawn and quartered for the integrity and courage of their differing beliefs. Her coterie of ministers and advisors sanctioned and indeed encouraged her actions. Power had to be absolute and to be seen to be absolute. Elizabeth had learnt her lessons about survival and supremacy through a harsh insecure childhood when she had been at the mercy of her father, who had ordered her mother's execution. Henry VIII, we all know, was a tyrant, and then he was closely followed by the reign of her half sister Mary Tudor, who was a religious bigot, probably as a result of her insecure and miserable childhood, the only girl child of a 'cast off' queen alone in her undeserved misery.

Curiously, some of the religious bigotry and racism that still sadly bedevils modern Scotland is the residue of that tumultuous period in Scots and English history. Within fifty years of the Union of the Crowns a civil war was waged, and a ruling but very foolish monarch, Charles I, was put to death publicly. After an unsatisfactory interregnum, his son Charles II was acclaimed king, but his brother, James II, soon after his succession, was deemed to be unsatisfactory and removed by the intervention of the king of Holland, William of Orange, who happened to be James's son in law.

Suspicion, terror, brutality and a cruel disregard for the ordinary man or woman's aspirations to live a life according to their beliefs and aptitudes was the norm centuries ago in much of Europe. Now we are witnessing the end of a brutal dictatorship in Iraq, after a war, the total consequences of which we will not be able to fathom for some time. Maybe that country's ethnic, tribal and religious divides will prevent true democracy as we in the West now enjoy but we hope it will evolve in the coming decades. It is also a fact that, in Anglo-Scottish history, it was the Union of the Crowns that led to further stability in our island nation, and the first real imperialistic forays as Great Britain.

Most of us would have considered Russia and China to be the last imperialists, but now the United States is making a very good job of demonstrating her super power strength. I hope she will have the maturity and wisdom to learn from the mistakes of others who have already been down that road. Dreadful, cruel, greedy psychopaths and megalomaniacs who appear to have dominated the world scene within the last 70 years have to be destroyed, be they in Europe, South East Asia, Russia, Africa or the Middle East, but one only hopes the Americans will have the honesty and generosity of spirit to achieve their goals and then allow an ancient race to find itself again in its own form of democracy, in what is considered the cradle of civilisation. Liberty and democracy are the two beacons of American belief, but they have the benefit of great wealth as a nation which naturally leads to great power. Liberty and democracy are concepts that are not yet recognised throughout most of the Middle East especially amongst those who have enjoyed considerable wealth in recent times. Yet intelligent thinkers in the Arab world consider a western version of democracy that stresses elections and free speech yet tolerates social and economic disparities, for example in health care and welfare in the United States, unhelpful to their progress. Forward-thinking Arabs want a greater chance to hold rulers to account for improvements in basic services and rights, within an Islamic tradition of consultation, non-discrimination, moderation and tolerance. I am convinced that theocracy has no place anywhere in this modern world.

Hindu scholarship, apparently, had little interest in history as such; mythology and sacred lore meant more and, thus, actually serve as the records of India's ancient past. Indian mythology is distinguished from that of most other lands, and certainly those in the West, by the fact that it is still part of the living culture of every level or society, as I have tried to explain. Over the millennia, invaders with superior military techniques have entered the subcontinent from the north-west and have largely been assimilated into, yet influenced, the more advanced but deep-rooted culture of the peoples they conquered. India is to my mind the sleeping giant of this new century with far more promise long term than China, who currently occupies the focus of attention commercially. If India's ancient value systems prevail and meld with the sensible desire for economic progress, she will be the colossus of the twenty-first century, but she must safeguard her wonderful status as the world's largest democracy and work actively towards achieving social and economic parity. If 'communalism' or religious divides continue to be actively promoted in Indian politics it will be so tragic and regressive. Recent history has demonstrated that economic and military strength is nothing without democracy, civil liberty and tolerance between races and religions.

With intelligent and well informed people, it is possible to talk all night, but we had a very early train to catch the following morning and, besides, we had little Yash in the car asleep. The various drivers had kept an eye on her but by the time we came out she was awake and shivering, although so good and uncomplaining. As I was travelling in Martin's jeep, I wrapped her in my pashmina and, on arriving home, carried her into the house. She was muttering away and rubbing her eyes and, finally, Annie and I were able to make out that she was upset at having missed the British 'Embassy' party! Sleep was indicated for us all.

CHAPTER FOUR

Fruition of my dream

Wertext e were up very early for the start of our quest to see tigers in their natural habitat. It was a bright sunny morning, with all of Delhi waking up to the detritus and let down feeling post Diwali but we were bright eyed and bushy tailed at the start of our journey. When Naveen arrived, we said our goodbyes to the household saying we would see them again in three weeks time and set off for New Delhi railway station.

It looked as if the whole of India had decided to travel but, no, this was just a normal morning for Indian Railways, though possibly there might have been a few travellers returning home after spending a family Diwali with relatives in Delhi. I looked around at the station which was shabby and dirty by our western standards, but the sweepers were working, and attempts had been made to encourage people to dispose of their litter in bins. The sheer size of the numbers that use the building and facilities, plus the normal heat and dust must make it a Herculean task to keep clean. I think a bit of good firm management would really help, along with good cleaning materials. As I was to see over and over again, the Indian idea of cleaning seems to have been subsumed by inertia. Merely rubbing a grubby damp cloth around a basin in the toilet compartment will not achieve a thing; whatever happened to the manufacture of Vim that old standby of my childhood, and perhaps a complete re-education in the utilisation thereof!

Naveen and the porter stood with us on the open platform awaiting the train. On the overhead electric cables Graham and I saw a number of large kingfishers. It was a delight, there in a sea of humanity to see such lovely birds quite calmly sunning their wings. It seemed to us a good omen for our forthcoming search for the tiger and other wonderful creatures of the Indian jungle. The train arrived on time and Naveen wished us well. We would not be seeing him again as he would be on his honeymoon. Sensible young man, he and his bride had chosen Corbett National Park for their honeymoon; that too was to be one of our destinations.

As we settled into our first class compartment the huge long train known as The Golden Temple Mail started slowly gliding by the famous sights of Delhi. I like to just sit and watch the daily life of the people all being played out in front of famous buildings like Humayan's Tomb and other historic relics of the past. The morning mist was lifting and these great buildings looked ghostly whereas near the track the bright sunshine was adding to the vitality of morning bustle. The compartment was comfortable, with air conditioning and reserved for just us. The attendant had brought clean white sheets with which I promptly made up the berths and thus we were able to relax and watch the countryside fly by now that the train was picking up speed. The attendant comes by regularly and asks if one wants breakfast, lunch or whatever. He also has bottles of mineral water for sale and there are metal containers in which to place these for safety. It was calming and fun. We had never stopped since our arrival in Delhi and here was an interlude in which to recharge the batteries.

In 2001, we had visited the York Railway Museum and so enjoyed it. One does not need to be a railway 'anorak' to enjoy that wonderful collection of engines, trains and railway memorabilia, but for us it was excellent fun. Now this journey reminded me of some of the trains I had looked at there. This was the modern way, but those in the museum showed what style the people in the fairly recent past had brought to a gentler age. I had taken some photographs of the various royal carriages and thought that really they were just a plusher version of the original Indian railway carriages in which I had travelled as a child. One's own w.c. compartment complete with sink was such a boon. Queen Victoria was not the only person to have had that privilege, all first class carriages until the 1970s were like that on Indian Railways. Now, however, one had to walk down to a public loo facility, which would have been fine had it been really clean. However, this is a whine that is being sung in our country too so I try not to be judgemental, but in India where there are so many wanting a simple job, however humble or repetitive, I cannot see how these little efficiencies are so difficult to achieve. Constantly one is told that Indian Railways is the world's largest employer after all!

The countryside looked neat and prosperous with village life going on its daily grind. It is one of the heartening things about travelling in India that once one leaves the big conurbations the countryside looks well ordered and beautiful and in this case there were granaries of cereals all full and fresh from the harvest. On this particular journey there are no great rivers to cross but the land is very attractive with ancient buildings and structures providing interest along with the herdsman and villagers to whom we would wave.

Bharatpur Junction is a clean and attractive station and one soon sees the reason for this. The famous Palace on Wheels train uses Bharatpur as its home. The beautiful train was sitting at a platform smartly painted and maintained in its cream and scarlet livery with intricate painted designs. The carriages are called Jaipur, Jodhpur, Kishangarh, Dungapur, Dholpur, Bundi, etc., named after the various royal fiefdoms that made up Rajputana as it was known, now more famously as Rajasthan. That is definitely a journey I would love to make, travel in style like days of old but with the added convenience of modern innovations.

We arrived at Sawai Madhopur station to be greeted by a car and travel representative. I wanted to visit various hotels and see them for myself. Both the Taj Group and Oberoi Group have very good hotels, the Oberoi hotel is luxurious, but there is a wide choice of standard hotels as well. Having been Diwali, the various places were almost fully booked and each of them has their strengths. However, knowing that Ranthambhore had been experiencing a severe drought for almost three years, I in no way wanted to contribute to that worrying state of affairs. Some five star properties give the impression that nothing is wrong, let's splash around in pools and jacuzzis having a luxurious hedonistic time – tigers, animals, drought, parched earth, weary villagers, what are these minor distractions! To visit a natural park and, if lucky, see some of the world's most beautiful animals, that because of the severity of the current climatic conditions are losing their natural habitat and being threatened by human population and then wallow in wall to wall luxury, either in buildings or tents, seemed obscene. We were booked to stay at a resort called Tiger Moon which is situated on the perimeter of the park in a very good setting. Graham and I liked it and found it very similar to those in which we had lived in Africa in the 1970s, again before game viewing became another luxury appointed competitive exercise. Tiger Moon has a rustic appearance with stone cottages, each with a roofed veranda, bedroom with sitting area and adequate shower, basin and w.c. en-suite. There are 32 cottages, a dining hall, which is open like a huge veranda, a bar, conference area and a swimming pool. The latter was empty because of the drought, which was entirely understandable.

Writing as I am now months later, I can thankfully report that Ranthambhore received a good rainfall this monsoon season of 2003, as did the whole of India. This has been a godsend for people and wildlife. I naturally care about both but am only too aware how crucial it was for the survival of the wildlife. In times of drought, the various prey species have a dreadful time. Predators like tiger, leopard and crocodile know that they have to come to the depleted water holes to drink and, being totally desperate and thus not as watchful as they might be, they are easy prey. Tigers and crocodiles have eyeballed each other, and I have seen a film of a tiger actually killing a crocodile. It is so difficult for females to raise cubs in these challenging conditions and they, after all, are the future for the species and the reserve.

Having quickly settled in to our room, we wanted to be out and about as quickly as possible. By now, it was late afternoon, the temperature was lovely and the surroundings looked wonderful in the mellow sunshine. Rakesh the naturalist took us on a walk through the back gate into the buffer zone of the park. This was very enjoyable as otherwise of course everything is done by jeep or canter, a sort of huge open jeep which has seating for quite a large number of people. Almost immediately we saw a small hawk which caught a chipmunk or tree rat. Then we spied a tree pie, a hare, mongoose, parakeets, avocets, ducks, a pipit owl, monkeys, a jungle babbler, and that was before we had walked 200 yards. We climbed on to a mound and looked at the small Jain temple with the setting sun behind it changing colour from gold to orange as it slowly went down behind the western horizon. It was a peaceful silent scene then gently interrupted by the tinkling of the goat bells from behind us. I turned round and there was the goatherd with his flock of goats with long floppy ears, dappled black and white coats and still bearing the decorations for Diwali. The local villagers were enacting a cow puja and celebrating with their buffaloes which also had painted horns. This being the buffer zone these people and their animals are entitled to be on the land, and we watched as the buffaloes made their way to the depleted water hole to wallow in contentment at the end of the day.

Ranthambhore is a beautiful park, and that was seeing it in appallingly dry conditions as a result of three years of failed monsoon. I have watched documentaries on the tiger filmed at Ranthambhore for the last twenty years and I knew it would be beautiful, but, sadly for us, the water holes and lakes were almost non existent and had a look of parched cracked earth. In the three and a half days we were there, one was almost continually covered in red dust. Driving in jeeps or canters the dust just blew up and over us and one could taste it on the tongue. Well, that was fine for us because we had had a good breakfast and could look forward to as much fluid as we could take at the end of a couple of hours, but consider the plight of all the animals who had to make do and go without. I look forward to visiting the park again in greener times because I am confident its haunting ancient beauty will be enhanced by water and lush vegetation and watching animals in their obvious contentment. The one advantage of the very dry period was being able to see quite clearly in the inches deep dust on the roads the startling fresh pug marks of tiger and other animals – this gave an element of drama to game viewing.

We visited Ranthambhore at the beginning of November 2002, but in September of the same year it had reached crisis point when over 400 villagers invaded Ranthambhore and brought in 4,000 head of cattle. They threatened to kill the tigers and destroy the park because their own cattle had no fodder or water outside of the park. A cry went up nationally and internationally from such distinguished people as Fateh Singh Rathore (the founder of the park and a committed conservationist) to people the world over to bring pressure on the local authorities and politicians. It is alleged that the local husband and wife political team connected to the Congress Party had urged the villagers to act in this manner. They stood to gain politically from this irresponsible and lawless behaviour because elections would be coming and they thought they would be seen in the light of benefactors to the 'untrained' minds of the local population. Many of the park invaders were armed and also threatened to use pesticides and indeed it is known that one tigress and two of her cubs were poisoned. Matters took an even greater turn for the worse and within two days 5,000 villagers and 15,000 head of cattle had moved in. The Field Director Mr G V Reddy was threatened and attacked. Mr Reddy is a good man, who was doing a good job and who was kind enough to allow me an interview in November 2002. He has since left the park and that is Ranthambhore's great loss. At that point, however, an amazing network came to life. Crossing all political parties, people including some of the most empowered businessmen in India, began to telephone the Prime Minister's Office and that of Sonia Gandhi, the Leader of the Opposition, to whose Congress Party the Chief Minister of Rajasthan, Mr Ashok Gehlor, belonged. Press, television and inspection teams including Dr Rajesh Gopal, Director of Project Tiger, all rushed to Ranthambhore. In the meantime, the Supreme Court sent contempt notices to the Chief Secretary of Rajasthan. The combined pressure proved to be too much for a system normally geared to do politicians' bidding. By September 20th, an armed force of over 200 policemen and forest staff evicted the people. The only Rajasthan politician who condemned the wicked expedient behaviour of the other politicians was Mrs Bina Kak, the Minister for Forests in Rajasthan.

Perhaps, in the last half century, the human race has in some instances mutated into a sub-species that should be called Homo Politicus. The world over it would seem politicians are reviled. In the UK, most young people now no longer want to aspire to be in parliament. In France, there is a similar feeling I discovered, and Italy is well known for its political problems. In India too, most of one's friends speak disparagingly about huge corruption, but outsiders have no solutions; these are Indian problems for India to solve. I know how depressed I was by the sorry tales I heard and I feel a sense of shame that this great land is letting itself down. Throughout the world at the moment, Indians are proving themselves to be so talented and capable, why do they not use their collective abilities to ensure that India takes its place as a country of efficiency with its democratic government taking responsibility for protection of the environment, wildlife and eco-tourism instead of allowing inertia and corruption to rule?

Expediency is the only word for this sorry tale. It was always going to happen. Year after year, humans abused their own lands, overgrazed it, cut down every last tree and then they wondered why they had so little water, fodder and fuel. What was worse, the powers that be had turned a blind eye when common grazing grounds were converted to industrial, urban or farm use. Ranthambhore Park, however, had been protected zealously and run well and nature had responded by providing grass, trees, water and food for wildlife. Not surprisingly tigers, leopards, deer, wild boar, bear and a huge number of bird species had thrived.

The tiger's real threat in the words of the conservation zoologist Ullas Karanth is lack of prey, more than poaching. He believes that cattle eating into the pastures of prey species such as deer, wild boar and gaur (the big bison) starves and kills these animals, which in turn starves the tiger. The root of the problem is habitat destruction and conversion of forest land to other uses and overgrazing. This can be summed up in two words: Population Pressure.

Project Tiger was founded in 1973 when wise men such as the late Guy Mountfort and others like Billy Arjan Singh and Fateh Singh Rathore realised that tigers in the sub continent were on the brink of extinction through hunting, poaching and population pressure. This was brought to the attention of Indira Gandhi, the then Prime Minister, who realised the enormity of the threat with about 1,800 tigers left throughout the country. Project Tiger was a central government project to focus on the crisis of the tiger and to provide additional money to various state governments to ensure special protection for the tiger and their varied habitats. In 1973, thirty years ago Project Tiger selected nine areas, which were both national parks and sanctuaries. In most cases, a Project Tiger Reserve is made up of a core central area which is a National Park that is surrounded by or adjacent to other areas that act like a buffer zone and can be Sanctuaries. Now Project Tiger receives 16 crore rupees (approximately 4 million dollars) for disbursal to state governments for use in 27 tiger reserves. The state governments probably spend an equal amount in the administration of these reserves.

When the villagers of Ranthambhore were moved out of the park in the 1970s, altogether 1,000 families involving between 6,000 and 7,000 people were relocated. Fateh Singh, who was then the park director, was brutally beaten and threatened. The solution found eventually was to tell the villagers that Vaghdeo, the Tiger God whom they worshipped as lord of the forest, would die unless they moved. It was an effective way of explaining to simple but devout people the reason for their imposed sacrifice, and it worked.

Some of the important national parks and sanctuaries in India are: Kanha, Bandhavgarh, Ranthambhore, Corbett, Panna, Pench, Gir, Bharatpur, Sariska, Dudhwa, Nagarahole, Bandipur, Periyar, Kaziranga, Sunderbans and a few which are not so well known. On this trip, we were visiting Ranthambhore, Bandhavgarh, Kanha and Corbett. I have visited Bharatpur, Panna, and Bandipur previously. I am also going to include a brief description of Gir, the home of the Asiatic Lion and Nagarahole, home to wild elephants.

"The tiger is the symbol of power, unbridled, elemental ... and he lives alone, unblemished, unmarred. The more you know about him, the more he gets into your imagination."

Billy Arjan Singh

Billy Arjan Singh and the late Guy Mountfort co-operated on a couple of books in 1972 to 1975 called 'On the Brink' and 'Back from the Brink'. These two books, which I read whilst living in South Africa inspired me and built on the knowledge of tigers that I had assimilated from infancy from my parents who thought them the king of beasts. In my extreme infancy, the late great Jim Corbett had still been living in North India and was a friend of my parents. Later in this book, I will describe the experience of visiting his little house, which is now a museum near Corbett National Park, which was named after him. So, tigers were in the blood as it were and now I was determined to do what little I could to help spread the word about this wonderful beast of myth and magic and true beauty, to try and help conserve them and their habitat for their future generations and those of mankind.

"A tiger is a large-hearted gentleman with boundless courage, and when he is exterminated – as exterminated he will be unless public opinion rallies to his support – India will be the poorer for having lost the finest of her Fauna."

Jim Corbett

The park covers more than 500 square miles or 1334 sq. km with a core area of 300 sq. km. The Aravalli Hills meet the Vindhya Hills in the park. There are 300 km of road networks. The normal annual rainfall is 800 mm but this is a dry deciduous and dry thorn forest. The population of Sawai Madhopur, the local town is over 77,690 according to a census of 12 years ago. Ranthambhore was once the shooting estate of the Maharajahs of Jaipur, and the Queen and Prince Philip went there during their official visit to India in 1961. I remember the press accounts of that visit because I was at boarding school and, in those days of loyal interest in the young Queen and her tours, we followed everything avidly. I was asked to create a little exhibition of her first huge trip to India and Pakistan. Even then I disapproved of Prince Philip shooting a tiger. It seemed to fly in the face of what the world was waking up to, that, without careful conservation, the planet's animals would face extinction through human exploitation, population pressure and obscenities like shooting for trophies. The royal couple would have done so much for the whole wildlife cause if they had declined the invitation to shoot but had enthusiastically taken up an opportunity for wildlife photography. However, thankfully, tiger shooting was banned in 1970 and Ranthambhore became a wildlife park. Along with its lakes and forests and wide open spaces, it has the added intriguing romantic beauty and interest of a great 17th century ruined Rajput fort crowning the great escarpment. This always gives photography in Ranthambhore an exotic allure and a sense of ancient peoples and their histories and dynasties that have come and gone but still the king of beasts thankfully reigns. For me, as a first time visitor, it seemed to be a perfect fusion of human civilisation with the still obvious feats of early engineering and building combining to create a backdrop for the current players: the tiger and all the other animals and beautiful birds that co-exist.

Ranthambore Fort was built in 944 AD and its huge walls measure several kilometres in circumference. It is a magical place for watching bird life and occasionally one may catch a glimpse of a leopard. One is allowed to visit in the middle of the day between game viewing drives that take place in the very early morning and afternoon. There is a temple dedicated to Ganesh and the area is covered in old water tanks (artificial lakes), *chhatris* (mausoleums), palaces and mosques. There are so many historic architectural and natural points that I could mention but this is not a guide book. In normal times with good rains, Rajbagh Lake is lovely. Biannually, in October and May, the lake is densely covered with beautiful lotus flowers and attendant lotus-eaters. This area of the park has the highest density of sambhar deer and marsh crocodiles. During the monsoon, these crocodiles lay their eggs in holes in the banks of the backwater pools of the lake and scores of newly-hatched crocodiles can be seen in the pools. We saw two crested serpent eagles and Rajbagh also has other birds of prey, such as the grey-headed fish eagle, the osprey, the crested hawk eagle and the brown fish owl.

The tiger, *Pantheris tigris*, has the following subspecies: Bengal, Siberian, South China, Sumatran and Indo-Chinese; the Caspian, Javan and Bali subspecies are extinct. A full grown tiger can be between 1.9 and 3.3 m from the nose to the tip of the tail. In ideal conditions, its life span is 15 to 18 years. The gestation period is 98 to 108 days and the tiger litter may be between 1 and 4 cubs in the wild.

In the early morning light (I would have liked to be even earlier) with the sun still coming up, there was still some coolness in the air. I looked around and thought how wonderful Rajbagh must be when rain washed and green as seen in so many excellent films, but now the lake beds were cracked by the recent summer's searing heat and drought and, where cool green water should have been, there were minute amounts of water at which the animals congregated. Tigers go very early in the morning to drink and their tracks were clearly evident along the roadway.

On that first trip, we saw scores of spotted chital deer, sambhar, nilgai, boar, some chinkara (Indian gazelle), monkeys, mongoose, owls, parakeets, tree pies, shrikes, vultures, kites, painted storks, pelicans, kingfishers, drongo, partridge, peacocks in flocks, bulbuls, bee-eaters and flycatchers, but the drive was nearing its end and we had not had the good fortune to see tiger. All the while, Rakesh and the other naturalist were scanning the undergrowth for tigers. Suddenly they pointed and we stopped.

Unbelievable, quite stunning and breathtaking, there were four tigers! They were all lying around, satiated and somnolent after feeding. We had been told that on the previous day the tigress had killed a sambhar so they would have had enough food for a day or two. The cubs were huge, about eleven months old and already magnificent. The mother tigress rolled over and lay on her back with her hind legs in the air displaying her stomach in a languid way, like a domestic cat. This was totally spellbinding for us all. Everyone was so excited and pleased with huge grins on their faces. Photography was not that easy with the excellent camouflage but we were just content to watch them sleeping or dozing with quick breathing or panting to cool themselves. It was for me a culmination of a dream and I just felt hugely privileged to be able to watch these wonderful animals. Graham felt exactly the same and I defy anyone to be blasé about such an experience. No-one I met was left unmoved. Through binoculars, I looked at the tigress and she opened her eyes just then and it seemed I was looking into her wonderful, round yellow eyes – quite

Tiger on the move – Ranthambhore

unbelievably moving. Suddenly, one of the cubs decided to move and walk about as if to show himself – that made the others move and thus provided superb photo opportunities. We continued to feast our eyes on the tiger family

Tigers at rest – Ranthambhore

which were approximately 13 metres away from us. At last, we reluctantly drove away and back to Tiger Moon for breakfast. There was a general air of elation and the naturalists were so pleased. The whole experience was of great interest but the tigers were the ultimate focus. Everything we saw was special, the sight of two chital stags fighting it out quite close to us, wild boar covering themselves in mud on the banks of the reduced lake, weaver birds in the palm trees, everything, but when one has seen the tiger, Oh! That is on a different level and those visual memories will live with me forever.

Chital Stag – Ranthambhore

Till the late 1980s, the tigers became more and more diurnal and the area became one of the finest in the world to see wild tigers. Then, in the 1990s, it was discovered that poaching was taking place and a poacher was caught with a tiger and a leopard skin. It is now thought that poaching gangs reduced Ranthambhore's tiger population by half. In the next few years, the alarm went up all over India and the complacency that had descended was shattered with the ugly truth that once again the tiger was a target for poachers selling their bones to the Chinese and the whole tiger population was under threat. The evil reality was that some wardens had colluded with this dreadful trade which also involved Tibetan traders; there are those in that supposedly saintly little nation that have little in common with their religious head the Dalai Lama. It is only in the last few years and the new millennium that tiger numbers are on the increase again because of vigilance and excellent field management. I am hoping that now that the Chinese government is co-operating with efforts to help save the South China Tiger (the South China Tiger will hopefully be the symbol for the Chinese Olympics) and the possible breeding in South Africa of these magnificent beasts, with hopefully subsequent translocation to China, that people in China will become aware of the futility of using animal bones for their cure-all medicines and the tiger's supposedly magical properties. Only vigilance and education combined with stringent punishments with hefty fines can possibly remedy this problem. Education and demonstrating to ordinary forest people and villagers how they can live and co-exist with wildlife is the long-term answer, but they also must benefit tangibly in some sound way and be made to think laterally about their own future. Now people are beginning to talk about reduction of the bovine population of sacred cows, but, whilst the animal is considered to be a sign of wealth and held sacred to the humble peasant, this is a huge challenge. In reality, there are millions of cows just surviving and not achieving a great deal by their lives. India is the largest milk producer in the world and this can be maintained in intensive farms for dairy/sweet *mitthai* production, but the average peasant farmer in rural Rajasthan has poor quality livestock. Buffaloes, however, have a greater input to the livestock worth of India, not being sacred they are used widely to provide 'beef' and of course they also provide milk.

Sambhar Deer – Ranthambhore

Everywhere in the developing world there is a challenge to educate people to have a tolerance of their environment and wildlife, be it Africa, Central and South America, South East Asia, Malaysian and Indonesian Borneo and, indeed Australia. India because of its vast population has the biggest challenge and it requires people of foresight and great integrity in government.

We had a quick but very welcome breakfast that was laid out in buffet style, then a rapid shower and change, which was essential in our opinion because of the dust. Rakesh said the canter was ready and we had indicated that we wanted to go round the fort at midday. Others had heard us make the arrangements and wanted to come too. It was fun and the fort was very interesting.

The fort was conquered by Ala-ud-din Khalji's army in 1031, and Akbar in 1569 but, for most of its existence, Ranthambhore has been under the control of Rajput dynasties. I found looking up at the skyline in the sunset or dawn light there was an ethereal quality to the ramparts and, then, on the second morning there, quite clearly silhouetted against the pale blue light of the dawn was a leopard, just looking down at us in silence. Quite magical!

Ranthambhore has one or two serious disadvantages with which it has to live as a wildlife park. Religious tourism or pilgrimage (after all, in the western world it is now realised that the Christian pilgrimages of the Middle Ages were in fact the first form of tourism) occurs every Wednesday and on the 4th day of the new moon every month. This results in tens of thousands of people entering the park each month. They come on foot and walk right around the circumference of the Ranthambhore fortress since this journey is their sacred pilgrimage to the temple of Lord Ganesh. Every September at the annual Ganesh festival one million people enter the park over two days. After a successful monsoon when the park's grassy areas are lush and green, the displaced villagers try to sneak in with their livestock for grazing. This of course has the inevitable consequence of some livestock being killed by tiger or leopard, for which compensation is demanded and given. Had the displaced villagers been adequately compensated for the removal and properly educated, or indoctrinated might be a better term, this annual dilemma might not occur. Sadly, in India as with so many things, events are mismanaged and developments lurch along in a half-baked way because of a lack of commitment.

For us from the West, so much of what we see and hear is frustrating and depressing and alien, like the monthly human invasion of a wildlife park, but that is the essence of India, that ancient customs and holy rites have to be respected and endured and allowed to co-exist with today's endeavour to maintain a wild but protected environment for endangered animals.

CHAPTER FIVE

More Tigers and
Some Simple Fun!

In the afternoon, we returned to the Park and saw everything but tiger, leopard or bear. A huge eagle close to us was a delight. The afternoon light is particularly nice and the warmth of the breeze was welcome in the open vehicles. Ranthambhore is popular and that is a very good thing in that it educates the people of India but the hustle and bustle can be a bit vexing; in true Indian style, it is noisy and inefficient and time-consuming. The naturalists do their best but even they become vexed with their Indian brethren.

Some Australians were annoyed because they felt they had been slightly short-changed in that they had booked a jeep but ended up in a canter; seeing the tigers, however, compensated fully, but Ranthambhore does need to address the problem of jeep quotas. The next morning, I awoke feeling very rough with a cold, Graham had one too so I imagine the flight out was to blame. We were glad we both felt the same way because we could feel miserable together which is better than one after the other; there is nothing worse than the person who has recovered returning to their normal 'chirpy' self whilst the other is now feeling half dead!

Rakesh sought me out and said urgently in Hindi that we should be ready to go; I was surprised as it was much earlier than the previous morning and seemed suspiciously efficient. I looked at the canters; one appeared full of women and the other totally empty. I looked Rakesh in the eye and said which one are you going in, and he just moved his eyes to the full one. I murmured that it was full and he said under his breath go in the front, there are two seats for you and sahib. Sweet thoughtful man, he stood the whole way. What a ride. We had hardly arrived in the park when we stopped urgently and Rakesh showed us the leopard moving on the top of the escarpment. It was stunning, the leopard cannot be mistaken for anything else – it is the way he holds his thick tail. Oh! It was so thrilling but did not last for long – the animal was about 400 to 500 metres away.

The drive was enjoyable, it always is at the start of a new day, a cold breeze and the light blue sky turning to pale gold as the sun rises. The noises of the various animals and birdsong, alarms from deer, the shrill of the peacock, the bell of a sambhar all contribute to a sense of anticipation and quiet enjoyment. Rakesh and the driver seemed to be concentrating on a particular area and had been tipped off that the tigress and her cubs had been seen drinking at a nearby pool. Their tenacity was rewarded.

Two cubs lying together could be seen about 20 metres away, but then they moved and came towards us. Well, it was astounding, one moved and sat so that without moving my head, just my eyes, I could see two tigers, one to the left and one to the right. We all just looked at them in hushed admiration. Then, the right hand tiger obviously thought to himself 'I had better humour these folk' and came towards us and veered to the right of the canter and threw himself down in the dusty road, just like our little Raju does in front of the fire. He gazed at us and then lay down completely. This lasted for a little while but boredom set in and he raised himself and looked at us or changed his position – he posed, there is no other word for it. All of us were so excited and happy; complete strangers, the female party were a group from Singapore made up of different nationalities who were only there for the one night and then going on to the Golden Triangle, but their elation led to friendly exchanges between us. I observed that a great deal of trouble had been taken to ensure to the best of the naturalists' ability that this group saw tiger, I have no idea what happened to the other guests and, at breakfast, I saw Indian guests, who had obviously not been out to the park, paying a lot of attention to their food. One wondered why they bothered to come at all. Ranthambhore is not on the way to somewhere, it does require special effort to visit it. I am so glad we did.

We were due to leave after breakfast. I had decided that I wanted to investigate another medium class hotel so that I could write about more than one experience. So, after breakfast and a shower, we said our farewells to the management. I explained that I wanted to do whatever I could to help promote and protect India's wildlife, and I made some suggestions to ensure guest satisfaction which were well received. Rakesh came to talk to me and it turned out that he is a Jat, and that his brother is serving in the army with the Jat Regiment, the same regiment as my late father, Frank Rose, was in, a wonderful coincidence. I have had a great loyalty to that regiment from infancy. In fact, I told Rakesh that on November 20th I would be a special guest of the Regiment along with Graham as I had been invited to present my book, *India: The Peacock's Call*, to them at their Annual Raising Day Reunion.

Raj, one of the management team, and Rakesh drove us in a jeep into Sawai Madhopur and delivered us to the Ranthambhore Regency Hotel. Ravendra Jain who owns the Regency and his staff made us very welcome. It too tries hard and provides good service and very good food. The gardens are pleasant with a swimming pool and one can live in the garden cottages or within the main building.

That afternoon, we joined a party of Indians who had hired a canter to take them to a local dam for an outing. This was an interesting experience because of the drive through the town and then on to the open road until we arrived at this rather charming artificial lake, which, because of the drought, was much reduced in size and, therefore, the fishermen in their boats were having great success. Watching yet another great sunset sitting on the dam wall with a slight breeze one was again reminded how pleasant truly rural India is – away from the inevitable squalor of the towns.

The Indian families were obviously all close friends and had come on a Diwali holiday together. It was lovely to see the interaction between them and, now that we had all been together for a little while, they wanted to talk and pressed us to accept some of their 'picnic' – we did not but only because we were looking forward to supper and, anyway, I am largely wheat-intolerant. On the return journey, it was dark with the new moon of Diwali shining as a slender crescent. The adults decided to sing and shyly started with a song called 'I love my India', after which they grew in confidence and sang very well until we reached the hotel. Passing through the town, the locals looked in wonder at this open canter full of singing Indians and two Europeans. A shy but happy interlude for us both, this sort of experience is important to gain an overall picture of modern India.

We had supper on the lawn and, despite feeling rather grim, we appreciated the good food and the Rajasthani musicians and a puppeteer who worked his puppets to the delight of the little ones amongst the guests. It was a family evening with tiny babies and toddlers and gossiping parents. Our colds ensured we departed for an early night.

The next morning, two British women whom we had met briefly and exchanged notes with appeared to have had an accident. The one had fallen out of a jeep when it came to a sudden halt and had landed on the concrete road and been concussed. This had not happened inside the park and the fit and healthy companion was by now quite worried, so we tried to help and explain to the hotel management who immediately called a doctor. Thankfully, she made a good recovery and it did not deter them from continuing to Sasan Gir. In fact, they very kindly sent me an account of their time in that fascinating place, home of the Asiatic Lion.

We, however, went out in a canter with a lot of Indians with their young children. We were worried as to how this was going to work but we communicated with them and shyly they responded and were eager to learn and see for themselves, and appreciate the importance of not making an endless chattering noise! This fourth drive for us went on an unfamiliar route and we saw everything but a tiger. You have to look closely and carefully. Suddenly, I spied a little owl sitting in a hole of a tree, then I realised that there was a second owl sitting right next to the first one; the camouflage was so good that it was difficult to spot him until he opened one eye. I murmured 'Mummy and Daddy owl' which delighted the little ones who all giggled and repeated it.

Sunset over a Jain Temple – Ranthambhore

Our group were so eager to see a tiger when suddenly we saw a group of vehicles and realised that there must be tiger in the vicinity and I urged them all to be totally silent. The monkeys were calling an alarm call, I thought, yes, it is going to happen again – but it did not. Certainly there was a tiger or tigers close by but they just kept out of sight. Eventually, the people in the other five canters started behaving rather badly, making a noise, gesticulating and almost demanding to see a tiger; well it did not happen and we were all disappointed. I felt bad for the others but they seemed to care less than I did though they would be leaving the next day.

We arrived back so late that we had to rush to our appointment with G V Reddy, the Field Director of Ranthambhore. It was good of him to see us and I explained my motivation, which he accepted, and promised to keep in touch by email. Graham and I were both depressed by the conditions in which his administration worked. To us Europeans with our smart sleek offices, this looked shabby and inefficient, but this is India and our western perceptions are constantly challenged. So much assaults the eye and the senses. I despair as to how anything operates in this huge country but it bumbles along tied up with string. One wonders if the great lumbering elephant that is India could be galvanised into a trot by the biting of millions of ants – the people. I don't know. Indians are very good at talking and complaining and blaming the corruption of their political leaders, 'from the top down' is the expression in constant use. I know it to be so but only they the people will be able to change it and not in my lifetime.

We departed by train for Bharatpur. There was some mix up or oversight in our reservations and though I had paid for first class air conditioned seats there were none for us and we had to go to three tiers 2nd class and oust someone from our seats. Graham put on an effective 'strop' which provided an interesting spectacle for other passengers, who then cautiously started to talk to us. We explained what had happened and they agreed that Indians are also 'ripped off'. Fortunately, the journey was only two and a half hours long, but the difference between first class and anything else is quite substantial. Apparently, Indian Railways is attempting to do away with first class travel, which I think is a shame, but, realistically, the average Indian probably finds 2nd class adequate and less of a drain on his modest income. I resolved to bring it up with the agents that had booked this particular part of our journey. What particularly annoyed me was that we had paid extra in that we had been compelled to pay for the seats from Surat on the West Coast of India, where the train had started. As a jovial Indian said 'A scam!'

The drive from Bharatpur's very nice railway station was pleasant in the afternoon sunshine. It was actually my birthday and Chandra Mahal, where we would be staying one night, is a pleasant place with good food. It was five years since I had visited and, though it is still good and clean, I felt that the usual Indian inertia had been allowed to creep in and the owner was not sufficiently motivated. She blamed a lot on 9/11, but then we consider that that outrage should encourage one to try harder. Knowing what wonderful textiles are available in Rajasthan I felt that with careful additions the place could look sumptuous and the Haveli's central courtyard should have a tinkling fountain and lots of lush plants to create an atmosphere of tranquillity and welcome. None of this would be expensive, but if one is going to run a guest house or small hotel there is the need to remain constantly alert to new ideas and renovation and have a 'can do' philosophy'. Now why should I demand that when in little old Peeblesshire one constantly encounters an 'aye been' attitude, i.e., always was that way! Scottish Tourism is full of horrors and people who seem to glower at guests and snarl 'no you can't have something to eat; it is five past two...' I had it happen to me the other day at a local hotel in Peebles, which is privately owned and a member of the Best Western Group. The disease must be catching because normally in restaurants in India people fall over themselves to oblige, whereas the local 'Indian' in Peebles, which serves good food is now running its business round its snarling waiters and losing customers daily.

The chef at Chandra Mahal was still cooking good food and we sat out on the lawn under the stars and they brought me a sort of birthday cake, which was so thoughtful and greatly appreciated. Earlier, we had gone and visited the little shop across from the Haveli with the idea of telephoning my mother and telling her all about the tigers. This was so efficient and easy and cheap. All over India one finds these tiny shops, some of them look like a hole in the wall. One dials and speaks, clear as a bell, and is presented with a modest bill that comes out of the machine like a normal cash receipt. Mummy was enchanted to hear of our tiger experiences and considered us very fortunate. Then we tarried and looked at some of the charming water colour paintings of birds that were for sale. These local artists produce wonderful work and when one has just encountered all this exotica first hand the enthusiasm to buy is large. We had bought a small painting of a tiger in Ranthambhore and now we bought one of kingfishers and a second of a kingfisher painted on to a very old government receipt, so that the stamp of Rajputana was evident – the paper would be about a hundred years old. Finally, we indulged ourselves and bought a large one of entwined peacocks and another large one of cockatoos. These now hang in one of our spare bedrooms which is decorated in Anokhi soft furnishings. Anokhi originated in Jaipur and now has shops in Delhi, Mumbai, probably Kolkata and Chennai, and one in London. The block work is all hand done in beautiful colours. I chose from their new design Indigo, which, as the name suggests, is largely blue. I love a blue and white theme and the other guest room is in yellow and white. Indigo has a special meaning for me because my French great grandparents had huge indigo estates in Eastern India and tragically died together with their youngest child when my grandmother Aline and her sisters were still children. It seemed appropriate to chose Indigo in memory of them. Anokhi sells such charming designs and for us the prices are very modest, so one is able to refurbish a room every four years or so if the sun fades the designs. My dear friend Mala

Sen, the author of The Bandit Queen and Death by Fire, periodically brings me things from the Mumbai shop, she too finds Clapham can be greatly cheered by additions of vibrant colour from Rajasthan.

Chandra Mahal is very well situated for a visit to Keoladeo Ghana Bird Sanctuary, which is commonly referred to as 'Bharatpur' like Ranthambhore or Kanha or Corbett. We had been there on a previous visit and we did not have time to make another visit on this occasion, but, oh, how I wish we had!. In 1733, the Maharaja of Bharatpur dammed several small rivers to create a marshland breeding ground for birds. A stone tablet in the reserve details the enormous number of ducks the royal guests then blasted from the sky – sometimes up to 4,500 in one day. The 29 sq. km area, of which about half is marshland, became a national park in 1983, having being declared a protected area in 1956. Now home to around 360 different species, Bharatpur is, without doubt, one of the finest bird sanctuaries in the world and has a thriving animal population. It is a tranquil beautiful place and totally absorbing even for visitors who are not addicted to bird watching. One must rise very very early and get out into the park by sunrise and watch everything coming to life, with the mist lifting off the water. The lakes and marshes provide a whole range of birds, ducks and geese, moorhens and jacanas, cormorants and darters, herons, storks and cranes. A speckled pond heron floats in perfect camouflage on a muddy pool, while just above, a kingfisher flashes turquoise through the dappled shade, a mated pair of grey and scarlet Saras cranes stick close together as they feed, and if you look overhead there are trees bulging with the nests of painted storks. India as a whole is home to some 1,200 species of bird, of which at least 400 are found in and around Rajasthan and about 360 species are in the bird sanctuary alone with annual visitors in the winter months, when the annual migratory species from as far a field as the Russian Steppes and Central Asia fly in to spend the winter. I love the little owls that are often only a couple of feet above one's head – they just look gravely at you and open and close one eye as if to say 'OK matey, I am real, now you have seen me, push off'.

The bird sanctuary does not allow motor vehicles within its boundaries, except on official business so one cycles around or is driven in a cycle rickshaw. This is a splendid gentle way to get around and adds to the tranquillity. That could never be a practical form of transport in a massive wildlife park with big carnivores but, here, in gentle little Keoladeo, it is superb. One can stay inside the park at the official hotel, but that is a personal choice. In my last book, *India: The Peacock's Call*, I recounted the amusing encounter with the owner of a cycle rickshaw who was so helpful to us – I wish Devi Singh, as I write, all blessings for his Diwali. He is a super alert young man whom I would love to meet again. May the goddess Lakshmi enter his home this year with good fortune.

There are good possibilities to see chital, nilgai and sambhar along the paths, plus otters, jackals and Indian black buck. The latter are so graceful and so well drawn in Rajput miniature paintings; they are often depicted with Lord Krishna and are considered sacred and protected. We saw a large number near Jodhpur when visiting the Bishnoi People. People do talk of seeing tiger in rare instances within the park. This presents a quandary really because then there is a potential threat to bird watchers who are cycling around in their innocence. I think I might very well fall off a bike into the water were I to be confronted by a full grown tiger or tigress on the path. However, this family has already had such an encounter. Mother, when my parents were still in the Indian Army with access to shooting blocks of forest, used to accompany my father and go out nearly every weekend to shoot fowl and buck for the pot. It is not something that I would now care to do but *shikar* was a normal accepted sport or pursuit in the late 1940s. I was taken on an elephant at the age of six weeks for a weekend shoot. On this particular occasion Mummy was walking along a jungle path and suddenly came face to face with a tiger. It must fairly concentrate the mind. She told me this story from infancy and it was probably the first influence on me as a child to revere and treasure tigers. On this occasion, the king of the jungle just looked, twitched his tail and turned off the path. Going behind a tree takes on a whole new meaning when there are those sorts of voyeurs about, don't you think?

I strongly urge a two or three day visit to the area which can combine a visit to Deeg, of which I wrote in the first book, and Fatehpur Sikri plus the Taj Mahal at Agra. Jaipur is not too far away and both Jaipur and Agra have good air connections to Delhi and Mumbai. In fact, a holiday starting in Delhi, staying at Tikli Bottom, then flying down to Agra, visiting the Taj Mahal over two days, plus the Red Fort and Sikandra's Tomb, etc. could then continue by car to Fatehpur Sikri which requires an afternoon, and two nights at Chandra Mahal. Two mornings in the sanctuary with a midday visit to Deeg could then be followed by a train trip down to Ranthambhore for the wonderful experience of that special place and then return to Bharatpur by train and go by car to Jaipur. From Jaipur, after as many days as one likes, fly back to Delhi, or on to Mumbai, or Jodhpur. It all depends on how much time a traveller has at his or her disposal. Two weeks would be a perfect amount to do this justice. When I see Golden Triangle tours advertised for nine days I know it will be disappointing, and as for anything less, well that is almost an insult and back to the old idea of travelling 'this is Tuesday, so it must be France .....'

On this occasion, we had to rise at four in the morning to leave at 0530 hours for a car journey to Agra to catch the Shatabdhi Express to Gwalior. That was a challenge, given the way we were feeling, but we started some antibiotic therapy which soon saw off the potential chest infections. The driver arrived from Agra and was another excellent fellow and nice to chat to about everything and anything. We were anxious not to miss our train but there was no danger of that and he arrived in Agra in good time and I said let us go and have breakfast at The Taj View hotel. The roads were full of army vehicles all streaming back from the north and the border with Pakistan. The Indian Army had been stood down after the threat of war receded, but their attempts to get everyone home for Diwali were not realistic and mile upon mile of military vehicles filled with troops were on this main road. Moving half a million men in a short time must be quite a logistical exercise and, while we waited for our train, the station platform was awash with soldiers and officers all waiting for their respective trains to go home and be reunited with their families.

This was the 9th November and the morrow would be Remembrance Day on the Sunday in Britain. I thought of what that means for so many people, and, now, writing after the second war in Iraq, there will be a special poignancy for so many again this year. Will it never end?

This was my second experience on The Shatabdhi Express, but Graham's first. It is comfortable and pleasant and reasonably efficient with good service. The speed eats into the long distances and it really was quite a relief to know that soon we would be staying in Gwalior for two nights in four/five star accommodation. It gives one a chance to recharge the batteries which were a bit low at this stage because of cold and antibiotic.

We arrived at Gwalior and were met by car and a travel agent and swiftly driven to the Usha Kiran Palace Hotel, which is now owned by the Taj Group. Until very recently, it had been owned by the Welcomgroup, but now the Taj Group have huge ambitions to remake it into a five-star luxury resort. The building is not that old and had been a palace belonging to the Maharajah of Gwalior. We were warmly greeted and shown to their best suite which was bliss, pure unadulterated bliss. I asked the bearer for tea and if someone would press some clothes and quickly do some *dhobi*, i.e., laundry. The bathroom was palatial with marble and first class plumbing and the Dobbie couple were in heaven, and promptly fell sound asleep. Five mornings in a row, we had risen at 0500 or earlier and with all the action and travel and cold this had taken its toll. However, a couple of hours later we were up and raring to go. I sent an apology to the guide who had been patiently waiting for us, and explained the reason for having kept him waiting. Now lunch was calling, but first I went and had a talk with the hotel's new management team. The Taj Group are one of India's most prestigious chains with hotels throughout Asia and one in London, along with some serviced apartments and two very elegant restaurants in London's West End. The management were charming and I am sure when the renovations are complete this will become a very good city break destination for Indians and others like ourselves who had come to see the various historic sights.

Vakil, our guide, was excellent and very good company and with a nice driver in an ancient Ambassador car we were able to see a great deal of Gwalior's attractions. It has to be said that at the moment it is an appallingly dirty city, but it has so much of interest to the visitor. The powers that be have designated it a 'Counter Magnet' city, and, thus, apparently, effort, initiative and money is going to be invested in transforming it. Now I understood why The Taj Group are prepared to spend seven crore of rupees on renovating Usha Kiran. Gwalior is famous for its annual music festival (which is similar to the annual Edinburgh Festival and what it generates as income for Edinburgh) and it has an annual trade fair at which one receives huge rebates for items purchased. There is a large military cantonment and it is a centre for textiles. Its pottery was famous at one time and it is a manufacturing centre for vehicle tyres. Coupled with all that is the fact that it is a hugely historical place and the current Prime Minister, Mr Vajpayee, hails from this city and is himself a noted poet.

Notwithstanding all those positives, travellers from Europe will not make a detour to come here unless it is substantially transformed. If however that is achieved with vision and determination, it will become a splendid destination for anyone and is a superb base for visiting Jhansi, Khajuraho, Sonagiri, Datia, Orchha, Shivpuri and Panna, the lovely game reserve which is very close to Khajuraho.

CHAPTER SIX

Historic Gwalior

V akil was good company as a guide. We have not yet encountered a bad or indifferent guide, but there is no doubt that one warms to particular personalities. Vakil was knowledgeable and had his own positive views about life in Gwalior: where India is going in terms of modernising, upkeep of her historical treasures and so forth. Our first destination, again in warm afternoon sunlight, was the Jai Vilas Palace. This is still the residence of the Scindia family who for over two centuries have been the ruling house of Gwalior. Maharajahs of Gwalior have played a significant part in Indian history for the last two hundred years, and have been taking an active part in politics in the last few decades. Tragically, the 10th Maharajah (though these titles are meant to be extinct now), Madhavrao III Scindia, was killed in a plane crash in 2001. This is, however, a wealthy family who still can and do wield considerable influence.

The Scindia Museum within the palace comprises some 35 rooms all laid out as if the residents had just left the room. Jai Vilas is an Italianate structure which combines the Tuscan and Corinthian architecture of the 19th century. I think there is an opportunity to renovate it sympathetically and improve on its presentation, as older and much more impressive buildings in Rajasthan are superbly presented. It could be that, because Gwalior is not on the major tourist trail yet, the Scindia family or their property management have not bothered to make the effort, which is a shame because they have a great deal that is worthy of interest and inspection. In the UK, where finance is a consideration in private ownership and folk are robbing Peter to pay Paul to maintain a

- 54 -

historic property, one sympathises, but Gwalior could seriously improve its presentation, and probably not incur a huge expense. Good management with close attention to detail under the eye of a good estate manager would achieve what is necessary.

The Durbar Hall is imposing and grand and dwarfed by two huge chandeliers, each weighing three and half tonnes. They were considered to be the largest chandeliers in the world when this palace was in its heyday. The story goes that ten elephants were taken on to the roof by means of a 500 metre long earth ramp to test the strength of the building before the chandeliers were hung. Quite a lot of the glass throughout was made in Murano famous for its Venetian glass. It is all in good condition and the huge reception rooms are impressive but, for me, not amazing because they resembled so many European, Italian Baroque or British palaces. One of the eye-catching treasures is an electrically driven silver train with cut glass wagons which served guests as it moved around on miniature silver rails on the huge dining table. This I had heard of from my father and other people, it brought a whole new dimension to 'passing the port' or more likely the whisky in India. There is also a silver set of bedroom furniture and Venetian glass was used for cradles and fountains in the courtyard; a Venetian cut glass swing which is used by the Scindia family to celebrate Lord Krishna's birthday must be unique. The Prince of Wales visited Gwalior in 1875 with an entourage of a thousand, which must have been a logistical nightmare for the family retainers and servants. The grand staircase taking one up to the Durbar Hall has Venetian glass banisters and a huge red glass chandelier. Venice must have made a huge impression on the designer of Jai Vilas.

It is an interesting museum and palace with odd corners that are fascinating and others that are just resting places for dusty relics of a bygone age. Because our museums and ancient houses in the UK are so well maintained and project the past so well I want that for their equivalent in India, but they must want it too and perhaps at the moment people have yet to have a comprehensive 'feel good' factor before they have a true respect for the past.

As we were going round, a large party of teenage school children entered and behaved in the customary way of all school parties, unless they are very controlled. They appeared to be interested in why we found it all so worthy of interest, but then some of the teenage boys spoke slightly disrespectfully and jostled me and Vakil exploded, so did I because I know a cheeky child when I see one, and in India never tolerate any nonsense; so I answered them crisply in Hindi, which provoked shocked silence. Usually, I have no gender challenges and, particularly now that I am in middle age, but, sadly, there are plenty who try to denigrate the female in India, particularly western women or girls. Some of this behaviour has been the response to foolish westerners wearing totally unsuitable clothing and their inappropriate behaviour. Indian youth at a certain level seem to have formed the opinion that all European women are loose with no morals and easy prey for 'eve teasing'. For this reason if anybody tries anything impertinent with me I react very severely whatever their age or circumstances. Apparently, American films with blatant sex grittily displayed are the reason. I am not so sure; to me it is an easy excuse. India is still looking at and reflecting on the fact that huge numbers of women are poorly treated and given no respect and exploited both within their homes and certainly in the outside world. Domestic violence is a huge issue as is female child exploitation and slavery of little girls. These are ugly issues with which this huge country must come to terms and change their culture. Atrocities against women, especially under-aged girls will never end unless women themselves really want it to. Behind every flagrant violation there is always another woman in the background abetting the violation. Women's organisations and a free press and all sorts of courageous people do speak up about these issues, but the Indian Government must take drastic steps and demonstrate to all levels of their society that they will not be seen as a modern respected country whilst there is any denigration of the female sex or barbaric customs like slavery. Political lip service is contemptible and most Indians see through that as it is. Mala Sen attacked this huge ugly problem in her book Death by Fire which talks of dowry death, female infanticide and widow burning or *sati*. It was very courageous of her to tackle such a controversial subject, but as her first book, *India's Bandit Queen, the true story of Phoolan Devi*, was also controversial, one realises she has the determination and commitment to stand up and be counted amongst her own countrymen and women. There are many such women throughout India but I assure you it must take enormous strength of character, particularly if the person continues to live in India and face the male hostility around her. All the progress made by India in various spheres will fade away and become meaningless whilst slavery is condoned in any form; how can India's political leaders even think of buying luxury aircraft to swan around the world to promote a supposed democracy when there is still a traffic in flesh of under-age females.

What I find so maddening about it is that the women perpetuate this lack of respect at certain levels of society by their indulgence of their male children. Since time immemorial, indulgent Indian mothers have lavished unquestioning love and devotion on baby boys growing into little boys into teenage youth and then spoilt young men. It would be quite understandable to say 'well this is how it was' but I know it is not *dharma*, i.e., duty, respect for convention, therefore this should change. The societies and countries where women are suppressed or humiliated or prevented from achieving are the societies in which currently democracy, a respect for the truth and a realistic approach to modernisation are extinguished, presumably because the men in those cultures feel threatened. Most of those countries have not developed well and once their various revenues are exhausted will have very little with which to satisfy their countrymen. What does it say for all those men? I am bemused because, of course, we all know that Sri Lanka followed by India were countries to have two of the first female prime ministers, the others being Israel and then Great Britain. Since then, women have largely taken their rightful place in the politics of their various nations. There is one further point related to this and then I will leave it; India has so many goddesses in the Hindu pantheon, the Ganges is Mother Ganga, India is thought of as a mother land, and the deity who bestows good fortune is after all a goddess, plus of course the deity responsible for death is a goddess!

Graham and I enjoyed ourselves and my photographs have come out very well. Vakil had so much to offer us that we had to eliminate some options. However, I also recommend the Sarod Ghar which is the beautiful ancestral home of the Bagnash family which is architecturally elegant, full of sculptural detail and well maintained. The family flourishes and the museum traces the rich musical legacy for which modern Gwalior is famous. This is a Muslim heritage and can trace its origins to the fame of Tansen who was the favourite musician of the Moghul Emperor Akbar, and the formation of the first formal school of Indian music was established in the palace of Man Singh. In the nineteenth and twentieth centuries, the Scindia family continued the tradition of royal patronage of the arts and music. The Bagnash family were very talented and a new instrument was born called the *sarod*. The sarod is a wooden plucked instrument and, as one wanders round the museum, recordings of sarod music give one a sense of the wealth of Indian classical music and its complexities.

The Scindia Chhatris are a short distance away and another form of egotistical memorial to the family's wealth and importance. Somehow, these chhatris reminded one of the Medici chapel and mausoleum in Florence. Since the beginning of time mankind has sought to secure his place in history by building mausoleums and these are not different. The carvings depict the regal lifestyle of a king and the little stone elephants beautifully carved with intricate detail surround the platform presumably to symbolise the power and wealth of the maharaja, but then there are panels depicting the life of the God Krishna surrounded by his many beauties and, of course, marble life-sized effigies of the maharajah and his three wives.

If you are interested it is possible to drive to Shivpuri, which was the former summer capital of the Scindias, 114 km south west of Gwalior where there are some more royal chhatris. Apparently, it is quite atmospheric in the evening when devotional music is played. I, however, did not consider it worth a day's visit and consulted Vakil who had been scheduled to take us there. He was so glad that I had this feeling because, of course, he has to do what he is told unless the client changes the itinerary. He feels that Shivpuri is overrated and was delighted that we had other more constructive plans, though sadly he would not be part of them as those destinations were quite far away from Gwalior. It could be that Shivpuri will have an injection of life with renovation and perhaps the little local national park will be reviewed and more species translocated to it but, currently, a whole day wasted would vex the average traveller, yet lots of guide books and tour companies persist in including it. I, however, knew about Sonagiri and Datia, and these are two places of which I will speak once we have thoroughly explored Gwalior. In Britain most of the travel companies are not knowledgeable about these two significant historic sites that can be visited one after the other as they are almost adjacent to each other.

Gwalior Fort is quite simply stunning and immense. However you approach Gwalior whether it be by air, rail or road, the ancient fortress dominates the scene as it has done for the past 1500 years. Rising sharply from the flat, arid plain is a 300 foot rocky escarpment of a very strong sandstone formation, and almost growing out of the surface and hardly distinguishable from the rock itself is the Fortress of Gwalior. It must have stood for hundreds of years like a great sentinel at the crossroads of India dominating a divide between the fertile plains of the north and the scrub lands of central India. All through Rajasthan, there are similar citadels and fortresses but this is huge, one and three quarter miles long, i.e., three km long from north to south, and 600 to 2,800 feet, i.e., 200 metres to 900 metres wide, the fort encompasses six palaces, three temples and several water tanks as well as a private boys' school and a new Sikh *gurudwara.*

Driving up a steep road through the gorge of the Urwahi valley, one passes a line of rock-cut Jain statues along the way. These are huge and actually better seen from a distance. The son et lumière which takes place at night is very effective and the narrative traces the history and culture of the fort accompanied by Indian music and, in the coloured lights, the whole place is romanticised making modern Gwalior a nonentity in the dark.

The earliest historical mention of the fort is found in an inscription on a temple of the sun built on the cliff top by Matricheta in the 15th year of the Huna conqueror Mihirakila, circa 525 AD. Legend has it that Suraj Sen a Rajput chieftain from Kotwal about 25 miles, i.e., 40 km, north of Gwalior, who suffered from leprosy, was out hunting one day and became separated from his followers. Climbing

Gwalior Fort

to the summit of the cliff on which the fortress now stands to try and locate his men, he met an old man called Gwalipa, who gave the thirsty chief a drink from the tank (water hole) near his hut. To the astonishment of the chieftain he was immediately cured of his disease and in return asked the sage to name a reward. He was instructed to enlarge and beautify the tank and to build a fortress on the hill. Suraj Sen immediately fulfilled the wise man's request and called the fort Gwaliawar, i.e., a boon or gift given by Gwalia or Gwalipa the wise man. The old man apparently was so flattered that he in turn renamed Suraj Sen Surajpal prophesying that his line should rule over the region until a prince should succeed whose name did not end in 'Pal'.

Three hundred and fifty years later, Gwalior was part of the kingdom of Kanauj, then under the powerful Pratihara King Mihira Bhoja who ruled over the greater part of India in that time. There are two inscriptions on the Chaturbhuj temple dated 875 and 876 to corroborate this. Gwalior continued to be ruled by Rajput dynasties, one of which the Kachhawahas, ruled over Gwalior for nearly two centuries and brought peace with the building of temples on the fort itself and in the neighbouring countryside. In 1232, Gwalior passed from the possession of another line of Pratiharas to Muslim rulers who had besieged the fort and vanquished the Rajputs. The royal ladies committed *jauhar*, the act of self-immolation rather than fall into the hands of Iltutmish's advancing army. To put it in context, Muhammad Ghuri had invaded India successfully but was assassinated in 1206, and though his kingdom did not survive in Afghanistan, his Indian provinces and the forts and palaces like that at Gwalior remained more or less intact in the hands of his Turkish general Qutb-ud-din Aibak. This ex-slave, who founded the Delhi Sultanate or The Slave Dynasty, was the first major Muslim ruler of the subcontinent. Gwalior remained in the possession of the Muslim rulers of Delhi from 1232 to 1398 but, during the confusion which followed yet another invasion of India by Timur (Tamerlane), the Tughluq dynasty came to an end and Gwalior reverted to Rajput rule.

Stone Statue outside Gwalior Fort

Rajput rule flourished throughout the fifteenth and some of the sixteenth centuries. It was during this time that most of the rock-cut Jain sculptures on the path leading up to the plateau were carved. The Tomar ruler Raja Man Sing who lived from 1486 to 1516 is especially remembered for his love of music and architecture. Shortly after Man Singh's death the fort was vanquished by Ibrahim Lodi and then it passed to the Moghuls when they succeeded the Lodi dynasty in Delhi. Under the Moghuls, it was regularly used as a prison and one of its prisoners was the younger brother of the Emperor Aurangzeb who had this particular brother killed by slow poisoning; he took sibling rivalry to new heights if one considered he killed his eldest brother and presented his head on a platter to his father Shah Jahan, whom he had imprisoned in the Red Fort at Agra.

In the mid eighteenth century the Marathas conquered the fort and the stronghold passed from victor to victor and the connection with the Scindia family starts from 1777. Rather surprisingly the British captured the fort in 1780 but handed it back to Chhatrapati Singh of Gohad. The Scindias retook the fort in 1783 only to have the British bombard and capture the fort again in 1804; however, it was restored to the Scindia family in 1805.

The Man Singh palace known as the Man Mandir is the finest of the six palaces and considered a remarkable and interesting example of a Hindu palace of an early age. The vast eastern front which measures approximately 100 metres in length and about 30 metres in height is relieved at regular intervals by six round towers crowned with domed cupolas. The southern face of Man Singh's palace is about 50 metres long and 20 metres high with three graceful towers. The entire palace wall is inlaid with enamelled tiles of blue, green and yellow, forming bands of mosaic, and depicts figures of men, ducks, elephants, tigers and plantain trees. On such a massive structure, it just gives a touch of delicacy and attention to detail. The main building is two storeys high, but there are three underground floors of apartments in the eastern section. It was here, in these gloomy, though amazingly well ventilated dungeons, which to my unease were full of squeaking bats, that the various prisoners were kept chained to massive pillars. Aurangzeb's brother Murad met a slow death by poppy poisoning, which saps the vitality and finally drives the victim mad.

I felt rather claustrophobic, partly, I suspect, because of the lingering chest infection, but I urged Graham and Vakil to take as long as they liked and I went and sat on a rampart and looked at all that was going on around me. A young boy approached me in a nice manner and we began a conversation, partly in Hindi and partly in English. Pawan was a delight, eager but not pushy. He is fatherless and he sells postcards at the fort in the afternoon to help the family but attends school in the mornings. We bought some of his postcards just to help; he would not have just accepted the money alone. Vakil obviously has a soft spot for him and talked of him with affection. It is when one meets young folk like that one yearns to help in a more substantial way; well we do through recognised charities sponsor children, grandparents and whole families, but an encounter like that touches the heart and the impulsive response is to give, but then where does one stop? Graham and I do not have infinite resources like most of us.

The palace next in order of merit is the Gujari Mahal standing at the foot of the fort rock, but within the lower fortifications. After entering the Badal Mahal gate, turn to the right and pass through two more gates and one comes face to face with Gujari Mahal. This was built by Raja Man Singh for his favourite queen, Mriganayana, a Gujari by caste. The legend goes that Man Singh was out hunting one day some miles from Gwalior when he encountered the beautiful, but low-born, Mriganayana and asked her to marry him. She would only consent on condition that he brought the waters that flowed by her beloved village to the palace he wished her to occupy. Nothing daunted, Man Singh built an underground channel which conveyed the stream, famous for its purity and curative properties, to the Gujari Mahal, which takes its name from Mriganayana's caste.

The Gujari Mahal is now the Museum. It has a plain exterior and is relieved by domed turrets. The configuration of the rooms is ideal because there are double-storey galleries that open into a courtyard which must have been life-saving in the intense heat of summer. It is well worth a visit because of all the antiquities housed in it and on the roof. The other two Hindu palaces and the two Muslim palaces are of little interest. There are numerous old temples on the fort but the major ones are the Gwalipa, Chaturbhuj, Larger and Smaller Sas Bahu, Mata Devi, the Jain temple and the Teli-ka Mandir.

The Sas Bahu Temples occupy a prominent position on the eastern face of the hill. Sas Bahu means mother in law and daughter in law, and is a popular name given to two similar objects such as temples, wells, etc., standing side by side. These are Hindu temples, not Jain as was widely thought. The larger one is dedicated to Vishnu. The doorway leading into the shrine is elaborately carved. Overhead, are the three principal Gods of the Hindu trimurthi, Brahma, the creator, at the left, Vishnu, the preserver, in the middle and Siva, the destroyer, on the right. Vishnu occupies the central position being the deity to whom the temple was dedicated. The smaller temple is also a shrine to Vishnu and, though quite small, is a very good example of the ornate style of temple architecture of the mediaeval age.

The Teli Ka Mandir or Oilman's Temple is situated a few metres to the west of the Gangola Tal, a water tank. It is the highest of all the buildings on the fort being over 35 metres in height. This is a nineth century Vishnu temple and it is peculiar in that the plan and design of its Sikhara (spire) is Dravidian which is commonly found in southern India. The rest of its intricate details are in Indo-Aryan style and the combination is odd.

Vakil told us of the British cemetery that forms the last resting place for British soldiers, who occupied the fort from 1858 to 1883. He knew of another cemetery, however, in which one of my Rose kinsman is buried, but this is down on the edge of the military cantonment and we went on to visit it. It was after the battle of Maharajpur in 1844 that the fort was garrisoned by British troops. It was handed over to Maharaja Jayaji Rao, when he came of age in 1853; and he held it till the rising of 1857 when it fell into the hands of the Sepoy forces. General Sir Hugh Rose vanquished the rebel army and took the surrender but this is the story not only of the Indian Mutiny or as I prefer to think of it The First War of Independence, but of a great heroine of India – the Rani of Jhansi.

Rani Lakshmi Bhai, is better known as the Rani or Queen of Jhansi. She was born into a Brahmin family and married Raja Gangadhar of Jhansi, but never bore him children. In 1853, the British tried to force her into retirement when widowed, along with her adopted baby son. The Rani retaliated in 1857 by personally leading her bodyguard of five hundred warriors to seize Jhansi Fort from the British. Jhansi is quite close in modern terms to Gwalior and we were to visit it in two days time. The British took 17 days to breach the walls of Jhansi Fort and it was a battle in which 5,000 were killed. The courageous Rani strapped her baby son to her back and somehow managed to escape from the vanquished fort and join the main rebel army at Gwalior, where she subsequently rode to her death dressed as a man wielding her sword in both hands and holding the reins of her horse in her mouth. With more than one Rose ancestor who played a part in the history of Gwalior, I naturally have a special interest in the area. The Rani of Jhansi is to India what Joan of Arc is to France and one will see splendid statues in many places in Northern India, but especially in Gwalior and Jhansi. I would strongly recommend John Master's book, *Night Runners of Bengal*, to explore this story fully.

Vakil remembered the way to the old Christian cemetery, which is not a normal tourist destination. There, in a sort of sombre isolation, were several tombs to fallen colonials, both civilian and military. We found the Rose tomb and pondered on the waste of his young life, but that is what we are still doing with current conflicts. The sun was setting and this romanticised a melancholy place that was overrun with straggly bushes and weeds, and was obviously used as a latrine by modern people who are oblivious to another religion's sanctified ground. I resolved to try and encourage someone in the military authorities to achieve a clean up and regular maintenance of the walled cemetery; curiously there are some modern graves and plinths and we wondered if they are in fact Christian, it was not obvious just by looking at them. At the end of a long day that started at 0400 hours, we were glad to return to the Usha Kiran Palace hotel. We bid Vakil good night and said we looked forward to the next day.

Usha Kiran Palace Hotel – Gwalior

At the hotel, it was so pleasant to sink down into our own lounge chairs in the suite and order a drink and then contemplate a good meal. Out in the hotel gardens, there were huge preparations for a forthcoming wedding. November onwards is the wedding season in India and pleasant gardens are usually the venue for these lengthy and huge rituals. I know western weddings have become a sort of social nightmare with huge economic burdens, but India takes the whole wedding business into a different stratosphere. The one being planned for this venue was no different, and in fact it looked as if some taste and discernment had been put into the outdoor stage set and scenery that was being shifted into place, along with all the hundreds of little lights that help to give these marriage gardens a sort of fairy tale atmosphere.

The next morning, after a leisurely start, Vakil took us to the Tomb of Ghaus Mohammed, an Afghan prince who helped Babur take Gwalior Fort. It is a fine example of early Moghul architecture but we were appalled at the dismal way in which we had to approach this pleasant monument. Truly, Gwalior will have to re-examine itself and make strenuous efforts to enhance its ancient buildings. At the moment, this charming building stands in a rather boring bit of bald lawn with a few flowering shrubs. The narrow lane in which to approach by car

The Tomb of Ghaus Mohammed

was full of the usual Indian squalor; it beggars belief that the Madhya Pradesh

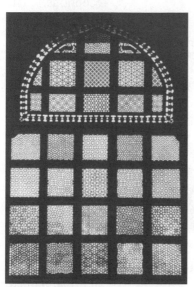

Exquisite stone carving at the Tomb of Ghaus Mohammed

Government and the local equivalent of a town council can leave everything in this mess, particularly as the garden also has a smaller, but immensely important, mausoleum, that of Tansen the famous musician who was the Emperor Akbar's favourite. Annually, performers and music lovers from all over India flock here for Gwalior's music festival in November and, to western eyes and thinking, this would be reason enough to ensure that the whole area was kept immaculately and served as a complement to the two elegant buildings. What adds insult to injury in my view is that, from what we were told and shown, Gwalior is a prosperous city, the comparison would be that of a place like York or Chester or Stirling not taking a pride in its history and appearance.

Vakil then took us to a shop that was especially opened for us. This happens often with guides and if they are not pushy about it we never mind. We are aware that they supplement their incomes with the percentage that the shopkeepers give them if a sale takes place. It was quite interesting and I bought an inexpensive *salwar chemise* which means a tunic and pants. It was to prove quite useful actually in the days ahead and I find that sort of costume very comfortable yet elegant.

After a sleepy afternoon, we piled back into the car and visited the Moti Mahal or Pearl Palace. Vakil was required to bribe some lowly government employee to enable us to go in. This is not even mentioned in the guide books. The Moti Mahal is now a local government office which just made my blood boil. In its day, it would have been elegant and attractive, perhaps a small palace for a royal lady – maybe a dowager, now it is nearly a wreck, nearly, but not quite. The government offices are dirty and dusty and to visit the rooms that Vakil wanted us to see we had to climb outside stairs and traverse a couple of flat roofs. They were covered in human excrement. I just could not believe it, yet we entered these two rooms and found something so worthwhile. They are totally painted in wonderful intricate murals and have panels and high-coloured glass ceilings that with the correct lighting would make them twinkle like jewels. My photographs have proved successful. I quite understand that the majority of the palace may be of no value and therefore suitable for administration, but the two rooms should be beautifully maintained and open for visitors, or hired out for

receptions. The Moti Mahal has a pleasant aspect on to an artificial lake, which was originally ornamental and has a ramp down to it by which elephants used to be taken to bathe. It would be such a lovely tourist attraction if the whole area was cleaned and maintained,

The Moti Mahal Palace – Gwalior. The Palace is now in decrepitude but has glorious inner rooms

the tank repaired and filled with clean water and lotus plants and a couple of elephants taken for their daily bath every afternoon. Instead, I tried to imagine

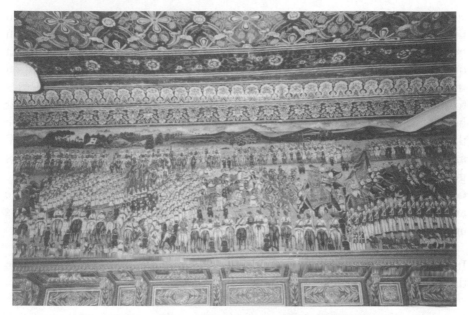

**Exquisite ceiling paintings in the Moti Mahal,
now a government office**

it in its glorious past with perhaps the maharajah's elephants being taken there for their daily dip by eager and protective mahawats. Vakil could see how angry we were with all the dilapidation and he said now we should understand his frustration at trying to do a good job as a guide.

As I write in October 2003, I am reading a big article in The Times under World News. 'India's maharajahs demand their palaces back'. How glad I am to read it. Having seen in Rajasthan where the various royal families have been able to maintain their strongholds and preserve them, I know that this could be crucial for India's tourism. In a move dubbed the 'Revenge of the rajahs' the royal families are going to court to demand the return of their forts and palaces on the ground that the Government has failed in its promise to preserve them.

The dispute over the royal properties dates back to 1947, when the princely states of Rajasthan, ruled by the royal houses under the British, were incorporated into an independent India. In the years that followed, the royal houses handed over or had taken from them, dozens of forts, palaces and other properties for government use. Others had to be handed over by maharajahs unable to look after them after the abolition of the civil list in the 1970s by the socialist-leaning Government of Indira Gandhi, which also took away their titles. Indira Gandhi seemed to hate the aristocracy of India and appeared to take a real vengeful pleasure in humiliating them.

Each family's case is slightly different. The one thing that they are all agreed upon is that the government has failed to look after the properties, indeed, in many cases, has misused them and, that as the royal families, they are best qualified to save them from ruin. Long before the government embarked on its recent privatisation campaign and started leasing former royal properties to the private sector, Rajasthan's thoroughly modern royals had shown their business sense by going into partnership with hotel and tourist groups to save their forts and palaces from decay. Interestingly, one of the most respected and distinguished royals, Maharajah Gaj Sing of Jodhpur says 'The country is going through a change … we are shedding the mantle of bogus socialism. The Government cannot look after these properties and they must recognise that we are now in a position to do so, perhaps in a way that was not possible 50 years ago.'

In Gwalior, some of this decay and government negligence is graphically on display. I am hoping that, with India now set to become an economic giant, that some of that wealth will be responsibly used in saving its architectural heritage. It is interesting to note that Russia is also doing the same thing after years of neglect. As I said at the beginning, the fact that Atal Behari Vajpayee actually originates from Gwalior and is a poet one would think would encourage him to subsidise the state government of Madhya Pradesh and require them to renovate and maintain the jewels in their tourist crown. Indeed, perhaps that is the reason for Gwalior being designated as a developing city. I do hope so.

CHAPTER SEVEN

Glorious Khajuraho and
Orchha, via Sonagiri and Datia

W e left Gwalior the following morning aboard the Shatabdhi Express for Jhansi. It was an efficient way to get there, but as I realised from looking out of the train window we would have to go back on our tracks by road to see both Sonagiri and Datia. Whilst I am, as it were, travelling through my memory it might be beneficial to point out that Gwalior makes a very good jumping off point for Khajuraho and the nearby wildlife park of Panna.

The easiest way to get to Khajuraho is on one of the daily flights from Delhi, via Agra, as indeed we had done five years previously, or from Varanasi. The Delhi Agra, Khajuraho Varanasi air route is usually very efficient, however, having said that, five years ago we had an unusual but slightly amusing experience, all of which I have chronicled in my first book, *India: The Peacock's Call*. Khajuraho is a small place and I think a jewel. It is hugely popular for honeymoons, weekends away and a gentle 'relax and recreation'. It is also easily reached from Jhansi to Satna by rail and, for that matter, by car from Gwalior. There is a hotel in Khajuraho to suit everyone, from five star properties to humble hostels. We had stayed in the Jass Oberoi, which I think now belongs to the Trident Group. It was excellent and so are the other five star establishments.

Khajuraho abounds in wonderful Hindu temples, immaculately restored after almost a thousand years of neglect. Indeed, some of the excavations continue with possibly the biggest yet to be unearthed being discovered in 1998–99 in the area of the Southern Group. If I have been ranting on about Gwalior's decay and neglect, then let me cheer you up by saying Khajuraho is an absolute must for a first time itinerary. The temples were built between the tenth and twelfth centuries AD and are justly famed for their sculpture – the delicate intricate detail depicts such sensuality and forthright eroticism. When I was growing up in the 1950s in India, Khajuraho was not yet a tourist destination and it is a source of puzzlement that these great architectural achievements of the Chandella Dynasty should have been abandoned and ignored until discovered by the British. Although, now, Khajuraho is easily accessed as I have explained, presumably the fact that it is 400 km southeast of Agra and the same distance from Varanasi (Benares) saved it from marauding armies and invaders and Muslim zealots who deliberately vandalised so many Hindu sites. Graham and I loved our one-night stay and would have liked to spend a couple more days just unwinding. When we visited, there was still a peaceful small-town atmosphere, which sadly might change but I hope not. Tourist 'tat' spoils anywhere be it Europe or Asia and I hope Khajuraho is not eventually subsumed by trinket shops. I should mention that it is a World Heritage Site which should ensure it keeps its beauty.

Very close to Khajuraho is the Panna Tiger Reserve. This too is a lovely peaceful wild destination and I am delighted to hear the good news that tiger numbers have increased at the Reserve from two to three per 100 sq. km to seven to eight in the same area. Panna is a most beautiful park with stunning water falls and a lake and is known as the emerald forest. It was made into a tiger reserve in 1994. This welcome rise in tiger numbers results from the implementation of new management techniques, in particular the use of radio-collars which has allowed close monitoring of the population. Dr Raghunandan Singh Chundawat, head of the tiger project at Panna says 'This close monitoring has allowed the radio-collared tigers to breed and increases the chances of cubs surviving to adulthood'. International fundraising and lobbying have been crucial, demonstrating how the integrated groups can lead to success in the face of political apathy and lack of institutional reform. The lake and waterfalls at Panna are especially lovely and I would encourage anyone who does not have a lot of time to spend to think of adding Panna to their itinerary because of its practical proximity to Khajuraho, which in no way diminishes its importance or enjoyment. To reach the other well known wildlife parks can take whole days of travelling, whereas at Panna it is close to an airport.

As our train approached its destination, Jhansi, I thought of all I had read about the off-the-beaten-track area of Bundelkhand. This area is defined by the Vindhya Hills and belonged to the Chandella Rajputs who built Khajuraho as I have already mentioned, but it abounds in historic relics: the Vishnu pilgrimage centre of Chitrakut, the massive astrologically aligned deserted fortress of Kalinjar, and its hills and valleys which even now are quite lawless and populated by bands of *dacoits*, dangerous outlaws and brigands who become the stuff of legend. Mala Sen's true story of Phoolan Devi brings it all vividly to life. This area was known as *bhagi* or rebel territory. Later on, in another chapter, I will talk of the Thugs and *thuggee* because it is also relevant to the area of Jabalpur where we plan to stay one night. As the train approached Jhansi, I could not help thinking that the famous Rani has been the female rebel of the nineteenth century and hugely respected and admired, but in the last few years of the twentieth century Phoolan Devi had reached another sort of fame or notoriety. She was not a Brahmin's daughter but low-caste Sudra and a peasant, yet she had challenged the Government's forces and had made them agree to her terms of surrender; having served a jail term in Gwalior, she then had gone on to become an MP for several years before her murder in July 2001. Her murderers have not yet been brought to justice, nor will that be the full story if it ever reaches the courts. This was perhaps India's female Robin Hood? In no way am I trying to trivialise this woman and her awful harsh childhood; she was born to poor but good parents, but life in desperate poverty trying to eke out a living has its own challenges and being married off to a cruel man when still a child herself, then being kidnapped and repeatedly raped by a gang of bandits fashioned her into a fearless bandit leader herself.

I know that the India I know and love as the Land of my birth is the same ancient but callous country in which huge inequalities and cruelty exists and that we in the West have not experienced this sort of barbarism, or certainly not since mediaeval times. There is something odd and timeless about visiting areas for their historic importance, but being brought to a standstill by the fact that there are people living in these areas in the shadow of buildings that go back at least six hundred years, but those living might as well be stuck in that time warp. Banditry, rape, murder, humiliation of females, bonded labour, extreme poverty, poor infrastructure with a population of a billion sits oddly with information technology, advanced medicine, gleaming hotels, bejewelled women and burgeoning wealth and sophistication. Sometimes I find it really hard to accept the dichotomy of this great land; I understand the reasons but I so want it to change for the poor and disadvantaged.

We arrived at Jhansi, which is 18 km away from Orchha which in its day had been the Bundela capital and remained important till 1742. Now, it is a deserted jungle ghost town and I was looking forward to our visit and spending one night. We were met by a car and driver. Gautham was very nice and a pleasure to be with and the air conditioned jeep was to prove excellent. We immediately set off for Sonagiri, which is 61 km southeast of Gwalior and we had seen some of its charming landmarks from the train. The road was reasonable and we made good time, just stopping for a pit stop and a bottled cool drink along the way. Sonagiri has 84 gleaming white shrines marking the spot where the legendary King Nanganang Kumar together with half a million of his followers achieved liberation from the cycle of rebirth. This is a site sacred to *Digambara* Jains which means clothed by the sky, i.e., naked! It is

Sonagiri's pure white Jain temples

apparently very popular as a special place of interest to visiting dignitaries like Bill Clinton and European presidents who are brought by helicopter. One drives into the village square and parks under a huge tree. There is a seminary where old Digambara monks talk and discuss religion with pilgrims. Nowadays, they appear to have clothed themselves. A young man offered to be our guide and we accepted, but I did not like him that much and he kept trying to talk in both French and English and making odd remarks – this was probably the first guide we had disliked. One has to take off one's shoes and walk the path barefoot. This is not a problem, being a Jain holy area everything is very clean and fresh and was a delight. My photographs have worked very well and Graham and I really enjoyed the walk up to the top temple which also gave us a splendid view of the surrounding countryside and, as the temperature was very pleasant and the sun shining, it was thoroughly enjoyable. When we returned to the base of the hillside, the guide tried to make us pay him a quite disproportionate sum, but we were very firm and in the end he grumbled rudely and walked away, He might have assisted Bill Clinton and Chancellor Kohl in their time but I really did not require his services but would have enjoyed his company if he had been like Vakil – as it was he was a nuisance!

On the return journey, we stopped at Datia. The majestic multi-storeyed palace at Datia was constructed at the height of the Bundela Dynasty's 'golden age'. It is considered to be one of the finest Rajput buildings in India. The Raj Bir Singh Deo Palace stands in the north of this little town which comprises narrow streets and has little attraction. This uninhabited but reasonably preserved palace is five storeys high and decorated with paintings and stone carving. The construction is clever because, though very gloomy at its entrance floor, it gradually becomes airy and light as one rises, but the construction has been thought out to provide maximum air and coolness in baking summer heat. When one reaches the top among its domes and cupolas there is a splendid view over the tank with its dhobi ghat and memorial chhatris. Sonagiri is visible in the distance. There is also a fort, the Bharat Garh and the home of the current

The Datia Palace has clever architectural features to ensure coolness

ruling family but we did not venture into either of these. Gautham drove us back to Jhansi and on to Orchha, where we arrived in the long shadows of the evening sunshine. It could not have been more beautiful.

Orchha mean 'hidden place' and it certainly lives up to that name. This deserted mediaeval town is in the middle of a jungle or forest on the banks of the Betwa River. Here lie ruined crumbling palaces, cenotaphs, temples, havelis which are being enveloped by the jungle. It gives one that odd feeling again, that here was a flourishing palace town, rather like Fatehpur Sikri, that must have been grand and important and now, man made structures are crumbling whilst all the while the jungle continues to grow around it.

Orchha graceful in its jungle decay

The Bundelas decided on this remote site because it is strategically placed on a curve of the Betwa River and presumed safe from the marauding of the Tuqluq dynasty that ruled in Delhi in the late fifteenth century. Raja Rudra Pratap started the fortifications and palaces and temples but he was killed in 1531 trying to wrestle a cow from the jaws of a tiger. After that untimely death, the dynasty had to rely on the Moghul rulers' tolerance but the most famous rajah, Bir Sing Deo, was an ambitious young man who managed to keep on the right side of the Moghuls, and indeed he ingratiated himself with the young man who was to become the Emperor Jahangir by sending him the head of one of his enemies on a platter. He was rewarded for his brutality by Jahangir who helped him to depose his elder brother Ram Shah. Bir Singh Deo ruled for 22 years and in that time erected 52 forts and palaces across the region including the fortress at Jhansi, the palace at Datia (of which I have written) and many of Orchha's finest palaces. He was killed in 1627 by bandits while returning from the Deccan with a camel train of booty.

You may now appreciate why I took the time to describe dacoits and bandits in such detail, they were there then and they are there now! Curiously, my own grandmother Aline Rose, as a very young woman, wrote a book called Bengal Dacoits and Tigers in co-operation with the daughter of the Maharajah of Baroda about a hundred years ago! We still have one white-ant eaten copy of this delightful book, for which Grandmother Aline painted the pictures. That young princess went on to become the Maharani of Cooch Behar and mother to the present Rajmata of Jaipur, Ayesha Jaipur. I never, sadly, knew my grandmother, but I like to think she would want me to write about India, and I do remember Ma Cooch Behar as she was universally known.

Driving through the living village of Orchha to approach the abandoned mediaeval area we were enchanted by the freshly painted village houses and shops. Everything here looked really attractive with much use of the bright blue and turquoise one sees so much of in Greece against the clean fresh white house walls. Graham and I were eager to arrive and explore.

Our destination was The Sheesh Mahal Palace which is owned by Madhya Pradesh Tourism Development Corporation. This was a case of the Sublime being followed by the Ridiculous, and then closely again by the Sublime! Sheesh Mahal is still being recommended by travel agents as the place to stay. Well, let me assure you that if you want an eccentric experience it is just fine, but not otherwise. The building was, in its heyday, the local rajah's country retreat and we had been assigned one of the two royal suites. The guide books still talk of it with enthusiasm when in fact they are wrong – this has passed its good days but, were its management to be given a hefty kick in the proverbial and supervised more closely, it could re-emerge as a good quiet little rest house. Currently, however, it is a crumbling old palace with shabby grubby steps, colonnaded dining/lounge area and lazy staff. Heritage eccentric would be my term for it! We found ourselves in a huge bedroom with sitting area, old-fashioned heavy furniture in a gloomy room 10 metres long by about 5 metres wide with a barrel vaulted high ceiling. Off this a marble passage led to an octagonal bathroom with its original fittings, a huge marble bath that was like a large sarcophagus with oblong flat base and one metre high sides. It would make an excellent lily pool. There was a basin set in ancient marble and then one went up a few steps to a w.c. – the ultimate 'loo with a view' set in its own added-on wooden structure. We hastily assured ourselves that it was positioned on sturdy steel girders. The best view from the suite was from the window behind the w.c. and to the right – the drop was easily 40 metres down!

Graham and I lay down and laughed – it was all so decayed yet atmospheric. The fan was hideous, incorporating four electric lights which mercifully one could turn off whilst still using the fan. Showering was just possible with an electric water heater that made all the difference. Refreshed we went out to have supper just outside our room. Ten years ago, this might have been attractive but now the shabby decay and lack of supervision made it a boring experience. The food, however, was fine and we stuck to vegetarian dishes. The waiter had to lurch up the steps from the kitchen and by the time it arrived it was cool. Still, we had not had lunch so we finished it all. Television was available but we decided on an early night. In the middle of the night we both woke with a start, the electricity had obviously gone off and when it restarted the fan made a noise like tin cans being swung around, but then settled down to a peaceful whirr!

Next morning we had some very welcome 'bed tea' and then a safe breakfast of tomato omelettes and more tea, and then set off to explore. A lot of renovation has been done and is still continuing but somehow their 'good ideas' become ineffectual in that they do not blend in, for example, huge electric street lamps that have been vandalised and are stark rusting structures. No-one would walk on these paths in the dark anyway. The paths are constructed, but rubble left on the side with gates off their hinges. Some of the renovation is very coarse and does not do justice to the fine architecture. There is no supervision or quality control. This is modern India's besetting sin. In the wide open spaces, again one saw human excrement in dollops and this is where tourists would walk, gazing upwards!

Please do not get me wrong, Orchha is a wonder but this should be sympathetically and carefully conserved, with proper attention to detail. Khajuraho proves that it can be achieved, but I have formed the impression that Madhya Pradesh has tried to climb on a tourist bandwagon but has allowed bureaucratic ineptitude, corruption and lethargy to drain its valuable tourist resources. What I saw made me ashamed of India and I passionately want to see it rated as a top tourist destination that will bring it prosperity with the resulting trickle down effect for all. However, the moment one steps outside private enterprise there appears to be no ethos or commitment.

The vultures wheeled high in the sky and then came and perched on the tips of the domes of the Jahangir Mahal. This is Orchha's most important building which again was built by Bir Singh Deo as a magnificent present for the Moghul emperor when he paid a state visit in the seventeenth century. These are a stunning set of ruins about four centuries old and everywhere one looks there is an ancient mausoleum or chhatri or temple with the trees and vines around. We chatted to other travellers who had come from Korea, USA, and France; they had all reached Orchha by different travel routes. Once Gautham arrived with the jeep we settled our bill and started off much to his surprise. He took us through the village to the old Lakshmi temple on a hill. This is a delight and the *chowkidar* or watchman chatted to us whilst showing us round. There are beautiful wall paintings in vegetable dyes, powdered marble plastering with depictions of the Ramayana, the Bhagavad Geeta and historical events of the nineteenth century, such as the siege of Gwalior. The detail is beautiful and charming and thankfully my photographs have proved successful. The temple had been robbed and vandalised years ago and the Lakshmi statue injured, thus the temple had to be abandoned and a new one built. The watchman was so nice and easy to talk with and glad that we appreciated his architectural gem.

**The saga of war and diplomacy at an abandoned
temple in Orchha**

On the way back from the temple, Gautham pointed out the Animal Clinic unaware that Graham is a vet. I explained to Gautham in Hindi and we asked to stop and pay a visit. The clinic consisted of a square piece of land of about one acre surrounded by a one and half metre stone wall which contained a double entrance gate, one half of which had been demolished, possibly by an enraged buffalo, but more likely by a careless tractor driver. In the middle of the property was the clinic itself consisting of two small rooms, one a dispensary. A cattle crush, a tree and several obligatory chairs completed the scene. There was one young vet plus his assistant, three others and one woman. The clinic is funded by the state. All the services were free for all species including dogs and pigs, although the latter were never presented for treatment. We were both made very welcome, but Graham could not help noticing that the vet did not actually seem to do anything physical – just instructed the others. Not for him the dubious delights of a country vet with his arm up to the shoulder feeling around from the back end of a cow. In our early married life, I well remember the appalling soiled clothes in which Graham would come home, but somehow it was not bad as cows are herbivores and the muck could be washed out very easily with lots of detergent. In India however, as ever, it would seem that '*Ao laago*' as I call it flourishes, that means roughly 'Come – do....!'

I enjoyed taking photographs in Orchha village and the charming colours have come out well. Gautham seemed surprised that we did not want to endlessly explore, but you see we had done a lot on foot before he arrived and we did not feel the need to go and inspect every nook and cranny. I just soaked up the ambience of this deserted place with its Chaturbhuj Temple, Unt Khana, Raja Mahal, Rai Praveen Mahal and Jahangir Mahal and Museum plus of course the Lakshmi Temple. It had rained gently in the morning and now cleared to warm sunshine. Sometimes, it is just good to stop and look around in silence.

Gautham at our request drove us to The Orchha Resort and, once there, we decided to go in and investigate. Now we had again arrived at the Sublime! How we had wished we had stayed here the previous night, as there was very little difference in the tariff! This hotel is a charming, well-maintained low-built complex of rooms opening onto an attractive swimming pool in the shape of a lotus flower with a central fountain. The terraces and gardens are elegant and the whole complex is sited on the banks of the river Betwa, with a sturdy wall providing a boundary over which one can view the river. Sitting later in the gentle warmth of the setting sun, which was slowly descending behind the huge memorial chhatris behind the hotel, the serene sound of water splashing from the pool fountain in front of me will be an abiding memory. The Betwa River itself is beautiful and clean and I loved looking out over it resting my arms on the wall. I was writing up my observations in diary form while Graham had a refreshing swim. The management of this hotel is excellent and pays enormous attention to detail. We took a room for the afternoon and were enchanted by the fittings that are all in marble with inlay, like the Taj Mahal. The cleanliness, vibrancy and elegance made this a very good place to stay with the addition of delicious food.

As well as the conventional rooms with well-appointed bathrooms, there is also a tented accommodation complex that is also attractive and presumably a bit cheaper. For us, this was a welcome find because we were not due to leave till the evening train from Jhansi, and, if one is hanging about in decayed surroundings, it can be a vexing experience. Gautham came back to collect us for an 18.30 departure to get us to Jhansi for the 19.25 train to Umeria, due to arrive there at 06.15 the next morning.

I have the most recent editions of two of the most famous guides to India and I am a little disappointed in that they still continue to include details about the charms of the Sheesh Mahal Palace and seem to be dismissive of The Orchha Resort. They should update their research, this was also evident by the fact that in a reference to the Bandit Queen they appear to be unaware that she had been murdered. Editions printed in 2001 and 2002 should not lack this sort of detail otherwise they become slightly unreliable. I have also come to appreciate that guide writers have an exaggerated sense of what can be enjoyable, rather like young Naveen saying hopefully 'This can also be fun?' Graham and I usually look at the cup as half full, but I suspect we fall into the large category of well-travelled middle-aged people who no longer want to experience 'eccentric' in the ablutions department, or see the waiter lurching along outside with the food being brought to us uncovered, where a passing bird or fly might render it unwise to eat!

Jhansi, similarly, on The Lonely Planet website had been described as 'a hole', but this was not our experience. The railway station is quite impressive architecturally and reasonably maintained. There is a big army cantonment and the civilian community is made up of half and half Christian and Muslim. Being an important railway junction, there is the evidence of the colonial era with good wide roads, fine old bungalows and Raj-type architecture, plus of course Jhansi Fort itself. This is interesting but in no way does it compare with Gwalior. The Rani Lakshmi Mahal, however, was the palace of the Rani of Jhansi, a sort of dower house, and is now a museum warehouse, but still charming and interesting. It is worth noting that it was the scene of an awful massacre by British troops in 1858 when they bayoneted all the occupants. So much is repeated of what the rebels had perpetrated on the British civilian population; it should be remembered that *in extremis* our soldiers behaved very badly too. Two wrongs do not make a right. Innocents inevitably pay a terrible price, as we have seen recently in Iraq, in Viet Nam and other war zones but, even when I was growing up in India, there was a foolish defensive attitude about the wrongs that British and European people perpetrated. Lord Attenborough showed this so delicately in his wonderful ageless film of Gandhi, which I watched again very recently.

As we stood waiting for the train, the platform was covered in sitting and sleeping bodies, some of whom answered a call of nature on the railway line. There was an unwholesome fragrance wafting up which was rather stronger than that from Venetian canals on a hot day! We boarded the air-conditioned second class sleeper without any problems. On this train, there was no alternative of first class. The porter and travel agent helped us settle in and as soon as the train was on its way the bedding was brought in and Graham and I settled ourselves down to relax and sleep. We could have read but it had been an eventful day and quite honestly the movement of the train was very soporific. Graham climbed onto the top bunk and I fervently hoped that no-one else would join us at the one stop en route to our destination. They did, however, and that amusing event I will describe in a following chapter. I had taken the precaution of arming myself with a little torch for any visits to the loo, and we took very good care of our luggage and placed it right under my bunk so that anyone trying to divest us of our belongings would probably wake me.

CHAPTER EIGHT

Earth's Proud Empires

A s I relaxed and tried to sleep, the day's events revolved in my visual memory and I knew that at some point I had thought of something which I wanted to explore mentally.

It came to me, that here in Hindu heartland where there is still a vibrant Christian community living alongside a Muslim community, plus of course the Jains, the Sikhs and the Buddhists, there is a microcosm of India, land of religious pluralism. Jhansi, as I said, is an important railway town and Indian Railways employ the largest workforce in the world, many of whom through their cross culture of being Anglo Indian are Christian. The railway community also was the home of great numbers of the Armenian community, and in my childhood I had been at school with quite a few children who belonged to the Armenian Christian Faith as well as the others mentioned. That is India's great wealth – its diverse people of many faiths.

Now, once again, we are reading about the tensions in Ayodhya, we recall only too well how impulsive action by some Muslims led to a massacre on the train bringing Hindu pilgrims back from Ayodhya and this, in turn, led to wholesale slaughter of Muslims, with huge political implications for the state of Gujarat. As if that is not enough, forces of evil, working in the name of Islam, plot and sometimes succeed in bombing innocent people such as happened in Mumbai in August 2003 and in the Indian Parliament in 2001.

Lying on my bunk in the dark with the lurching of the train and the continuous clicking sound of the wheels on the track I thought of all the train journeys I had done in India since I was a toddler. The excitement, anticipation and sheer enjoyment of it all when I was young and the family had a complete carriage to itself. I was but a babe when at Partition angry mobs from both religions, Hindu and Muslim, killed with hate and lust and set trains on fire. My parents, however, recounted it all to me and showed me sombre places where atrocities had taken place; moreover, they knew people who had lost sons to this terror. Please, India, do not be deflected from your destiny. You are to the world a beacon of democracy and religious pluralism and tolerance; do not allow politicians to encourage, for the sake of expediency, any other path.

The words of my favourite evening hymn came into my mind:

The day thou gavest, Lord, is ended;
The darkness falls at thy behest;
To thee our morning hymns ascended;
Thy praise shall sanctify our rest.

So be it, Lord, thy throne shall never,
Like earth's proud empires pass away.
Thy kingdom stands and grows for ever,
Till all thy creatures own thy sway.

There is something very comforting about those words but, in fact, they could be a hymn from any religion or all of them. I like the idea of the latter though and proudly sing them as a Christian myself.

Which leads me on to the subject of another proud empire passing away – to use a figure of speech. All over India, there are the architectural relics of lost empires but Madhya Pradesh has two of great note. One is Orchha and the other is Mandu.

Mandu is situated at the edge of the Vindhya Range and overlooks the Narmada River. Once known as Shadiabad 'The Citadel of Joy' it was the pleasure resort and capital of the rulers of Malwa for nearly a thousand years. We were not visiting Mandu on this occasion simply because there was not enough time but, let me assure you, it is beautiful, particularly in the monsoon or soon after. All the vegetation springs to life after the parched summer heat and, like Orchha, it becomes a haven of green with great ghostly buildings.

For practicality, one is best to fly into Indore from either Delhi or Mumbai and then go by car for the last 98 km of the journey. Indore is a dull city but prosperous, a sort of Indian Detroit with cars, scooters, tractors and other machinery being manufactured locally. It is situated on the confluence of the Kham and Saraswati rivers and was unremarkable until it became the capital of the Holkar dynasty. Malhar Rao, the chief, managed to accrue significant pieces of land and, in time, Malhar Rao's daughter in law, Ahilya Bai, took over control of the state which became vast and stretched as far as the Ganges and the Punjab. The rani was a superb ruler, praised by contemporary British diplomats, and, not being content with creating modern Indore, went on to build a whole series of temples, palaces and *dharamsalas* (rest houses for pilgrims) throughout the country. She died in 1795 and her four grandsons destroyed a great deal of her legacy by dragging the state into a civil war and then a war with the Marathas and the East India Company. Finally, the dynasty was left with a much smaller dominion and the prosperous capital of Indore. In Mumbai in November 2002, I was delighted to meet the current Maharani of Indore, Usha Malhotra, at a dinner party – a graceful intelligent lady. Indore is now hugely prosperous and there are many five-star hotels, shopping malls and signs of affluence. Honda, Bajaj Autos, Hindustan Motors and Eicher tractors are all manufactured in the industrial estates nearby. It is Madhya Pradesh's most prosperous city, though Bhopal is the capital.

It is thought that Mandu became a fortified hilltop from around the sixth century AD, when it was known as Mandapa-Durga or Durga's Hall of Worship; this, in time, was distilled into Mandu. By the eleventh century it was strategically important when the Paramaras moved their capital from Ujjain to Dhar which is 35 km north, but it eventually fell to the army of the Sultans of Delhi in 1305. The Sultanate, however, continued to have its hands full fighting off the Mongol Hordes from the North and the Afghan governor of Mandu seized the chance to make it his own independent kingdom. He died prematurely but his son went on to reign for 27 years and Mandu became Hoshang Shah's royal capital and acquired some of the finest Islamic monuments in the whole of Asia. Successive rulers built more palaces and the place prospered and entered its golden age under the Khaljis but, by 1526, the Sultan of Gujarat found it an easy target and gradually it decayed until it was deserted by 1732.

It is worth recalling that Sir Thomas Roe, the ambassador of King James I of Britain passed through the gate on the Emperor Jahangir's triumphal procession of 500 elephants. James became King of England in 1603, exactly four hundred years ago when he succeeded to the English crown on the death of Queen Elizabeth I in March 1603. This year, 2003, has seen the commemoration of the Union of the Crowns here in Scotland. A couple of years later in 1607 the first settlement of a few hundred people took place in Jamestown in Virginia in the New World, now known as the United States of America. The Dutch East India Company had received its charter in 1602. As all these world changing events were taking place, Mandu was enjoying the height of prosperity and yet, a hundred years later, it was abandoned. As I said 'earth's proud empires fade away...'.

Hoshang Shah's Tomb was, apparently, the first marble structure in the country. Emperor Shah Jahan is said to have sent master builders to study it before starting to build the Taj Mahal. The Jami Masjid is patterned on the great mosque at Damascus and is, perhaps, the finest example of Afghan architecture in India. The Asharfi Mahal is known as the palace of gold coins and Mahmud Kalji's victory tower.

The city is still haunted by the love story of Rupmati and Baz Bahadur, and Baz Bahadur built the queen a pavilion on a crest of a hill on the southern side overlooking the Narmada River, which looks especially beautiful on a night of the full moon. The Hindola Mahal or Swinging Palace derives its name from the leaning walls of the palace that resembles a swing. The palace combines immense proportions with a simple design. Finally, the Jahaz Mahal, as its name suggests is The Ship Palace because it resembles a ship and is about 130 metres long and 17 metres wide, double storey with domes and balconies and is built between two lakes. Today so much is derelict, but one can see what was beautiful and the turquoise tiles that are still in evidence must have looked lovely together with the blue ceramic tiles that plastered the Afghan style domes.

Returning to my theme of earth's proud empires, the most moving example is the Nil Kanth Palace, which was an old temple dedicated to Shiva which the Moghuls converted into a water pavilion. Emperor Akbar used it as a royal retreat and Persian verses remind one that despite victories and empires there is a futility to material achievement. This is the most wonderful place from which to watch the sun set.

Watching the sun rise and then set is something of which I never tire in India. Sunsets are wonderful all over the world and touch the soul, but, for me, somehow there is a spirituality in India at the start of a new day with the *pujari* calling on his Hindu deities and the *muezzin* calling the Muslims to their devotions. Then at the day's end, with a glorious sunset, I just thank my God for all that I have been allowed to experience. For all its noise and confusion in this overcrowded land, one is able to find peace and solitude and contemplation quite easily.

Ujjain is a holy city of India just 55 km away from Indore and a venue of the mammoth Kumbh Mela, which is held here once in twelve years. The Kumbh Mela is considered one of the most sacred of all Hindu festivals, and is held every three years in rotation between the four pilgrim cities of Nashik, Allahabad, Haridwar and Ujjain. This year it was the turn of Nashik to hold the Khumb Mela between August and September and it is considered a great honour to play host to the event which attracts the largest gatherings of people in the world.

The origins of the Kumbh Mela go back to the time when the *devas*, or gods and the *ashuras*, or demons decided to set aside their eternal differences and work together to retrieve the nectar of immortality by churning the ocean using a giant serpent as the rope. When finally the waters released their ultimate treasure, a great fight broke out between the two sides, each one trying to wrest the pitcher from the other.

During the fierce battle, a few drops of the immortal elixir fell at four different places in India: Prayag (Allahabad), Nashik, Ujjain and Haridwar. Ever since, when the configuration of the stars and planets are just right, it is believed that the waters of the rivers that flow through these sacred cities turn into nectar. A dip in the water during this time, it is said, heals and cleanses the soul and body and accrues merit equivalent to bathing in the River Ganges for 60,000 years.

Ujjain, in my opinion, would be a place that devout Hindus would want to visit. Those of us who are interested, recall the huge mela that took place at Allahabad three years ago, truly it was astonishing and the BBC actually made a current affairs programme visiting the mela every evening for one week. The logistics of such an event put anything held in the UK to shame!

Sleep continued to evade me and the theme of railway journeys remained in my mind and I thought of what had probably been my very favourite journey as a child, going by train overnight to the sea. Thought process is a funny thing and, possibly because I had thought of Mandu and Ujjain, this led me to remember Puri in the state of Orissa. Orissa is east of Madhya Pradesh and south of West Bengal; therefore, when we lived in Calcutta or Kolkata as it now is known, Puri was the obvious destination for a seaside holiday. Puri is also considered a holy city and has some very interesting places to visit in and around it. Orissa is a state in which there is extreme poverty coupled with great cultural heritage and some good wildlife areas. As a child none of this invaded my consciousness but as a teenager and now mature adult I realise that Orissa is another of India's dichotomous regions where there is a wealth of wonderful architecture related to Hinduism and yet the tribal people eke out a living on rice growing which ends in a feast or famine outcome because having a huge coastline the state is prone to receiving devastating cyclonic weather. The *adivasi* or tribal people have been on this land for thousands of years and are descended from the aboriginal inhabitants of pre-Aryan times. Now, tourism has exploited them by making them the subject of tourist routes and there are also many 'advancement programmes' many of which have achieved little, and certainly the revenue from tourism has not trickled down to the very people it exploits.

Ashoka, the most distinguished of the Mauryan dynasty, descended on Orissa in the third century BC and slew everyone in his path. It is said that this carnage may have led to his conversion to Buddhism but the fortified city of Sisupalgarh, which is near modern Bhubaneswar the capital of Orissa, became his stronghold. After the Mauryan dynasty declined, the area experienced resurgence before coming under the heel of the Chedi dynasty, followers of the Jain faith. Gradually, this too waned and the area entered a dark age and Buddhism and Jainism diminished to be overtaken by Brahmanism with an emphasis on the god Shiva. Since those times, Hinduism has been the predominant religion fortified by various Hindu dynasties which created some of the finest artistic and architectural achievement devoted to their faith in the whole of south Asia. In the twelfth century AD, the Ganga dynasty created the magnificent temples at Bhubaneswar, Puri and Konarak. These temples are the one with which I am most familiar having visited them as a teenager.

The Simlipal National Park in the north of the state is similar to those in Madhya Pradesh, forested by *sal* trees with spectacular scenery and with a wealth of animals, birds and reptiles. I believe there are tigers there along with elephants but this area is so difficult to reach that I am told it would require extreme dedication on the part of the wildlife enthusiast. From a selfish point of view, I am quite glad because it has more chance of retaining its wild nature and, thus, naturally conserving the animals. The Chilika Lakes, however, are quite near Bhubaneswar and, in winter, the huge salt water lagoon becomes a bird watcher's paradise and easily accessible by train from Kolkata to Bhubaneswar. The Bhita Kanika Sanctuary is the third important conservation area where the giant Olive Ridley marine turtles go to nest. These giants migrate here in February and March from as far away as the South American coast. Having witnessed turtles nesting on Turtle Island in the Sulu Sea off the coast of Sabah in North Borneo, I can imagine the pleasure one would experience here. Turtle Island is only a foot above sea level and tiny and very strictly controlled. Snorkelling off the beach was pure delight and then watching these great creatures lumber out of the water in the dark (we were only allowed one torch) and laboriously dig their holes and lay up to a hundred eggs and then slowly lurch back into the sea was quite emotional. In the dawn light, we saw the various tiny turtles that had hatched the previous night, offspring of another maternal giant, scrabble their way down to the waves. The keepers take them down very very early so as to avoid the various sea birds that would hunt them for food once the sun has risen. The Ionian Island of Zakynthos also has a turtle haven, but there they have to compete with beach tourism and I do not really rate their chances in the decades to come.

Bhubaneswar has a wealth of temples but, of the five hundred that remain, there are only a few that are of real interest. These are easily accessed by a car with driver or, more cheaply and with charm, by a rickshaw. One is able to see and appreciate over a thousand years of temple architecture but yet appreciate that they are living places of worship. In the Hindu religion, temples can become objects of worship as opposed to other faiths that create buildings in which to conduct their worship. Anyone wishing to investigate this area should buy an up-to-date guide book because it is 40 years since I visited and nothing remains the same. However, it is worth saying that a short distance from Bhubaneswar, there are some important caves at Udaigiri and Khandagiri. The caves were the home to a community of Jain monks about two thousand years ago and though not in the same league as those in the Deccan or at Bhimbetka, near Bhopal, they are of interest. At Dhauli just off the main road to Puri, is an even older monument; the edict of Ashoka commemorating the battle in 260 BC to which I referred where he reportedly slew up to 150,000 people. There is a stupa at Dhauli commemorating Ashoka's change of heart to a peaceful spiritual path as preached by Buddha and in the edict inscribed on the rock nearby part of the inscription reads 'All men are my children...' plus advice on how to treat animals. This site is on the route taken by Japanese and other Eastern races who adhere to Buddhism and the Japanese have apparently erected a new stupa which slightly overshadows the original memorial. We were to meet large parties of Asians on the Buddhist Trail at Bhimbetka and Sanchi in a few days time.

Puri has so many happy memories for me and for my family. The company house could be rented either as a whole or one floor, it being double storey with four large suites to each floor plus a lounge and dining area with veranda or terrace. Two weeks at Puri was pure bliss for people of all ages. The house which belonged to a Hindu rajah had been furnished simply to provide comfortable but not luxurious accommodation and with four bedrooms, or maybe the whole house, a jolly party could have some good fun. I know that it still exists and can therefore imagine that various families from the ITC Group are having just as good a seaside holiday as we did long years ago. The emphasis was on swimming in the sea; walking on the beach; eating good plain food, which largely consisted of very fresh fish, cooked by one's own cook; and reading books and playing board games or scrabble. The Puri temples and those of Bhubaneswar were a magnet for those interested in history and the finest of them all is at Konarak. Today's holidaymakers would have the addition of television.

The Jagannath temple at Puri is right in the middle of the town and very high and it seems almost incongruous that it rises out of some mean streets, but that is how the town has developed. The spectacular religious festival that is centred on this temple is the annual Rath yatra. This huge temple is one of the four holy *dhams* or 'abodes of the divine' which entices pilgrims to spend three days and nights praying to the god Jagannath. The present temple was built in the early twelfth century. I have a memory of walking about in the courtyards and little shrines – westerners and non-believers are not actually allowed in the temple itself. The Car Festival takes place in July and August depending on the full moon. The immense chariots (or cars) are draped with brightly coloured cloth and Lord Jagannath and his brother and sister deities are placed on their chariots and dragged by 4200 honoured devotees through the assembled multitudes to the summer home 1.5 km away. The chariots process down the main road accompanied by elephants, the local rajah and several little bands of musicians. It takes eight hours to haul the deities to their summer resting place and, after a nine day holiday, the whole procession is performed in reverse and the deities returned to their permanent resting place, the temple!

As far as I can work out Lord Jagganath is yet another incarnation of Lord Vishnu in his well-known role as Krishna but the pilgrims take it all very seriously and, from time to time, fatalities occur when pilgrims throw themselves in the path of the chariot and are crushed. The English word Juggernaut is derived from the chariot of Jagganath and we take it to mean a massive destructible vehicle, of which we see plenty, unfortunately, on Britain's roads.

I actually did not enjoy my visits to these temples partly, I think, because at sixteen I was too young to appreciate that they are symbols of another huge ancient faith. Now, I can respect the Hindu Faith and accept that millions the world over derive comfort from their devotions and beliefs but, at that time, newly confirmed in the Christian Faith it seemed rather sinister and confusing and not very clean. Moreover, in the temple courtyards, there were cows left to roam and be fed by the devout but these animals appeared to have extra legs grafted on to them – presumably to inculcate greater devotion in the untrained mind that would gaze and assimilate them as divine. As a mature adult and student of history one knows that in the Christian Faith medieval pilgrimages were encouraged to inculcate a similar devotion and all manner of saints' bones and extremities were sold to the innocent gullible illiterate pilgrims of the early Middle Ages. At the tender age of sixteen, I have to say it all seemed repelling and cheap and exploitative.

We did, however, go by jeep to visit the Sun Temple at Konarak and that too was amazing. They say that if you visit only one temple in Orissa it should be Konarak. It stands carefully renovated and preserved having been allowed to fall into neglect over four hundred years ago. At the beginning of the twentieth century, when it was rediscovered, the British authorities ensured it was sympathetically renovated and Lord Ronaldshay wrote of the newly revealed temple 'one of the most stupendous buildings in India, which rears itself aloft, a pile of overwhelming grandeur even in its decay'. The temple represents a colossal chariot for the sun god Surya and a team of seven galloping horses and twenty-four finely carved wheels line the walls of a raised platform. There are also the most extraordinary erotic sculptures of entwined couples, rather as one has seen at Khajuraho, apparently putting the advice of the Kamasutra into practice. I was only sixteen when I saw this and was so astonished and embarrassed that I found it difficult to look at the various males in the party. The world has changed a great deal in the intervening forty years but in 1962 modesty still reigned, and I was not yet aware of the Kamasutra! It seems likely that the Konarak erotic art was a kind of metaphor for the ecstatic bliss experienced by the soul when it fuses with the divine cosmos, which is a fundamental belief of Tantra, and everywhere you look at Khajuraho's wonderful temples.

The myth is that Samba, one of Krishna's sons was caught spying on his stepmothers whilst they were bathing in the river. Krishna was enraged at his son's infamy and cursed him with leprosy and expelled him from the home. Twelve years later, Surya, The Sun God, who is also the divine healer of skin complaints, took pity on the young man and cured him, in return for which Samba built a temple dedicated to the sun god. The more prosaic story is that the temple was built in the thirteenth century by a Ganga monarch.

When we visited Konarak it was little known outside Orissa and Kolkata and, therefore, there was no tourist tat, I do not know what is currently there, but consider that we probably enjoyed it for its simplicity as yet another relic of a past dynasty.

I have been told that Orissa is still recovering from the devastating cyclone of 1999, but that strangely Puri was not affected. I am glad; at least my memory of the huge beach can still be fairly accurate. In today's terms it would probably not be considered a safe beach but, at that time, we would go swimming three times every day accompanied by a fisherman wearing the traditional pointed hat. The hat I understood protected them from the fierce rays of the sun but also helped in protecting the head from the massive waves, as the point deflected the blow to the head as one swam through them. I have never again been so fearless in a big sea and, though I enjoy swimming in the sea these days, I take care to swim in more protected waters or bays which are also devoid of any sharks. Sharks were evident on Puri's beaches and, on one memorable day when only ten, my father urgently told me to get out and pointed to a huge fin not all that far away. Shark menace is a huge problem on the beaches in Southern Africa and I would only now swim where there are shark nets. In Mexico earlier this year, we enjoyed our sea swimming enormously, but this was behind a wonderful little reef, which encouraged masses of brightly coloured little fish and the odd small barracuda but no sharks. The snorkelling was superb. Puri's fishermen would bring their boats in at about noon. The boats were simple wooden catamarans and the excitement of seeing the catch was great. Din, our cook, would stroll down from the house and Mother and he would purchase fish for lunch and dinner. It was so good, simply fried or grilled fish with lemon and a few vegetables. When fish is as fresh as that it needs no sauce or adornment, just a hint of butter and a squeeze of lemon – there was never any left!

Puri will have a host of hotels by now and be a really vibrant holiday place for Bengalis from Kolkata's overcrowded conurbation; I, however, will not go back as I prefer my happy memories of a golden time in my family life.

CHAPTER NINE

Bandhavgarh Wildlife Park

At 06.15 hours our train pulled into the little station at Umariya. It was a fleeting stop so we were already at the door eager to descend. In the cold, misty, dawn light, I looked around and shook myself, partly to dispel the aches and pains of a long night but also because here I was in the very heart of India but, had it not been for the vibrant vigorous blossoms of the bougainvilleas on the little station building, I might have been in Surrey. The architecture is so typically that of Victorian railway buildings. People were scurrying around and I noticed one or two other Europeans who had also travelled on our train with presumably the same objective – to visit Bandhavgarh National Park. The platform and surrounding area is well kept and attractive. I was jolly glad of my pullover; early morning in Madhya Pradesh from November till February can be really chilly.

A driver presented himself and said he was Raju and would we please go with him, which we did thankfully. Arrangements that work are wonderful but, occasionally, something goes wrong and then, depending on how remote a place one finds oneself in, it demands some lateral thinking. Raju was driving an ancient Ambassador car. A cursory glance from Graham and the feel to my aching back left us in no doubt that car had well and truly paid its dues on India's roads. The journey to Bandhavgarh is about 30 kilometres but it was not comfortable, and I tried to firmly put the vexed question of the car to the back of my mind whilst I enjoyed the scenery and drank in the experience of approaching one of the more remote wildlife parks, but perhaps over all it became my favourite.

In summer in Britain, we are used to a very early dawn, but that actually never happens in India and, thus, the locals take their time to rise. As the sun ascended in the East like a huge orange orb, the mist dispersed and one could see the fields, gradually giving way to jungle. At the roadside were little hamlets where very few were stirring. Winding the car window down, I caught sounds of the *pujari* calling the spiritual to the rituals of a new day; several *pye* (pariah) dogs wandered around and barked at our car. Old men were starting their ablutions or contemplations. The little houses were simple but clean and attractive with interesting wall painting mostly in bright blue and white – this bright blue seems to be the favourite traditional colour for house decoration in Madhya Pradesh.

Graham and I were delighted with it all and looking forward to the day ahead. It has to be said that the night had not been totally peaceful. This particular train from Jhansi only offers second class air-conditioned compartments. Initially, there had only been the two of us in the compartment but, at a midnight stop, two men had entered and switched on the overhead light and seated themselves noisily. The one astoundingly sat on my feet on the bottom bunk. And when I moved said cheekily 'You don't mind?' I did but I let it pass at first. Now this was odd; if he was entitled to one of the other two berths he should have just sat on the lower one or made his way up to the top one. Above me, Graham was sound asleep. I looked up and the Indian sort of glanced at me and continued his noisy fulsome chattering. It was quite obvious to me that he was trying terribly hard to impress the other older man who was sitting opposite me and was well dressed. An unlovable pair because, aside from talking loudly, they began to 'burp' from both ends. I really was quite vexed and suddenly sat up and with machine gun speed in Hindi requested coldly that he might like to go and sit in his own seat. Well, he was so astounded that he jumped up and hit his head on the underneath of Graham's bunk and said 'sorry for disturbing' and shot off! The other man followed and that thankfully was the last of them.

Graham and I pondered it all laughing in the car and I came to the conclusion that perhaps they had not bought tickets and had slipped the attendant some cash and been shown into our compartment. When he had sat on my feet deliberately – there could be no question about a slumbering body in a grey blanket – he was just taking liberties and maybe thought I was a 'young inexperienced' backpacker. These are the sort of challenges a single woman can face in India and it would be naïve to underestimate them. Not everyone would have the advantage of Hindi but stand up for yourself with firmness and courtesy and that usually confounds that sort of oaf.

We were booked in at Tiger Trails on the edge of the national park. It was a delightful setting with the village fields bordering the encampment and the fringes of the park alongside. The staff welcomed us warmly and we asked for a tray of tea and tomato omelettes. It seems in India that I only really function with my breakfast of those two items and, wherever possible, some papaya. The little lodges were attractive, built out of stone and brick, and comfortable but simple. The sun was shining, the sky was blue, the parakeets darting about and it all felt very good. There is a charming large pool with water lilies and a small chuckling stream emptying in at one side near to our cottage. Because we were in the buffer zone of the park, one heard jackal and other creatures at night; there was no-one else about except the staff. The bearer was a friendly fellow and, in no time at all, we were talking. Rajan the Conservationist came over and introduced himself and asked if we would like to go on a nature walk and visit one of the nearby villages. Naturally, we said yes.

Set amongst the Vindhyan Hills of Madhya Pradesh, Bandhavgarh has an area of 1161.471 sq. km, of which 624.752 sq. km. is the core of the National Park, with approximately 47 tigers and 33 leopards. The prey species comprise chital, sambhar, barking deer, nilgai, chinkara, wild pig, chowsingha, langur monkeys and rhesus macaque monkeys. There are over 70 species of butterflies in this paradise of streams, marshes, woodland and wildflower meadows. In the water pools, there are dragonflies and damsel flies.

The legend is that Lord Rama bequeathed the fort to his brother Laxmana, hence the name 'Bandhavgarh' which means brother's fort. At the base of the fort is a monolithic reclining statue of Lord Vishnu, 35 feet long lying on the seven hooded snake, known as Sheshshaiyya and also statues of all the incarnations of Lord Vishnu (who, you may recall from my simple explanation of Diwali, is one of the three great deities).

The predators are tiger, leopard, wild dog, wolf and jackal. The lesser predators are fox, jungle cat, ratel, palm civet and mongoose. Besides that, there are sloth bear, porcupine, Indian pangolin and a variety of bats.

Bandhavgarh was the favourite hunting reserve of ex-rulers of the state of Rewa, hence it remained protected from poaching and illicit felling. After the abolition of the princely states, the degradation of this area reached alarming proportions and the late Maharajah of Rewa prevailed upon the government of Madhya Pradesh to declare an area of 105 sq. km as National Park in 1968. This was extended to 450 sq. km in 1982 and, in 1993, it was declared a Tiger Reserve under Project Tiger.

Lord Vishnu's ancient statue in recumbent position – Bandhavgarh

The birdlife is plentiful with more than 250 species of birds. The raptors are the crested serpent eagle, shaheen falcon, Bonnelli's eagle, shikra, marsh and hen harriers. Peafowls, painted and grey partridge, red jungle fowl, sarus crane, lesser adjutant stork, large racket tailed drongo, brown fish owl, paradise fly catcher, green pigeon and parakeets can all be seen.

In the evening, a paraffin lamp is brought to every cottage as the electricity goes off intermittently because Madhya Pradesh has not acted prudently about its utilities. It is essential on this sort of trip to have your own torch. The en suite bathrooms are simple but provide hot water for a good shower plus basin and w.c. We found the facilities very comfortable. If you require something more luxurious, there are other establishments but I found this pleasant and the cooking proved to be good and wholesome and with fresh ingredients. Because of the intermittent current, the management do not rely on freezers, so, though it is simple Indian cooking, it is good and thoughtfully presented considering the limitations imposed on the cook. The bearer serves one carefully and engages one in conversation if you allow him, which we did. They are mostly so eager to please and want to know about the world away from India. Sometimes, I am vexed by the way Indians treat hotel staff. Their abrupt and dismissive manner just contributes to the poor individual having what we would consider a 'bad day'. I saw some bad behaviour in various places and usually the assertive guest was large, fat and throwing his body weight about as well as his dubious intellectual capacities. Indian women can be just as bad; some who have visited us here in Britain also annoy me. I long to tread on their toes and say 'Just who do you think you are to treat your fellow human beings like that?' but usually good manners prevents me in this country and in India it would be very unwise to interfere in what very sadly seems almost the norm.

Rajan appeared very soon after breakfast and the three of us went off on the nature trail that takes one to a nearby village. The birdlife was good and noisy with plenty to see and Rajan pointed out species and tried to fill us in about local conditions. The village fields were well maintained and the crops were largely lentils and cereals. This was a neat beautiful little village in its ancient simplicity of immaculately kept, freshly painted houses and raised terrace areas. On almost every roof of terracotta tiles, there were pumpkin plants basking in the late autumn sunshine. In one property, a pair of oxen were trudging round a pole, threshing the rice, which is later laid out to dry. Village women were picking over the rice and leaving it in neat round formations to dry in the sunshine. The *sarpanch*, the village head man came to greet us and have a formal conversation. He enquired as to whether we would like to visit a home and we replied yes, very much. I am not sure if it was his own but everything was fresh and clean and I was invited to take photographs. One shy teenager darted away to comb her hair and then asked if I would photograph her. I understood her Hindi and replied of course. This led to photographs of all the family and I have sent her copies with enlargements of herself. The little home had a beautiful swept courtyard with a *tulsi* plant growing in the middle. Tulsi is an Indian form of basil and essential to have in a household. The village

The author with the eldest daughter near the home's Tulsi plant

Village cattle threshing wheat as they have done for centuries

well was ancient and Rajan said that records show it had been in existence for 900 years, the construction was of bricks in a herring-bone pattern. Alongside it, was a terrace with a temple, the stonework of which was from the eleventh century and carved with gods and goddesses. In British historical terms, that means since the time of William the Conqueror in 1066.

Tribal village woman and her beautiful home – Bandhavgarh

The State has recognised the fact that the success of wildlife conservation depends a great deal on the support and respect awarded to the conservation areas by the neighbouring indigenous population. The State Government is trying to bring the indigenous communities into the national mainstream of progress and prosperity and, thus, they have become involved as 'stakeholders', and policies are implemented through select micro institutions such as Forest Protection Committees, Village Forest Committees and Eco-development Committees. The initial response from the target people is good.

Madhya Pradesh has an effective Protected Area network of about 10,862 sq. km, harbouring nine National Parks and 25 Wildlife Sanctuaries. Community pressures on managed forests and protected areas have increased considerably, as we have seen in earlier chapters on Ranthambore. According to one estimate, there are almost 100 million forest dwellers in India. Besides this, forests are a source of livelihood for another 275 million. In western terms, that is a total figure equal to the population of the whole of Europe. Village communities depend upon forests for their day-to-day needs. In earlier colonial times, the forest management principles were essentially rooted in a policy of commercial exploitation. Gradually, thankfully, this is changing. It is absolutely essential that the needs of indigenous peoples are considered and that they are involved in the conservation and management of wildlife, to ensure both the survival of the animals and the forests. Plants, animals and human beings have co-evolved and are inseparable owing to their interdependence. Therefore, the ailments of forests also affect the wild fauna. This, therefore, calls for a holistic view to redress the situation. Any strategy advocating a dichotomy would be myopic, since almost 70% of India's wild fauna thrives outside the Protected Area system in regular forests.

Whilst walking back to the lodge, I was thinking about a good friend. He runs a registered charity called LifeForce Charitable Trust. The aims of LifeForce are to help educate the Forest Guards and encourage them to appreciate and respect the job which they are paid to do. By doing this, they hope to help conserve the tiger throughout Madhya Pradesh. Our friend works in collaboration with the Forest Department of Madhya Pradesh and spends as much time as he can afford out in India himself. "To preserve the Tiger is to preserve your Family" is one of his quotations when talking to the guards. In his careful presentations, with written notes in both Hindi and English accompanied by simple drawings, he attempts to show how wildlife has declined in the last century and why. A cynic would say that what he is doing in his small organisation is 'a spit in the ocean'. So be it, but do remember Gandhiji's saying 'if we all do a little then a lot will be achieved". Actually, in this modern rapacious world, whoever we are that is the best advice to follow – whatever your own interest and commitment.

I am going to quote a little from one of LifeForce's notes: "…so, in a very real sense, you are doing one of the most important jobs in the world. Thinking and caring people all around the world admire and respect what you do. To them you are heroes. I will quote from Indira Gandhi about Project Tiger 'the interest in conservation is not a sentimental one but a rediscovery of a truth well known to our ancient sages. The Indian tradition teaches us that all forms of life – human, animal and plant – are so closely interlinked that disturbance in one gives rise to imbalance in the other. Nature is beautifully balanced. Each little thing has its own place, its duty and special utility. Any disturbance creates a chain reaction which may not be visible for some time'….." Thus does LifeForce try to inspire simple men to do their work well with commitment and devotion and enjoyment.

To quote from The Upanishads (the Vedic literature written in 500 BC, dealing with the nature of the soul and ultimate reality): 'This universe is the creation of the Supreme Power meant for the benefit of all His creations. Individual species must, therefore, learn to enjoy its benefits by forming a part of the system in close relation with other species. Let not any one species encroach upon the other's rights'. It seems to twenty first century thinking that we are just re-discovering this truth and calling it 'ecology'.

Rajan, Graham and I walked back quietly the way we had come and, in the process, saw tailor birds, a serpent eagle, a shrike, an Indian roller, and the usual bulbuls and jungle babblers plus a little wren.

It was still quite early in the day and the children were taking themselves to school, either on foot or, for the privileged few, by bicycle. We came across one of the young teenaged girls we had seen earlier. Rajan asked why she was not going to school and she shyly replied that her duties at home had been decreed by her father to be more important. Whether Rajan was truly vexed, or just showed that to be the case for our benefit I would not know but he said he would speak to her father and rectify the situation. That is just a small example of the discrimination that is still experienced by some females in India. I hope that Rajan did do what he promised. That young girl's face lit up when he spoke, and her aspirations will be to better herself through education. Graham and I reflected that there are so many here in Britain who regularly 'wag' school despite everything being provided – they have not a clue how advantaged they are – and yet, in the country areas of Scotland one can still meet old men and women who had to leave school at fourteen. They had no real career choices in those days; it was domestic service, down the mines, armed forces or the police, or a local mill for large numbers of people. Sixty years has made a great change in our own country, hopefully progress will contribute to significant cultural change in the next half century for Indians.

I felt that I had been on the move constantly for the last eighteen hours and the veranda of our cottage was a welcome respite from all this activity. Lying in the sunshine with the gentle country noises and the constant noise of the little waterfall was very soothing and rather reluctantly I went off to have lunch in the dining area. It was, however, to be a very fortuitous meeting. The only other people present were the distinguished photographer and his companion of whom we had heard from the waiter. Harshad Patel and Anil Juwarkar proved to be very friendly and in no time at all we had discovered several areas of mutual interest, but most especially the conservation of Indian wildlife. Harshad Patel had a book called *The Vanishing Herds* published in the early 1970s by Macmillan. His subjects were the various beasts and birds of African wildlife. Recently he has set up and registered a charitable foundation in India called 'The Vanishing Herds Foundation'. The Foundation's objectives are to establish facilities for undertaking education, training and consultancy in the sphere of wildlife conservation and its environment, and to undertake research on wildlife and its ecosystems and all matters relating to conservation. The aim is also to promote eco-tourism, and to provide a forum to support the initiatives of individuals, institutions and academic bodies and to co-operate with them by exchange of information and personnel.

I felt myself very fortunate to have come upon these two men and we had such a good time. Lunch was good as a foursome and we heard about Sasan Gir – the wildlife park in Southern Gujarat near to which the project is based, on land purchased by the Foundation for this very purpose. The Asiatic lion is Harshad's great obsession, along with tiger, leopard, cheetah and all the other magnificent beasts of the jungle. Anil is the Project Manager for much of the work that will be undertaken to establish the foundation, and he is wonderfully funny and vastly amusing as a raconteur. His father is a very talented painter. I have had the good fortune to be asked to speak on behalf of Vanishing Herds in London and, thus, help encourage contributions to their very worthwhile aims. The charity now has official recognition with the Charity Commissioners in the UK and the equivalent status in the USA. In India, this had been previously established.

The jeeps awaited us and Harshad invited us to accompany them. We declined, thinking that we should not intrude on their very serious photography. I wish we had. On their return, we heard of the tigress with four four-month old cubs that they had had the opportunity to photograph. Nevertheless, we had a very enjoyable and interesting time.

Bandhavgarh is so different from Ranthambore and so beautiful. I was very struck with the outlines of the green-covered hills and rocky escarpment in the early afternoon sunlight. Whenever one saw it, be it late evening as the dusk approached or in the dawn light, it was thoroughly mesmerising with its quiet serene beauty. We were fortunate to be there whilst the elephant grass was flowering so the lovely meadows or *maidans* were covered in the elephant-high white plumes of the grass which gave a sort of silvery wavy appearances to the forest clearings. The monsoon rains had been good so the jungle was green and not parched like Ranthambore. The trees are plentiful and majestic with sal, saja, mahua, achar, amla, dhaoria and bamboo. There were pools in jungle glades and flowing streams of clear clean water and interesting ravines of rock and dry river beds with sandy bottoms. Elephants are used to track tiger and it was a great pleasure to be so close to these huge docile creatures which are such favourites with us. Jeeps are the only form of motorised transport which was nice and so much more intimate.

The next morning, it was cold at 0500 hours and in the chilly sunrise I was very glad of a thick blanket round my shoulders as the jeep sped away to the park gates. We joined up as a foursome with a naturalist plus driver. We seriously quartered the park and enjoyed ourselves but saw no tiger, though repeatedly came across fresh pug marks. Then suddenly someone on an elephant spotted a tiger but he or she chose to wander off in a direction that avoided all the various jeeps. We returned a little disconsolate. Graham and I kept reminding ourselves how lucky we had been in Ranthambore to see tiger on our first outing – in all we had experienced seven tiger sightings in extraordinary close up.

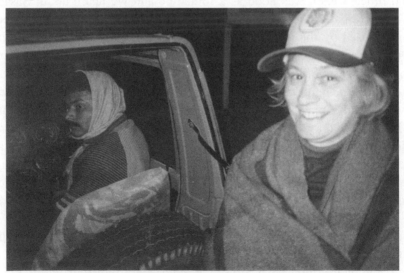

**The author in blankets against the
chill morning air – Bandhavgarh National Park.**

Harshad and Anil said their farewells and left for Kanha National Park, to which we were also headed on the next day. In the meantime, I followed through on the unsatisfactory car. I spoke to Travel House long distance and suggested to Sunil Hasija that this vehicle was not going to last the distance for our forthcoming hundreds of kilometres and nor did we consider it safe. He arranged for a replacement vehicle to be with us for the following morning. We explained to Raju the driver that it was no reflection on his driving, but that we could not contemplate so many hours in the old Ambassador. It was also important to make this point to his superiors as his livelihood could depend on a bad report. I would not hesitate to give a bad report if it was merited, but this was not the case. We gave him a tip and he waited till the replacement arrived the next day. The whole thing was an interesting exercise, that did not surprise me, because the local transport *wallahs* heard about it and tried to understandably exploit the system, but it is always better to stick with the people one knows, and Travel House has never let us down.

After a delicious lunch, we went back to the park. It was an exquisite afternoon and I thought I had taken some superb photographs – indeed, I probably had – but next morning disaster struck and at a crucial time the film jammed. Despite bringing it home to experts, it was all lost. I will try and describe the picture that meant so much to me in words.

Bandhavgarh has a particular jungle glade with wide still pools which one approaches over a concrete low bridge – what I recall was referred to as an Irish bridge in my youth. We crossed it many times, but each time I loved it because if the driver approached slowly and quietly the birdlife and the deer could be observed drinking peacefully. This particular time as we came to the bridge, I noticed from my side of the jeep that there was a tiny little Kingfisher sitting on the edge of the concrete. The little bird was only four inches in height. He seemed lost to the sights and sounds of us humans. He looked from side to side for the fish he was attempting to catch. I was sitting in the jeep perhaps three feet away and he seemed unconcerned, just tilting his head left to right. It was a magical moment and we just sat and watched him and photographed. The water was gurgling under the bridge; there was some bird sound but otherwise just the contented noises of Graham, myself, the naturalist and driver. He did not fly away; it was we who finally moved on. That was one of the most beautiful moments of my entire trip. A jungle glade, limpid water, peace, and the company of an exquisite little bird who felt unthreatened by us humans, just going about his daily business - truly this was the heart of my beloved India. The evening shadows lengthened and the jungle became cool and quiet but, regrettably, we did not see tiger. The naturalists were so crestfallen. That, however, is the point; no-one can guarantee tiger sightings.

We saw a leopard's pug marks, and those of a bear. There was the usual beautiful, graceful chital, sambhar, barking deer, langur monkeys, wild boar and a Bonnelli's eagle plus hornbills and peacocks. As we drove home in the gloaming, we talked of the little kingfisher and recalled the big ones on Delhi railway station and those at Ranthambore but we had never seen one so small – his miniscule size seemed to emphasise his iridescent beauty. Suddenly, an owl swooped low over the jeep and with the half moon in the deep blue sky above him it was a beautiful end to the day. A hot shower and some refreshing tea were very welcome after over three hours in the confines of the jeep.

Jungle glade and pool – Bandhavgarh National Park

At night, there are strange sounds, which are the noises the villagers make from their hides to frighten away the animals from their crops – it can be a bit startling but one soon adjusts. Early starts require early bedtimes, and if one is alone as we were for the second night there is nothing really to do but retire to the bedroom and read with the night calls continuing all around one. The jungle in this ancient land, with relics of long gone kingdoms is all around one, and except for STD dialling, which is so cheap, and efficient satellite dishes here and there, plus efficient water pumps, life seems to go on pretty much as it has always done; the children do go to school, or at least the majority do, but it is simple village life close to the land and its animals. I slept well that night and only stirred when I heard the familiar knock to the door which was the wake up call with a very welcome tray of tea very early the next morning.

CHAPTER TEN

The Ultimate Thrill

O n our last morning we were so determined to try and see a tiger that, when the waiter brought the tea, we leapt out of bed and dressed in double-quick time, swallowed a scalding cup of tea and strode out to the jeep. It was still dark and so cold. Alwin and Mukesh were impressed and said that, if we arrived at the gate first, it could be that we might pick up the first fresh clues as to a tiger's whereabouts.

That early morning drive was full of anticipation and, just to reward us, we had hardly left the camp but we saw a big jungle cat on the side of the road; he appeared to be going home to bed just as we had vacated ours! Then, we saw a jackal loping along and his eyes reflected our headlights as we passed. I said to Graham that I had a good feeling about this morning and, sure enough, we were at the gates of the park first and thus able to pick up the fresh signs of the pre-dawn activity.

Almost immediately, in the barely pink dawn light, we heard the various alarm calls. Mukesh spotted the very fresh pug marks of a big tiger and the peafowl were calling shrilly, then a sambhar started to 'bell' urgently and we knew we were so close to something. I looked round and there behind us, about thirty feet away, a big tigress came out of the grass and proceeded to cross the road behind us. The excitement was immense and Alwin and Mukesh were talking rapidly deciding what to do; out of the morning mist we saw an elephant coming up the road as fast as possible and the *mahawat* (elephant keeper and controller) was given gesticulatory instructions, so she plunged into the undergrowth after the tigress. All the while, the sambhar continued to bell and other deer started to respond; the anticipation was immense. Suddenly, coming from the right was another elephant. We beckoned urgently to the *mahawat* who rapidly brought the great beast right up to the open jeep.

Alwin said to me 'Get on Ma'am get on, follow the tiger'. The huge animal stood as close as possible and Graham leapt on her back. I thought rapidly – I have more than one serious back injury from my youth – but the adrenalin

kicked in and I leapt on to the metal side of the jeep and then on to the roll bar and with Graham's helping hand on to the howdah. Graham made room for me and then whispered urgently that he had found a huge spider and flicked it off. I looked at him closely – it is not like Graham to wind me up about spiders, and in these circumstances! Meanwhile the occupants of another jeep realising what was about to happen had arrived and were also climbing on the elephant. The elephant started to move off in a rapid swaying gait; I bent down and started to remove my shoes whilst Graham looked on incredulously and asked what I was thinking of, but I

Elephant used for tiger tracking Bandhavgarh National Park

explained as the huge animal purposefully moved through the undergrowth that I was castigating myself for having put on my 'slip ons' that morning in an act of laziness. I put this very nice pair of shoes under my bottom – better squashed than no shoes at all when the action started!

Our *mahawat* knew what he was doing and the elephant Bandhani quickened her pace. Meanwhile, the first elephant, who we later found out was called Jaisari, started trumpeting noisily – it was alarming and exciting, she was wheeling around either out of aggression towards the tigress or because she had slightly 'lost the plot'. Bandhani pressed on until there she was, the magnificent beast, the tigress standing looking at us just 10 feet away. She stood her ground and just looked – it was spell-binding. The American behind me stood up, in his excitement and I, very precisely and shortly, told him to sit down or risk unbalancing the elephant to everyone's detriment, or perhaps decapitating himself on a low branch! Being a really nice chap he apologised and, subsequently, Barry Snyder and I have kept in touch. We were all four trying frantically to photograph the tigress and the *mahawat* very expertly turned the elephant from side to side. I could not think why the tigress had remained and then all became clear. She suddenly pounced, there was a scream and we saw her prey, a little chital fawn whose neck she had efficiently broken. I had a pang of sadness for such a little life lost, but this was the jungle and tigers have to eat. Still, the tigress remained with her prey in her mouth and looked at us, but finally she turned around and walked away. With one last look at us she bounded away to eat her breakfast.

A tigress seen from an elephant – Bandhavgarh National Park

Bandhani made her way back to the jungle track with all of us elated and congratulating the *mahawat* on his expertise. As we walked out, there was a branch – quite a stout one – in our way. He gave the order and Bandhani just broke the branch effortlessly and ambled on. It had been an unforgettable experience. I stroked Bandhani's rough hairy sides and took a photo of her face; her eyes with their three-inch long eye lashes were so patient and beautiful. Then, to my horror, I found that the film had stuck – truly a trying moment – but fortunately Graham had also been photographing and managed some good shots. It was so sad to lose all that material on a 400-speed film, including the shots of the little kingfisher of the previous evening. Barry Snyder and I exchanged addresses on a scruffy bit of paper foraged out of Alwin's pocket and he promised to send me copies of his own photographs which he very sweetly did.

I questioned Graham again closely about the famous spider; he replied that it had been huge about four inches (10 centimetres) across and bright yellow with yellow and white legs and he only had time to flick it off the elephant's back just before I sat down on it! He admitted to having felt a bit panicky about it! No wonder, I think I would have gone into vertical take off had I seen it first! I subsequently heard from Barry that he had an opportunity to ride on the elephant again and saw the same tigress and took even better photographs. We, in our jeep, were feeling so pleased with ourselves. As we drove away we grinned at everyone and I saw some glum faces. Yes, I know it is not all about seeing tiger but believe me it is such an electrifying experience and definitely the cherry on the cake.

As we were making our way out of the park we came across a crowd of jeeps obviously hoping to make a sighting. An elephant went into the undergrowth and, when I followed it with my binoculars, I saw two young tiger cubs quite clearly. However, the *mahawat* returned saying that he had come across the cubs resting and, rightly, he was not going to allow them to be disturbed. We returned to camp victorious and everyone came out to meet us and saw by our

Tiger – Bandhavgarh National Park

big grins and thumbs up that something very good had happened. Then, it was into the hot shower, a change, a quick pack and some welcome breakfast before saying our farewells.

Fortunately, the new driver and Toyota Qualis 4 x 4 air-conditioned jeep had arrived. The driver's name was Gudu and he was such a good chap. He greeted me as if he knew me so I enquired carefully. 'Oh, Ma'am, I saw you at Gwalior at the Usha Karan Palace Hotel?' Well, I then realised he had been driving the Americans who had been fellow hotel guests and I was able to say that of course I remembered. Poor fellow, he had driven through the night from Khajuraho to get to us and seemed quite exhausted. However, we struck an immediate rapport and finally started on our journey to Kanha, which was going to be long in hours, because, though the distance was only 240 km, the road was known to be bad.

This whole eastern area of Madhya Pradesh is truly *adivasi* or tribal country. The villages of the Gond and Barga tribes dot the hills and valleys. As we had seen on our drive from Umariya, the village houses are painted in white and turquoise or ultramarine blue, maybe azure would be a more accurate description. These roadside villages were often enchanting with these neat bright freshly painted dwellings, each with their own forecourt having been smoothed with clay, coloured round the edges – all swept and clean. From time to time as we drove through, one saw women carefully wiping down their forecourts and refreshing the painting with what seemed similar to the clay slip with which I decorated my pottery at school. Wherever they can, everything is kept fresh and clean, but, a few feet away there can be a midden, or at the end of the village a huge mound of discarded plastic. India is only too well aware what a mixed blessing plastic has been. Whereas in the past people would have used cloth or paper bags now it is all plastic and, thus, not at all eco-friendly and a complete eyesore. The Government is trying to dissuade folk from using plastic bags but the habit is as ingrained as it is here in the West and I think they may have to be very courageous and ban them, or allow India to slowly be submerged under this wretched stuff.

In medieval Europe where people 'slopped out', there must have been the same effluent and mess but, in our sanitised western eyes, it is especially awful and one yearns to make them adopt hygienic practices. It has to be said that the day village Indians stop 'dumping' near to their doorsteps India will have taken a giant leap forward. The countryside was beautiful and carefully husbanded. Crops of lentil, mustard, rice and grains of all sorts were neatly laid out in colourful fields. We drove along escarpments, through valleys and wide jungle and forestry. Several villages were having their respective weekly bazaars and the people converging on the central road were colourfully and smartly dressed. Thank goodness we were passing through in the afternoon, otherwise the congestion would have held us up. The afternoon sunshine gave a gloss to a long drive but I had reached my goal – the heart of India.

When one is travelling long distances by road, it is easy to chat for a while and observe the passing countryside but, inevitably, as a couple, we lapse into a comfortable silence, with the odd encouraging word to the driver, in this case Gudu who spoke a lot of sense whenever we asked his views on life in general. It is good when there is a comfortable relaxed feeling and also security in sensing that were an emergency to arise we would all deal with it well together. Believe me, though the traffic is not really heavy in this central heartland, some of the driving is pretty atrocious and from time to time one heaves a sigh of enormous relief when some drama is avoided – in the nick of time. Of course, we carry the sensible medical kits with a fresh sealed drip system for each of us, but one is a long way from modern hospitals and it has to be faced there is always an element of risk in this sort of journey but then, on the other hand, I might be run down in Edinburgh or Graham could be involved in a crash on the M6. We, however, do use the safety belts provided and not all Indians are scrupulous about this precaution. However, I soon sensed that Gudu was good at his job so I could fall into a reverie as the shadows lengthened and think about the area and anticipate the next few days.

The map of India has changed in the time I had been absent. In November 2000, Chhattisgarh had become a separate state, having devolved from Madhya Pradesh, which hitherto had been the largest state in India. At roughly the same time, Bihar had shed a huge area that is now the separate state of Jharkand and, in the north, Uttar Pradesh had given up its northern reaches to the new state of Uttaranchal. Bihar and Uttar Pradesh were both states in which I had lived in my childhood and I was interested that India seemed to be still evolving in its semi-autonomous form of state government. Was it all that different from what we in Scotland had recently done, devolution in 1999 with a new version of a Scottish Parliament? Now, four years later, we will go to the polls in a few days and deliver a verdict on these last few years of self-government in Scotland.

Chhattisgarh however is not really on the beaten track for travellers and we did not have the time to go and research it personally but, from talking to people and reading about it, I am aware that it is going to play a significant part in India's progress economically. It is in mineral wealth terms India's richest state with 28 varieties of major minerals, including diamonds. Along with two other states, it has almost all the coal deposits in India, which has contributed to its wealth. All the tin ore and a fifth of the iron ore is here and there are also rich deposits of bauxite, limestone, dolomite and corundum. The state's information technology sector is superior with efficient providers of high bandwidth allowing for high internet speeds, which is more than can be said for our part of the Scottish Borders! For the traveller, what is of great interest is that one third of Chhattisgarh's population is tribal, mostly in the thickly forested areas of the North and South. The central plains of Chhattisgarh are known as the 'rice bowl' of Central India. Female literacy has doubled in the last decade to reach the national average, and the gender ratio is just below that of Kerala, the only state where women outnumber men.

Bastar in the south of the state and on the borders of the state of Orissa, is a huge tract of land that is larger than Belgium or Kerala, covering an area of 40,000 sq. km, actually about the size of Switzerland. It is difficult to reach but, I am assured, richly repays the effort to do so. One of these days, I shall make that effort but, realistically, I find I cannot be away from home for more than one month at a time. The forests are primeval and, in the Kangar Valley, is India's largest national biosphere reserve in which nature has been left totally undisturbed by man. The water falls of Teerathgarh at a height of 250 metres or the equally spectacular Chitrakoot Falls on the Indravati River are quite special. I suppose it is the sheer inaccessibility of Bastar that lends it enchantment. This is home to the famous bison horn Madias, who dance and beat their drums at folk festivals in India and abroad. The famous mynah bird also originates here in the hills and, well I remember, my mother's favourite mynah that almost perfected the tune of The Merry Widow Waltz, which he heard so often in my school holidays!

I have already mentioned that Madhya Pradesh is known to have a significant tribal – *adavasi* – population and this falls into three distinct tribal groups. The most numerous are the Gonds, who once ruled much of the land of Madhya Pradesh centuries ago, and, after whom, Gondwana, the central portion, came to be known. They inhabited the Satpura and Kymore Ranges and their major branches, the Madias and the Muria Gonds live in Bastar, which is now in Chhattisgarh. I will talk about the Gonds a little later with some relevant history at another point in the journey. From what I have gleaned, Chhattisgarh's tourism is still in a fledgling state but the ethos is good and not the rather dismal disinterested inertia of so many state tourism enterprises throughout India. There is a lot to see in the form of wildlife parks and virgin forests, waterfalls as I have mentioned, and the Kotamsar and Kailash caves plus some ancient temples. Tribal art and handicrafts are particularly beautiful and interesting. This is a lost world waiting to be discovered but only I fervently hope with care and consideration. It is worth reflecting that, in my youth, Khajuraho was not known but look how it has developed into a gem of a tourist destination. I think this could be the future for the area of Bastar and its capital of Jagdalpur.

We arrived at Mandla and knew that the major portion of our drive was accomplished. After deciding on one of the many tiny STD shops, I was able to telephone my mother and tell her all about the morning's excitement with the tiger. It seemed incredible that the last time she and I had been on an elephant together was in 1952 in Bandipur Wildlife Park, and we had just seen a tiger quietly slinking away; now, 50 years later, Graham and I were having such wonderful experiences and amassing memories that will stay with us for ever.

The 15 km of road towards Kanha was superb, a typical example of the fact that when India sets her mind to do something she does it very well. Apparently, this stretch of road had been laid at a time when the late Rajiv Gandhi was going to visit some local institution; because the road was in a dreadful state, the powers that be decided to rebuild that particular stretch for his visit. Rajiv Gandhi died tragically in May 1991 and here we were in November 2002 and the road was superb, eleven years later. It just fills one with frustration and disappointment that the state government cannot prioritise and achieve the same for the rest of Madhya Pradesh's roads – they are in dire need of improvement. I have recently read in India Today, the very worth while Indian weekly, that Madhya Pradesh is now aware of its transport infrastructure's weakness and is resolved to improve matters. They could achieve this within two years if they were sufficiently committed to the idea. I am confident the benefits would be exponential.

CHAPTER ELEVEN

Another Glorious Tigress and a Charming Elephant!

F inally, in the golden afternoon sunlight, we crossed the upper reaches of the Narmada River. This is one of India's seven sacred rivers along with the Ganges, Yamuna, Saraswati (which is underground), Godavari, Sindhu and Kaveri.

"O Holy Mother Ganges! O Yamuna! O Godavari! Saraswati! O Narmada! Sindhu! Kaveri! May you all be pleased to be manifest in these waters with which I shall purify myself" (Prayer to the Seven Sacred Rivers recited by every devout Hindu at the time of taking his bath) – that is an English translation of the prayer.

I had never been over the Narmada or on its banks, though I had seen it at Mandu. That made it rather special for me as I have experienced the Ganges or *Ganga* and the Jumna or *Yamuna* and the Godavari in Southern India. Near to the source of the Narmada, it is quite beautiful and timeless with many artificial small tanks as they are called in India, really artificial ponds on the banks of which are several small good-looking towns. I imagine its actual source will be as lovely as that of other mighty waterways all over the world. Sadly, currently this is a subject of huge controversy as the various state governments have sought to harness it in a huge dam project running through Gujarat, Maharashtra and Madhya Pradesh, where a series of 30 mega dams, 135 medium and 3000 small dams are being constructed. Up to half a million people are expected to be displaced by the project and the lives of a further 21 million who depend on the ecology of the valley will also be affected. The largest dam, the *Sardar Sarovar* had been held up by a legal stay on construction but this had been removed in 2000 by the Supreme Court. This decision will allow approximately 245 more villages to be flooded and many of their inhabitants have pledged to drown when the waters are finally released. Arundhati Roy, the Booker Prize winner for her book *The God of Small Things* has spoken out strenuously about the scheme and, as is quite normal in India, there is a huge army of volunteers working to rescind the decision. But, with so many big businesses and political futures enmeshed in the project, it is unlikely that the millions of dispossessed and relocated villagers will have any real success. Certainly The World Bank which had originally pledged 450 million dollars towards the project withdrew when an independent report stated that all those who would be fundamentally affected could not possibly be resettled or rehabilitated adequately and that the full consequences to the environment had not been adequately addressed.

Writing about this dilemma for modern India between its ancient past and thrusting new endeavours I am reminded of a most beautiful poem that I once read and found so moving.

Hospitality in the Narayana, by Hitopadesa (written in the 12 century A.D).
The Book of Good Counsels:

> *"Bar thy door not to the stranger,*
> *Be he friend or be he foe,*
> *For the tree will shade the woodman*
> *While his axe doth lay it low.*
>
> *Greeting fair and room to rest;*
> *Fire and water from the well*
> *Simple gifts – are freely given*
> *In the house where good men dwell.*
>
> *Young, or bent with many winters;*
> *Rich or poor, what'er thy guest,*
> *Honour him for thine own honour*
> *Better is he than the best.*
>
> *Pity them that ask thy pity;*
> *Who are thou to stint thy hoard?*
> *When the holy moon shines equal*
> *On the leper and the lord!*
>
> *When thy gate is roughly fastened,*
> *And the asker turns away,*
> *Thence he bears the good deeds with him,*
> *And his sins on thee doth lay."*

These sentiments just say it all. Ancient heartland, village life, time-honoured cultures may all be swept away with the dam waters. Up until now not all India's dam schemes have proved beneficial, sometimes, third world expediency returns to haunt a country. Sadly, whoever is in power locally and centrally inevitably has a personal axe to grind. The age of true altruism has gone it would seem and, in mature years, I now realise that not even the most high minded politician in any country in the world actually possesses this rare quality. Philanthropists, yes; politicians, no!

Thankfully, we reached our destination after a very attractive approach. The Banjar River flows on the perimeter of the park and is lovely: wide with huge rocks and boulders. In the evening sun with its long shadows, everything looked so tranquil and one could see women washing clothes and others bathing. Our chosen spot, Kipling Camp, was in walking distance of the river and afforded us much pleasure as you will discover! Kipling belongs to Bob Wright of Tollygunge Club fame in Calcutta or Kolkota (as I must learn to call it). Sadly, Bob could not be there to greet us as he is a man of senior years and in frail health and had to return by train to see his medical consultants in Kolkota. I was so sorry to miss him and remember him from over 40 years ago when his children and I were but teenagers. He, however, had charming people running the whole outfit in the shape of Margie Watts Carter and Aditya Dev. Kipling's star attraction is Tara, the lovely elephant made famous by Mark Shand in his delightful book *Travels On My Elephant.*

Kipling Camp's dining and convivial area

Gudu said farewell and went off for a very well-earned rest. I enquired what arrangements he had made and he assured me that all was well and he would see us in two days time. I have no doubt he had a pleasant spell, in which he found time to use the beautiful river to wash his precious new 4 by 4; he took such pride in its smart appearance. Kipling Camp is configured in a cluster of simple cottages with a continuous veranda. The rooms are very basic but attractive, with their own bathrooms. There is a larger building which is laid out as a sitting area, dining area and bar. During the day, lunch is taken at a long table under the trees. The evening meal is under a roof to escape the dew and, because it gets quite cool, one needs a sweater or shawl. There are clever round fireplaces, which essentially are a deep cement circular lip in which a wood fire is lit, round which one can sit and socialise. Because it is the brainchild of a European, the décor or ambience is more western in style, as if one had wandered on to someone's charming veranda of long ago with quirky humour and photographs that are relevant, plus books by authors who have visited, most important of all Mark Shand, who still owns Tara who lives in her elephant house a few metres away.

After a welcome shower and change, we went out to meet up with the other guest. Mark Ponniah is a charming Australian of Sri Lankan Tamil origin, proud of both his heritages and utterly devoted to wildlife. It was a pleasure to get to know him. Margie and Aditya and others joined us three. It was a pleasant and relaxed gathering followed by some welcome dinner. A few hundred metres away is Wild Chalet, which is also a very nice set up with individual cottages and dining hall right on the banks of the Banjar River, a truly delightful spot. I did not go and inspect the various other camps and lodgings which I am sure are just fine. Wild Chalet belongs to the group Indian Adventures which also owns Tiger Trails at Bandhavgarh and Tiger Moon at Ranthambhore, at both of which we stayed. They have another establishment called Bison River in Dandeli down in South India. I think they are good value for money. I have been informed that Margie and Aditya have since gone on to another place but I am optimistic that Kipling will endure. My only advice would be for the cook to be very firmly directed to cook Indian food, at which he must be reasonably competent. His venture into European cuisine was eccentric and not very toothsome! In the wilds of a huge wildlife park in India's heartland, the ingredients for British or western cuisine are not readily available. Long years ago, wonderful *khansamas* cooked utterly astonishing French and British food, the secrets of which had been handed down father to son. Indeed, our beloved Din, who was my parents' cook, as a young man had worked for my maternal grandfather Ord as a sort of sous-chef under his own father, Joe, the cook; he was just brilliant. I wish I had had the wisdom to learn the secrets of some of his fabulous dishes. The old man and I had an excellent relationship, rather like having an Indian grandfather, but he did not think to teach me and my head was too full of teenage delights and ambitions. Mummy and I still apparently get a faraway look in our eyes when reminiscing about his chicken cutlets, aloo (i.e. potato) chops and chicken dumpo. This last dish was only made for important dinner parties being a chicken within a chicken within a chicken with a sort of rich cream quenelle stuffing – obviously French in its origins. I am sure chicken dumpo had a much more elegant name in its original French form.

Rising at 0500 hours the next morning, we were cold and needed extra sweaters and blankets with which to envelop ourselves. Aditya had ordered cold omelettes and *aloo parathas* with fruit for our breakfast which was to be taken within the park at a designated picnic and comfort halt.

Kanha, considered the king of the parks nestles in the Central Indian Highlands; it is a world-class natural heritage site. There is justifiable pride in it being the first Sanctuary of the country having been established in 1935. Now, it has an area of 1838 sq. km of which 940 sq. km. is core, a national park, and 898 sq. km is a buffer zone.

The wildlife spectrum includes tiger, panther (leopard), wild dog, bison, barasingha, sambhar, cheetal, chousingha, nilgai, sloth bear, wild boar, langur monkeys and other species of mammals and reptiles, besides around 300 species of birdlife.

The floral splendour includes sal, saja, bija, jamun, mahua, semal, amla, tendu, dhaman, palas, kusum, arjun, dhaora, harra, bahera, lendia and bamboo, apart from unquantifiable species of grasses and ground flora.

Kanha is so large that one has to take breakfast and refreshment with one in the jeep. Aditya is an expert and dedicated conservationist and took immense trouble taking us out and showing us, or attempting to show us, all its attractions. It is stunning in its immensity and the park was by no means full and noisy as had been the case at Ranthambhore. Graham and I enjoyed ourselves immensely and at the picnic stop met up with Harshad Patel and Anil Juwarkar who were by this time staying at Wild Chalet next door to Kipling. We asked them over for a drink that evening. I also met up with Barry Snyder who had been with us on the elephant in Bandhavgarh. He too is passionate about the world's wildlife.

We visited the Kanha Centre which is quite good with a well-organised information and educational centre. They could, however, improve on their merchandising. All of that side of things is still very amateur in Indian parks, as opposed to our National Trust properties and great gardens and countryside parks. If the efficiency with which the Indian Army is run could somehow permeate the Wildlife and Forestry Departments then I am sure it would all take a huge step forward. In the UK, we know how important 'ethos' is to an organisation and, if one has people thinking 'job for life', an inertia sets in. India has a vast amount of that thinking sadly but, then, so did we in our own way. Nationalised industries in the UK in the years following World War II and before the 1980s, were famous for just lumbering along. India is now aware of these problems and seems to be trying to tackle it but one requires people of the stature of the late great J R D Tata, to be enticed in to head national institutions. J R D Tata most famously ran Air India International in the 1950 and 60s and made it so enviable at that time – a true flagship carrier. To turn things around and move constructively forward, it requires government dedication and, at last, we are beginning to see that appearing. The new President of India, President Kamal, although himself a scientist, has a dedication to conservation; perhaps he will gather round him some good leaders of vision and integrity.

In the afternoon, after a well-earned shower and lunch under the dappled shade of huge sal trees, we had a treat in store. The tradition at Kipling is that Tara the elephant walks down to the river with her mahawat and second mahawat. She ambled through camp and we caught up with her on the water's edge. She

Tara's daily bathing ritual in Banjar river

needed no urging to wade in and we saw her sinking in, deeper and deeper till only her head and trunk are visible. Oh! Was this a happy big elephant! She was such a darling, rather like an elephantine toddler enjoying her bath. She completely submerged and blew bubbles through her trunk, which looked like a periscope curling and kinking out of the water. Then, a contented eye appeared and looked at us, and finally, with a whooshing noise, she rolled over. We just sat on the boulders as close as was sensibly possible and crowed with delight. Mark decided to swim quite close to her – and him a biologist who should be quite aware of some of the water parasites that abound! Finally, the mahawat called and told her to get out – this took a further 15 minutes as she pretended she had not heard him and waded off deeper into the river. Tara looked on defiantly and he one minute scolded and then cajoled her. At last, she very reluctantly got up and waded to the shore. Then, she was told to lie down and this was where our job began. Truly, it was one of the most enjoyable experiences of my trip. I waded in and started to scrub this great creature along with her mahawats, each of us using a brush. Graham joined us. She just lay there and I stroked her ears and patted her head and just loved scratching her trunk, the tip of which is pink and tactile like a forefinger and thumb. I kept talking to her and telling her she was both shower and blow dryer all in one

The serious business of helping to scrub Tara

because of course she scooped up water and squirted it out, and then blew. She took my fingers in the tip of her trunk gently, just watching with one attentive eye. She liked to feel all round my various rings like a curious toddler might. On reflection, it was just like playing with my little grandsons, her gentle movements all the time belying her great size and strength.

When one side was all scrubbed she was told to get up and lie down showing the other side. Regretfully, finally the bath was finished and she was cajoled to get out, which she did slowly and reluctantly. Then, Tara went and stood on a great boulder to sun and dry herself. We took the opportunity to have tea from a flask. The next bit was pure delight! She was given a stick, about a foot (30 cm) long with which she proceeded to give herself a pedicure. I know it sounds a bit rich, but that is exactly what one saw, this wonderful huge animal picking up her feet one at a time, and scratching between her toes, the stick of course being manipulated very dextrously in her trunk. At one stage, she seemed to be standing on two feet, one front and one back. She was then fed and given tit bits and told to turn round and sun the other side. Sadly, the ritual being accomplished she walked off to be saddled up with a howdah. Tying the girth straps just right is vital. Once this was accomplished, we were invited to get on and then Tara ambled gently back to Kipling in the glow of the setting sun. It was a precious interlude and Graham, Mark and I just loved it.

Clean and contented Tara carries Aline and Graham home for tea!

Graham asked me to ask the mahawat about elephant diseases but the only thing he was prepared to admit to was that she can catch worms from eating earth. Graham wanted to know if males were castrated and whether their testicles were internal. I said firmly that, never mind that I do not know all the Hindi for that sort of conversation (after all not an average topic), I was not going to attempt indelicate subjects with a strange Indian mahawat! Graham later found out a lot of what he wanted to know from Aditya but is now determined to bone up on veterinary knowledge pertaining to elephants. On arrival back at camp, Tara let us down and ambled off to her own house. Mark Shand comes to see her as often as he can manage and had arranged to have her new house built for her.

Later on in the evening, Harshad and Anil came over from Wild Chalet with Eric, who runs it, a nice knowledgeable man. We had a splendid evening with much talk and laughter. Harshad very generously offered me one of his tiger photographs for this book, which is so typical of his generosity (Harshad's photographs are on pages 128-131). They both explained the aims and aspirations of The Vanishing Herds Foundation to the others present. In the last month as I write in 2003, the Foundation has been registered here in the UK and also in the US. It was originally officially given charitable status in India. Now, however, serious fundraising can take place and a website is being designed, which, when completed to Harshad's satisfaction, I will arrange to have linked to my own website and do everything I can to promote its ideas. I have been appointed a director of The Vanishing Herds Foundation Ltd in the UK and am now a UK trustee.

Harshad Patel with Aline, Graham and others at Kipling

The following morning something amusing happened. The bearer came with a wake up call of tea and fruit. Somehow I thought something was wrong and looked at my watch – 03.45 hours! So I went on to the veranda where Mark was already sitting smoking. When I questioned the time he too was astonished. Graham had not moved. I just went back to bed but, of course, could not sleep. The poor young bearer came back with a further tray of tea, madly apologetic, so I just said '*koi bath ne*' which means it doesn't matter/it is of no consequence. The embarrassed young man had got us all up an hour too early.

In the cold morning air, were we glad of the blankets round us in the jeep. It was a pleasant morning with picnic breakfast on the plateau. Lovely and peaceful and one can see for miles with not a building in sight. When we

Sunrise at Kanha

returned from the upland, we saw a number of animals, the usual chital, sambhar, gaur (a herd of them actually, which was wonderful). Gaur are the mighty bison with magnificent horns and huge breadth of shoulder. Then, there was muntjac (the hog deer), wild boar, monkeys, owls, an eagle, two jackals and some peacocks.

Aditya received word that a tigress had been sighted and that elephants were available on which to ride and see her close up. This we did with alacrity. Apparently, some purists feel it is in some way prostituting wildlife viewing. What nonsense! As we had already experienced, seeing tiger at close range from an elephant is one of the most visually splendid experiences one can hope to have, like swimming with dolphins and snorkelling in restricted areas with plentiful sea life. These are life enhancing experiences that have never in my observation from experiences around the world left the individual unmoved. Be it in Mexico, the Caribbean, India, Borneo or Viet Nam, Africa or Europe, close encounters with the world's wonderful creatures is something to be valued and will always stay in one's visual and sometimes tactile memory as with dolphins. Indeed, provided the animal is in no way badly treated or exploited, it is the way to educate people, and the privileged who travel, as to how fortunate we are to share this planet with other creatures.

A swift climb onto the back of Hemawati took us right up to the tigress lying camouflaged in the long grass. Oh, she was magnificent. We just gazed from about 10 feet away and clicked our cameras. She yawned and panted, and slightly moved about. My film ran out and Mark very generously gave me another 400 speed film. Try changing a film on a shifting elephant with everyone craning to see a tiger! However, the Tiger God smiled on me. It was successfully accomplished and I was able to take some potentially excellent shots with a zoom lens. We all had a great feeling of elation because the experience must have lasted about 15 minutes or more and then the elephant walked back to the jeep for us to dismount. We heard that the tigress was moving and had risen. All the while another wildlife enthusiast had been on the ground shooting film with a video. We found his behaviour rather odd: this is not an open air zoo and that tigress is not tame. Yes, she knew that she was not threatened by any of us and that her needs are respected and catered for but she is a wild animal and would be unpredictable if spooked. Our pedestrian visitor was behaving as if we had been watching 'the greater crested warbler' or some such bird. People appear to get carried away and lose touch with reality.

Graham, Mark and I were so happy. Curiously, there was a young girl out from Scotland who was helping at Kipling along with us on the elephant. She was experiencing her first sighting of big game in sublime surroundings and behaved in such an odd mute way that all of us just rolled our eyes. Perhaps these youngsters are so blasé that they are underwhelmed by what enriches the rest of us, which is, rather sadly, their loss. We were grateful that Aditya took so much trouble with us and we all returned elated to camp for a quick change and lunch and then departure. It was a happy occasion and Mark wanted to come with us in the 4 by 4 as far as Jabalpur, from where he would be catching a train up to Delhi. We were very glad to have him along and said our farewells and had a last pat on Tara's trunk as she ambled past for her bathing ritual, I wish I could have stayed longer but you know sometimes that is the right time to depart and have the most wonderful memories forever.

Jabalpur must have been a charming city once. It is still a prosperous bustling place and HQ for the Indian Army Madhya Pradesh/Orissa Command. The British established the military cantonment and administrative centre in 1819 and there are still English medium schools and hospitals as well as a mission presence. The drive from Kanha was pleasant but all of three and a half to four hours; however, talking between friends sitting in comparative comfort and safety with Gudu driving into the westering sun was pleasant. The army was much in evidence with so many thousands of troops newly returned from the frontier after the relaxation of hostilities between India and Pakistan. There are so many Raj era buildings, some of which are in beautiful condition but others have been allowed to decay totally, which seems odd in a country where renovate, repair, recycle could be the second name. We passed an elegant central war memorial in the middle of the old-style wide suburban road. I just

Contented tiger – Kanha

A magnificent tiger at close range – Kanha

managed to read the inscription "In memory of All the Men of all classes and creeds who sacrificed their lives …" I could not read the full inscription but that most poignant of phrases sums up the sacrifice of so many in the twentieth century. For me, it tied in so fittingly with the dedication by HM The Queen of The Memorial Gates to the Commonwealth War Dead of the Two World Wars. This had taken place on 6th November 2002 and had been the culmination of a five-year ambition for Baroness Shreela Flather, herself an Indian who sits in the House of Lords. Those of us with links to the Indian Army consider it should have happened long ago. What is interesting, however, is that the bulk of donations came from within the UK, and sadly some of India's most wealthy people, including those who frequent The Indian Merchants' Chamber in Mumbai and those who have achieved notoriety recently in Britain with political cronyism gave absolutely nothing. Actually, it is one of the unpleasant sides to India's wealth and progress that, although there are some great philanthropists, a huge number of reasonably successful people are apparently totally self-absorbed and unwilling to 'give back'. Indeed, I was to witness some of this again in Mumbai. All countries have these complacent folk who are only too ready to buy self-enhancing favours but, somehow, I thought that giving towards a memorial for the War Dead would transcend their petty ambitions. Here, in Scotland, one observes with some cynicism those who join charitable or voluntary committees for the 'social enhancement' factor. Inevitably, they are the people who find it challenging to turn up regularly to meetings or get stuck in to the washing up or whatever boring essential is part of the fundraising or social activity.

I have returned to this chapter on 11th November 2003 because in yesterday's edition of The Times I found the following excellent article by Jack Straw, the current Foreign Secretary.

Wear a poppy, too, for these forgotten legions of Asia

"Why are they here? What have they ever done for us? Is a cry I hear less often than I did 25 years ago ... on the day before Armistice Day, there is one very good answer (of many) to this question. 'They' fought and died for 'Us' in very large numbers in both world wars, and I might add, 'We' have never given sufficient acknowledgement to 'Them' in the decades that followed. …..By the end of the First World War, 1,100,000 people from British India – now India, Pakistan and Bangladesh – had served overseas, at a cost of 60,000 dead. Some 9,200 such soldiers won decorations, including 11 VCs. In the Second World War, the Indian Army had two and a half million men, the largest volunteer army the world has ever seen. And 87,000 died for us … And the Indians and Pakistanis who died in the mud along with their comrades from Blackburn and

Accrington and Burnley and across Britain no doubt asked all the time: 'Why are we here?' The simple answer is that we are all part of humankind: but above and beyond that, the lives and histories of Britain and South Asia have been intertwined for centuries. And, whatever people may feel 'They' owe 'Us', we owe them a great deal for dying thousands of miles from their homes, for us."

At last, there is some recognition that is so long overdue.

Our hotel in Jabalpur, the Kalchuria could be good but, being run by Madhya Pradesh Tourism, it is dire. However, remembering young Naveen's words 'this can be fun?', we looked on the bright side which was that the room was reasonably well appointed. The desk clerk warned us, however, that from 06.30 hours the next morning, the electricity would be off. This is a huge problem in Madhya Pradesh. Due to the state government's lack of vision through the years, the grid cannot supply all its customers on a continuous basis. What it must cost in terms of productivity lost is unimaginable. I resolved to jump in the shower and wash and dry my hair at that minute! Mark had also taken a room and we met up for drink after which he wanted to give us dinner but, as I have said the place was appalling, so we took an auto rickshaw to another, The Sandyria, for some supper. The restaurant was busy and there were one or two other foreigners. The food was good; however, just as we had finished Graham said 'look at that!' A little mouse had appeared and was eating all the crumbs under the adjoining table. I told the waiters that 'a chota chua' was there and we received the distinct impression that it wasn't the first time that they had seen him. We were glad that we had already eaten and indeed came to no harm. He was a dear little mouse rather like the ones Raju brings in at home that, if possible, we scoop them up in a special plastic jug and let them go in the garden or over our neighbour's wall. These are the hazards of having an excellent mouser for a pet. Sometimes he eats them but mostly I am successful in retrieving them and taking them to safety. He used to bring in the odd little bunny; I once found one cowering under a bedcover in the spare room and just scooped up the frightened creature and took him out (well away from Graham's vegetable garden!) The next morning, we departed at 06.30 hours having said our farewells to Mark the night before with a promise to visit him and his mother in Australia.

I should, however, say more about Jabalpur, although, at first glance, it is not a prepossessing place. Nearby, the Narmada gouged out a gorge of marble rocks that is truly a sight, particularly in the moonlight; for us it was a full moon. This is quite a tourist attraction but my mother had told me about them and that, in the early days without tourist tat, they were really beautiful. For me, the charm increases the less people there are milling around.

The former capital of this area was at Tripuri about 9 km west. That site was occupied around 2000 BC onwards and rose to prominence because of the lucrative trade route through the fertile Narmada Valley. The Kushanas who were contemporary to the start of the Christian era were followed by the Satavahanas, but these dynasties frittered away their power and wealth. The Kalchuri dynasty brought the area to prominence and their martial endeavours enabled successive rulers to extend their borders westwards. Finally, they too were swept aside by The Gonds who were descendants of Tripuri's original inhabitants, tribal people. Gond rule gradually spread down the Narmada to Bhopal before it was met by the force of one of Akbar's famous governors, Asaf Khan, in 1564. Rani Durgavati put up a fearsome resistance but was overwhelmed by the imperial army and Asaf Khan was installed as the region's overlord. This was the area known as Gondwana. The area is also well known through the stories of Kipling's Jungle Book and Mowgli stories. I grew up on these stories and so for me it was very special to have visited the forests, parkland, ravines and plateau that inspired Kipling to write his timeless classic that no doubt in due course I will read to my little grandsons, Piers and William. I do not, however, like the fact that Kipling made the tiger into a 'baddy'. That might have served in his time but today the tigers are the victims of man's inhumanity and greed and exploitation. Sher Khan was the name of the tiger 'baddy' against whom all of the jungle conspired to keep Mowgli safe. Well, now, many of us are happy to conspire and work tirelessly to help keep the tiger population safe from extinction in the great wild places of India. Once again, having seen these beautiful beasts in their remarkable bright colouring; having looked into their wonderful yellow/green eyes and seen and heard them pant and yawn and stretch and above all trust us, my friends, I am committed to helping preserve them in the best way I know how, by writing.

Jabalpur has a few places of interest including the Rani Durgavati Museum. Three kilometres west of the centre there are some pleasant bathing ghats, banyan trees and a row of crumbling Hindu shrines. A little further away, there are a couple of immaculately whitewashed Jain temples, much as we had seen at Sonagiri earlier. At Tilwara Ghat there are a handful of shrines which mark the spot where Gandhiji's ashes were scattered after his brutal assassination. His ashes were also scattered into the Ganga Yamuna confluence and, I do not know, but maybe even a portion of his ashes were strewn in the Godavari river. That special, little, courageous man and his writings and thoughts continue to inspire me, a child of Indian Independence; how he would have hated the suspicion, hatred and dreadful violence that are being demonstrated worldwide by evil men who have turned a great religion and doctrine on its head. He always looked for the good in all religions and he hated any form of communalism or sectarianism within India.

Gandhiji's words on Tolerance were:

> *I do not want a kingdom, salvation or heaven;*
> *What I want is to remove the troubles of the oppressed*
> *and the poor.*
> *I do not want my house to be walled in all sides and my*
> *windows to be stuffed.*
> *I want the cultures of all lands to be blown about my*
> *house, as freely as possible.*
> *But I refuse to be blown off my feet by any, I refuse to*
> *live in other people's houses as an Interloper, a beggar*
> *or a slave.*

The majestic Tiger

The Indian Leopard

Flamingos

The beautiful but threatened Asiatic Lion

Sambhar Deer

Indian Rhino

Elephants on the roadside, 1956

A young Aline wins first prize as The Queen of Hearts. Fancy dress party, Christmas Day 1950, Bihar

Aline as a young girl stroking a Sambhar Deer, 1954

CHAPTER TWELVE

The Long Bad Road to Bhopal

In October 2003 in The Times of London, I read a tiny article in the 'This Life' column which I shall quote verbatim: 'A civil servant has requested permission to kill himself in protest at the corruption and bureaucracy of an Indian state government. Vinod Shukla, under-secretary in the Madhya Pradesh finance department said: "I am fed up with the present system where honest officers are being sidelined for reasons best known to the higher-ups. I am prepared for the final act." The government's home, finance and administration departments have been asked to advise the governor on whether suicide is a workplace issue.'

Pigeons are coming home to roost for the Chief Minister Digvijay Singh who represents the Congress Party, led by Sonia Gandhi, heir to her late husband, mother in law, and grandfather in law Pandit Nehru. Madhya Pradesh is about to go to elections, as is Rajasthan and the likely winner is a woman candidate from the BJP, the Bharatia Janata Party which is the governing party, currently headed by Prime Minister Atal Behari Vajpayee. Apparently, the electorate are completely disillusioned with Digvijay Singh because he has enjoyed two terms of office and still the state suffers from severe power shortages, as we experienced, and appalling infrastructure, to which I have also referred. Both politicians are going through all sorts of politically expedient hoops, the BJP candidate enveloping herself in a religious 'holier than thou' mantle, but the truth is that the voters of Madhya Pradesh have woken up to the fact that they are as a state collectively needlessly backward in comparison to others because of inertia, corruption and inefficiency. I am heartened that all this has come to the fore in this forthcoming election, and again it reinforces my belief that, given an opportunity, democracy is the only way forward, even when faced with India's huge challenges. Indians, I am proud to say, know this to be true.

Ahead of us lay at least a seven-hour road journey to Bhopal. This is not something I would suggest to other travellers but, as I want to write about the heart of India, I have to do the research and just flying in and out or rushing by in a train does not give one sufficient experience and knowledge of an area; however fleetingly I visited it, at least we experienced much of what there is to see and do. Part of the main road to Bhopal is good but most of it is awful. As ever, the Indian countryside is both interesting and beautiful but the little towns are pretty dreary because of their poverty and squalor. Typical of government initiatives, one sees signs all over the big 'metro' cities and some smaller ones saying 'Say no to plastic'. Well, it will need some courageous action on the part of the Central Government to ban the use of plastic. We in the West have our own litter and refuse problems. Indians vets report that so many animals die from obstruction caused by eating plastic. It is worth reflecting that, in our own sanitised western culture, we are littering the earth with an annual use of more than 20 million disposable nappies in the USA alone. The UK will proportionately be just as bad, the first disposable nappy has not yet degraded. The bottom end of a baby is the least agreeable side of parenthood but we have made it all so easy at what cost to our global environment? In the past, Indians used cloth bags and then perhaps brown paper but in our modern triple-wrap society it is a nightmare.

The roads of Madhya Pradesh hid a huge sinister secret for hundreds of years. The goddess Kali was the deity of the Thugs who practised the ancient sinister wicked order of *thuggee*. Shiva, the destroyer, the agent of death and destruction without which growth and rebirth could not take place is one of the Trimurthi of gods. He is represented with either one or four faces. His matted hair is said to carry Ganga, the goddess of the river Ganges in it. His consort is Parvati, the beautiful daughter of the Himalaya and considered to be the perfect wife. She is also a form of the mother goddess Devi, whose body is India, and also appears as Durga the terrible (with a great following in Eastern India, particularly in West Bengal), and she also appears as Kali, the fiercest and to my mind most repulsive of deities. Durga is a mighty goddess with the combined power and strength of Brahma, Vishnu and Shiva – thought of as Shakti. Legend has it that the gods were impotent to quell a powerful demon in the guise of a black water buffalo. When their combined wrath condensed it became Durga. To her each of the gods gave his most powerful weapon. She decapitated the buffalo demon and slew the devil within. It is Durga who is supposed to have created

Kali who sprang fully formed from Durga's forehead. To incur the wrath of Kali is a terrible mistake within the Hindu belief.

Having lived a lot of my young life in West Bengal where Durga Puja and worship of Kali is strong, I find it totally repelling. Kali was the deity of the thugs. Up until 1830 when Colonel William Sleeman, later knighted, set his mind to ridding India's roads from the horror and nightmare of *thuggee*, travel in large parts of the sub-continent was very dangerous. Essentially, they were a secret sect of bandits and Kali worshippers who used to express their devotion to Kali, the jet-black four armed goddess of death, often depicted splattered with blood and with a necklace of skulls round her neck and a belt of dead men's hands.

These murderers would fall in with innocent travellers on the main roads, most especially in what we know as Madhya Pradesh. They would gain the confidence of the unwary, throttle them with the notorious silk scarf (*rumal* in Hindi) and any pieces of the corpse not required for rituals were dumped in wells or buried in large pits.

Fear of retribution and a belief that this was the will of this all powerful goddess forced village head men and local rulers to turn a blind eye and allow the killings to continue for generations. Sleeman acted with great strength and guile and with effective ruthlessness. Working through informers, who were promised leniency for themselves, he was able to capture 4000 thugs during a twenty-year campaign. Some of these murderers had notched up over 300 victims each. Special courts sent 400 convicted thugs to the gallows and many more to jail in the penal colonies on the Andaman Islands. The informers mostly ended up in a reform school in Jabalpur, from where we were travelling. Interestingly, as late as the 1960s, when roads were being widened in this part of the country, the contractors would come across the remains of ancient pits of murdered travellers.

I told you about bandits at an earlier stage in the book when talking about the late Phulan Devi, the Bandit Queen, but thugs were part of India's evil past and probably the supreme example of how simple illiterate people can be drawn into something so sinister and bad by indoctrination – but then it was Christianity that was referred to 'as the opium of the masses'; any religion or cult it seems can be so powerfully enforced to subvert untrained minds of humble people who live so close to the land that their whole lives become an existence with timely interruptions of ritual and menace. In the full glare of the noon sun with women working on the roads, fetching and filling potholes – yes, that is what they are doing in Madhya Pradesh using hands not machinery, one needs to pinch oneself to imagine murder and menace at the start of the twenty-first century. However, we have seen several bizarre cults in the last twenty years in which mass suicide and other sorts of horrors have played a part, so really a cult of ritual mass murder to appease a blood-thirsty deity less than two hundred years ago in an ancient land where religion used to govern every aspect of living is not that extreme. The word 'thug' is well known in the English language sadly; British 'thugs' are mercifully not necessarily murderers, just persons intent on violence and intimidation, but that is how the word came into our language.

As we neared Bhopal, the road did improve and the three of us cheered up at the prospect of an attractive destination. Gudu was able to find tea on the roadside but we did not trust the tea and could only find some bottled lemonade and a very primitive latrine at the top of the café owner's house; meanwhile the café customers were all glued to the cricket on the television – forever India, the two extremes of sophistication and squalor!

About 45 km southeast of Bhopal, one takes a secondary road to Bhimbetka. Discovered in 1957, this is one of the world's largest collections of prehistoric rock art. This is South Asia's equivalent of the caves at Lascaux in southwest France and Altamira in Spain, or the aboriginal paintings found in Australia. The earlier paintings are thought to have been done about 12,000 years ago. The second more prolific phase is about 8,000 to 5,000 BC. Quite simply these drawing or paintings are wonderful in their similarity to present day creatures: elephants, bison, wild boar, antelope and even what appear to be tigers. This Mesolithic era, i.e., Stone Age, art is astounding and all the more so because of its location in these open caves of huge rocks and boulders that look down onto the plain below. Both the Upper Palaeolithic era drawings and the later Mesolithic art fills one with awe because one begins to appreciate how the whole area must have been teeming with wildlife which is now largely confined to designated areas. It was sunny and rather windy and the *chowkidar* was a decent chap who took a lot of trouble to explain and show us all that there is to see. The area is reasonably well preserved, but open to the elements and free of charge; one simply pays some *baksheesh* to the watchmen on departure. Not many people take the trouble to come but, curiously, again it is those on the Buddhist Trail that form the bulk of the tourists, and we encountered some Japanese or Koreans as we were leaving.

Last year in October, the day before I departed for India, I came across an article in The Times reporting the discovery of wonderful rock art at Shankargarh, near Allahabad in Uttar Pradesh. Apparently, the local villagers had known about the local cave art but events took over when they found labourers trying

Bhimbetka's ancient rock art

to hew huge rocks off the boulders to sell for silica. They ran for the nearest police superintendent and when Superintendent Vijay Kumar arrived and saw the art he was amazed and knew that this was a hugely important find. Local experts summoned to examine the paintings said they may be between 10,000 and 30,000 years old. If their assessment can be confirmed it would rival Bhimbetka or maybe indeed surpass those that we have seen. The discovery was even more significant because, within a deeper set of caves, archaeologists discovered further treasures, more red ochre paint sketches and drawings and some detailed diagrams of the internal organs of animals. The ground was littered with what appeared to be tools used by the pre-historic occupants of the caves. No doubt, in time, this will become a tourist destination but, apart from building a road to access it, I think it is unlikely to be spoiled and exploited because Bhimbetka is still very simple and untouched. Tourists bound for hedonistic pleasures do not go miles out of their way to see obscure prehistoric sites, thankfully; thus these wild ancient places will retain their beauty and mystery for the rest of us.

Pachmarhi is a hill station reasonably close to Bhimbetka. It was only discovered in 1857, i.e., a century before Bhimbetka, by the explorer and big game hunter, Captain Forsyth. Again, this plateau is littered with similar rock paintings but one would have to search them out. Pachmarhi, however, is an attractive little place to which city folk go to escape the heat of the plains in summer. The town is 1000 metres above sea level and thus very cool and the architectural legacy of the Raj is evident in the colonial bungalows, church with spire and parade grounds and garden atmosphere. The Satpura National

Park to the north and west of the town encompasses a 600 sq. km swathe of sal, teak and bamboo forest. The park has bison (gaur), barking deer, sambhar, barasingha, jackals, wild dogs and a few tigers and leopards.

LifeForce, the wildlife charity, about which I have already written, does a lot of constructive work at Satpura Tiger Reserve. Our friend who is dedicated to conservation reports that, whilst the 2002 monsoon was not the heaviest, the vegetation was lush and green, large herds of sambhar and other herbivores were present, providing a good prey base for many carnivores: wild dog, smaller wild cats, civets, leopard and tiger. Five tigers were seen socialising very unusually and remaining together beyond a casual encounter. In November and December 2002, a tigress and cubs were seen in the forest only 3 km from the LifeForce base. Problems with poaching do, sadly, continue and, though the poachers were caught and await trial, whatever the legal outcome, the damage is done.

LifeForce has a litter patrol and tries to educate both the local population and visitors how persistent and widespread litter produces a breeding ground for harmful bacteria, which causes death of animals and despoils the natural beauty. The charity gives strategic support for the tribal people and villagers as part of community-based conservation. This year alone, ten tube wells have been drilled to provide water for drinking, bathing and irrigation. In areas where tube well bores did not find water, stop dams and lakes, provided by Lifeforce, have served the same purpose.

During the LifeForce medical camp in the forest, when over 600 people were treated by four doctors from Mumbai, it became apparent that a basic knowledge of hygiene, nutrition and malaria could prevent many problems. As a result LifeForce has organised, funded and delivered Health and Hygiene Workshops to the tribal people as part of eco-development programmes to encourage and establish co-operation between the Forest Department and the villagers. The Forest Department has been very supportive of all these initiatives. The charity even arranges for the attendance of a female gynaecologist.

Graham and I are only too well aware how all this takes huge effort and organisation and the charity has very modest funds but is run by someone who is dedicated and passionate about his work. He firmly believes that only by helping the local human population to thrive through simple education will one convince them not to prey on the wildlife and not to be seduced by the expedient idea of poaching. The key stone for conservation is education and provision of fundamentals such as medicine so that local doctors can treat the tribals and scheduled caste peoples.

Pachmarhi is a good destination in the winter months for those seeking a trekking destination perhaps with wildlife excursions. We were going to go and stay at LifeForce's simple camp but shortage of funds has resulted in this being closed down. However, there are a number of small guest houses and hotels and I would say that this is an attractive destination for those who like going off the beaten track.

Driving on to Bhopal, we became thoughtful about the infamous tragedy that took place there in 1984, when thousands of people were gassed and even more thousands died of respiratory complications in the following years. The deserted forlorn complex that belongs to Union Carbide still stands on the main approach road. This was the world's worst industrial disaster. Late at night on 2nd December 1984 a lethal cloud of methyl isocynate (MIC), a toxic chemical used in the manufacture of pesticides, exploded. A few weeks ago, on the Discovery Channel, Graham and I watched a documentary detailing the events that led up to the disaster and how fundamental safety regulations were ignored and the management were known to be negligent. A cost-cutting exercise to reduce the daily costs of maintaining the chemical at a temperature of zero degrees was introduced; this saved $40 per day. This is a highly reactive chemical and by reducing the pressure, the danger was heightened and then water entered Tank 610 through badly maintained and leaking valves. This combination triggered a massive reaction. The explosion was dispersed on the cool winds of the night throughout the densely populated residential districts and shanty settlements. Official figures appeared to minimise the enormity of the disaster but it is now known that at least 1600 people died instantly and 6000 died in the aftermath but that figure has now risen to 20,000 years after the incident. Over 500,000 people were exposed to the gas, of whom about one-fifth have been left with chronic respiratory problems. This was not a nuclear accident like Chernobyl but its consequences have been just as awful with health problems being inherited by children born after the disaster.

Whilst we were in Bhopal, Greenpeace activists tried to enter the premises of the Union Carbide complex but were arrested. The plan had been to enter the factory complex and start cleaning the poisonous chemicals which are still allegedly contaminating the environment and drinking water of the area. Even 20 years after the gas tragedy, there are several thousands of tons of lethal, poisonous chemicals lying around in the factory. This is all seeping into the ground, spreading at a minimum rate of 300 metres to 700 metres radius per year. As I said earlier, by now at least 20,000 people have been directly affected. Despite the campaigners' best efforts, neither Union Carbide, nor Dow Chemical Company, a US multinational which acquired the Union

Carbide company in February of 2001, or the state government of Madhya Pradesh has shown interest in removing the toxic liquids.

The management responsible for this disaster was ultimately American and removed themselves quickly from the scene. Shamefully, the Indian Government was bought off by a payment that in no way compensated for the suffering and death of the ordinary people. To this day, neither the Indian or American management has been brought to a court of law to stand trial for negligence on a vast scale. This is where, habitually, the Indian Government loses the respect of its average decent voter because it was only in 1989 that Union Carbide paid the equivalent of Rs15,000 to each adult victim – this is a paltry sum of about £215! It did not cover all the eventualities of each person's suffering.

There are two unlikely heroines of the Bhopal tragedy called Rashida Bee and Champa Devi Shukla. Both these wonderful people suffered dreadfully in terms of family loss and continuing ill health. In 2002, the women organised a 19-day hunger strike in Delhi, demanding that Warren Anderson, the former Union Carbide chief executive, face a criminal trial in Bhopal. In 2003, they collected 5,000 brooms from survivors living around the factory and delivered them to Dow's headquarters in Mumbai; they called it the 'Beat Dow with a broom' campaign. Now, they have finally achieved international recognition, which they deserve for their dogged refusal to let poverty deny justice to the people of Bhopal.

At the risk of sounding very judgemental, I think that the US was and is uncaring of disasters that happen to other peoples or cultures, yet in September 2001 they had visited on them one of history's most carefully calculated evil acts. The 3,000 people that died then are about one seventh of the figure that was affected by the Bhopal tragedy, which can be laid at the feet of one of their countryman. But, it was far away, to 'some little old villagers in a backward state of a backward land ….. Gee man, life is cheap out there!' What price a life, suffering, loss of parents and social devastation; these are lessons that maybe they have learnt collectively as a nation since 9/11, but I do not believe it. My experience with the US has shown me that, sadly and to their great detriment, Americans only really care when 'Americans' are involved. Those Americans that travel and work abroad broaden their thinking but a huge majority appear to have tunnel vision and seem to want to live their lives in a 'Disneyed gloss'. We were in Mexico earlier this year and saw once again that the exported idea of glamorous men and women that Hollywood portrays is a complete myth; the majority of the American holiday makers were obese, scruffy and determined to feed their faces to the detriment of their health and the astonished amusement of other races and cultures. Exotic Mayan civilisation, stunning snorkelling, wonderful dolphins, hell no, let's just stuff in another hamburger with fries. After all, it is eleven o'clock and we finished breakfast at half past nine! I sound cruel, but I might as well tell it as I saw it.

Bhopal is a pleasant city built round two lakes, and there is something reminiscent of Udaipur in Rajasthan. It is flourishing now and has tried to put the harsh memory of its tragedy behind it. Essentially, it was a Muslim city with a Muslim ruler and has all sorts of areas that are of interest plus a number of excellent museums. Again, were it to be really carefully cleaned and renovated this would have great potential as a week-end destination with so many historic sights on its doorstep, plus a number of good hotels and restaurants. We were booked in at the Noor us Sabah, the old palace of the Begum that is now a Welcomgroup Heritage Hotel. It stands on a hill with a simply stunning view across the lakes. We were shown to an executive suite with its own terrace looking on to the view. Everything was lovely and such a superb sublime contrast from the previous night in Jabalpur! We told Gudu to go off and have a good rest and we went in search of food. It was early afternoon but as yet we had not managed to eat breakfast, let alone lunch so we settled for yet another

Sunset over the lake at Bhopal

tomato omelette, papaya and coke and tea. A journey that started at 0630 hours and ended at about 1500 without anything to eat and only a lukewarm bottled lemonade had left us tired and dehydrated. However, we were elated; this last part of the journey had potentially been a bit of a risk because of no real accommodation or aid on the way. Thank goodness for the good jeep and Gudu. Furthermore, we had managed to fit in Bhimbetka, a definite plus.

Taking it easy and enjoying the luxury of our suite, we watched the sun set over the lake. Dinner, taken on the terrace, was good and we settled for an early night as the next day was going to be very long and active. In the morning, we would go to Sanchi which I have long wanted to see, followed by lunch and museums and some shopping and then catch a plane to Delhi late in the evening. Graham, however, bumped into some doctors, who were attending a medical conference within the hotel, and they warmly invited him to participate, however, he only spent a few minutes with them before retreating. The moon was at the height of fullness and looked lovely in its silver glory with reflections on the still water of the lake. I had managed some good sunset photos and I would rise early and call for tea and watch the sunrise the next day.

CHAPTER THIRTEEN

Sanchi and the Surroundings
of Bhopal

After a reasonably leisurely rise, with time spent in contemplation looking at the beautiful lake and the use of a luxurious pink marble bathroom and shower we were ready to face the world. I had managed to speak with Naveen in Delhi just to confirm some arrangements and wish him well for his wedding on the morrow. At one stage, it had looked as if we would have to leave at mid-day on the Indian Airlines flight back to Delhi and thus miss our visit to Sanchi. This was so annoying because it was partly the reason for coming all this way, yet we could not afford to miss the only plane out that day as we had a much anticipated appointment with the Jat Regiment in Bareilly on the following day. However, for whatever reason Indian Airlines rescheduled their departure till late in the evening and thus we had a full day to enjoy everything around us.

Gudu, who was also feeling fit and refreshed drove us the forty-six kilometres to Sanchi. Its stupas, monasteries, temples and pillars date from the 3rd century BC are so precious that it was declared A World Heritage site. Again, it was a beautifully clear day and that helps to enhance a special memory. Sanchi not only houses the most perfect and well preserved stupas but also offers the visitor a chance to see, all at once, the genesis, flowering and decay of Buddhist art and architecture over a period of about 1,500 years, from the 3rd century BC to the 12th century AD – virtually the entire era of Indian Buddhism.

The site is well maintained and dotted with vibrant bougainvilleas and other flowering shrubs. Looking down from the hilltop one can see all around one, rather like Bhimbetka, which is so much older. Graham and I really enjoyed ourselves and found the cleanliness, manicured garden and lack of people very enjoyable.

Sanchi had no actual connection with Gautama Buddha during his lifetime, nor was it the focus of any significant event in the history of Buddhism. The great Mauryan Emperor, Ashoka, who lived in the 3rd century (and of whom I have spoken with regard to Orissa) is thought to have founded the great religious establishment at Sanchi and erected a monolithic pillar as well – you may recall his edict in Orissa?

Ashoka's second wife, Devi, who belonged to the Vidisha dynasty was probably the cause of this flat-topped hill becoming a centre for Buddhism. By the 14th century, however, the beautiful structures of Sanchi were deserted and went unnoticed. It was only in 1818 that the site was re-discovered by chance by a British army officer, General Taylor. Sadly, amateur archaeologists and treasure hunters were allowed to ravage the site until, in 1881, a Major Cole initiated appropriate restoration work. Between 1912 and 1919, the structures were carefully repaired and restored to their present condition under the supervision of Sir John Marshall, and today they form part of the rich cultural heritage of Madhya Pradesh. It seems almost unbelievable that a century passed before actual restoration was embarked upon.

As one approaches the apex of the hill, one sees the big Stupa 1, which is the most fascinating structure on the site. This was actually built by Emperor Ashoka and it is thought to be the oldest stone structure in India; 36.5 metres in diameter and 16.4 metres high, with a massive hemispherical dome, the stupa's original much smaller version is entombed within the structure we see now. There is a very thick layer of lime plaster, which was added a century later, acting as an outer shell. A third of the way up there is a raised terrace, enclosed by a railing which is meant for ritual *pradakshina* (Buddhist circumambulation of the monument). The hemispherical mound known as a *stupa* has been central to Buddhist worship since the sixth century BC when Buddha was alive, but of the half dozen sites dotted around India only Sanchi has survived. The stupa is encircled by a stone railing, that is a larger heavier version of that on the terrace to which I have referred. There are four entrances through magnificently carved *toranas* (gateways). These gateways were erected in 35 BC and are among the finest examples of Buddhist art in India. Both sides of each torana are covered with prolific and consistently exquisite carvings depicting scenes from the life of the Buddha. Following traditional practice, the Buddha is not depicted in human form, instead emblems such as an empty throne, a riderless horse, or a wheel are used to depict him. A pair of footprints or the 'Bo' tree may also indicate his presence. In one scene, represented by a Bo tree, he is seen ascending a road to heaven. Archaeologists believe the craftsmen who

The Great Stupa at Sanchi, the earliest Buddhist building in India

fashioned these toranas, or at least carved the detail may have been craftsmen in ivory because the detail is so intricate. The four toranas face north, south, east and west, and the southern torana is the main entrance. My photography has worked amazingly well and, thus, I have documented the intricate carvings

A *Torana* (gateway) against the winter sky at Sanchi

pictorially. I could write a whole chapter on the detail but this is not a guide book so suffice to say that Graham and I were both enchanted and impressed

by the stories told in stone, the careful symbolism and the beauty and grace of the whole edifice.

We sat on the stump of Ashoka's pillar and enjoyed the shade. Ashoka erected columns such as this all over his empire to mark sacred sites and pilgrims' trails. It is made out of sandstone known as Chunar because it comes from a quarry of the same name on the banks of the Ganges near Varanasi. It was originally crowned by a magnificent lion capital but that is now housed in the state museum and the inscription etched around its base is in the Brahmi script, recording Ashoka's edicts in Pali, the early Buddhist language and forerunner of Sanskrit. The Ashoka pillar is a symbol of India's nationhood and an iconic symbol for all Indians. The second stupa is also remarkable

**Intricate carvings on a
Torana (gateway), Sanchi**

and I had difficulty in deciding when to stop taking photographs. The clarity of the day with the bright blue sky made such a wonderful backdrop to it all.

Sanchi draws visitors all year round but it really comes alive in late November (we were there on 19th November 2002); the temperature is just right and the festival of Chaitygiri Vihara takes place annually at this time. During this period, hundreds of Buddhist monks and pilgrims converge on Sanchi and the relics of two of the Buddha's early disciples, Sari Puttha and Maha Moggallana, are brought out for display. The relics were discovered in the third stupa in 1853 and are kept in the *vihara* or monastery for the rest of the year.

Sanchi is surrounded by other sites of interest, at one of which, Vidisha, 10 km from Sanchi and deserted after the sixth century AD, there are ruins of a

Brahmanical shrine dedicated to Vishnu and dated not later than 2 BC. The cement in the foundation bricks here reveals lime mortar, the first known example of the use of cement in India.

A general view of the ruins at Sanchi

The Heliodorus Pillar dates from 140 BC given by a Bactrian-Greek ambassador from Taxila, which was the capital city of Gandhara (now in the northwest frontier region of Pakistan). The shaft has an inscription dedicating it to Vishnu's father Vasudeva. Apparently, Heliodorus converted to the local cult that worshipped Vishnu. It is known locally as the Khamb Baba pillar. The Udaygiri Caves, about 5 km from Vidisha, are Hindu and Jain rock art shrines that have carvings dating from the fourth to sixth centuries AD. Raisen, on the road to Bhopal, 23 km south of Sanchi, is a huge and colourful hilltop fort with temples, cannons, 40 wells, three palaces and a large tank. At Sonari, there are a further eight stupas and at Andher, discovered after Sanchi, there are three small stupas that are well preserved.

Quite beyond our reach in one day, there is another example of superb Hindu temple architecture at Neelkantheswara, built in 1080 AD by the Paramara king Udayadita. It took 22 years to complete but is similar to Khajuraho, though perhaps more restrained in the subjects of its sculpture. Reasonably close by, there are a number of Jain temples with huge significance for the followers of the Jain Faith but tourism is not developed in this part of the country and to reach Oon and Bawangaja and Khargone one is just as well to travel from Indore. It has to be said though that these rich architectural religious sites are for the very dedicated traveller.

Graham and I returned to Bhopal exhausted but happy at having the opportunity to experience this wealth of antiquity. This great land never fails to amaze me, vast fortresses, temples, cities, mausoleums, rock art, wildlife, flora, cuisine, music, textiles and crafts keep presenting themselves as new and thought-provoking experiences. Along with all that are the people, mostly happy, spiritual and getting on with their lives. Yes, I know only too well about the suffering, deprivation and poverty that is part and parcel of India's billion population. I care deeply about it and never dismiss it totally from my mind but, truly, there is such a wealth of wonder for anyone to assimilate and enjoy. My advice to the westerner is to enjoy and take away some of all this in your heart and mind and demonstrate your caring by giving to a reputable organisation – there are so many NGOs (non-governmental organisations) that are constantly requiring our help.

Whenever I return from a long morning of sightseeing I feel quite dehydrated and long for an ice cold coke with lots of lemon and ice. In a reputable hotel such as the Noor us Sabah, the ice is no danger but in lots of other places I would not adulterate my bottled drink. It was great to just stretch out and enjoy the quiet of our suite where someone had thoughtfully put a vase of flowers and left me a gift. After a light lunch, we were ready to go out again and see the various places of interest or, at least, make a choice between them and then do a bit of shopping. There are, as I say, a number of places worthy of interest including the Birla Mandir Museum, which houses some of the finest stone sculpture to be found in Madhya Pradesh. There is Bharat Bhavan which is considered to be provincial India's most outstanding arts centre. One of the interesting exhibits is that of the adivasi art. The Gond painter Jangarh Singh Shyam was featured in Mark Tully's well known book '*No Full Stops in India*', which I would recommend to anyone visiting India for the first time. There are a number of his works on display.

For us the main attraction is The Museum of Man which is the attempt to tell the story of India's indigenous minorities, the *adivasis* or 'original inhabitants'. I have already spoken of the tribal people and the gradual erosion of their traditional culture, this sadly continues with more and more of the modern brutal world impacting on their way of life. Modern governments always feel embarrassed by what they think of as anachronisms, but I wish they would value them for what they are, people who link us all to our original roots and cultures. They deserve our respect and help, not ridicule. Specialist adivasi men and women were brought in to construct and depict their own particular way of life and this hillside 'page of history and culture' is in marked contrast to the noisy teeming city below. Here, in the West, we do this sort of exhibition very well and produce atmospheric depictions of ancient times. In India, one has to realise that the exhibition is depicting ancient and modern, i.e., some of what still exists. Even here in Biggar, very near to where I live, we have wonderful little museums, indeed, it is considered to be the king of museum towns in Scotland, despite its small population, but they all depict activities and actions of past times; in India, there is the realisation that the time is not yet past. I do not know what the future holds for India's adivasis but I pray that governments will respect them and not bully them and exploit them needlessly. Even in Botswana we recently heard of coercion towards the Bushmen of the Kalahari by their own government, who wished to relocate them from their natural living and hunting grounds into some barren suburban site. I think, with the world's help, the Bushmen won that round. Let us hope influential men and women seek to help the adivasi populations of India.

Gudu took us to shop at the Madhya Pradesh State Cottage Industries. This was an interesting exercise. First, we realised that it would be good to have some rupees in cash, our original sum having dwindled. This was absolutely no problem. We went to a small air-conditioned office, glass walled with a locked door, which was opened by a security guard. He inspects you and realizes that you want to use the ATM and unlocks the door and leaves you to your machinations. It could not be easier, out pops the cash after the usual procedure that one would follow anywhere. The Cottage Industries had not, however, yet opened, though it was long past the hour! The security guard realised that we wanted to enter and, though it was nothing to do with him, he spoke sharply to some young people whom he presumably recognised as staff and told them to hurry up and open the shop for us. The usual inertia, lack of motivation and I suspect pure boredom was reigning. We enjoyed ourselves and bought several gifts for Christmas plus one or two other things including some wonderful curtaining. It was ridiculously cheap and yet so good – it cost about a pound for a metre. Graham, bless him, valiantly carried the ten metre package out to the jeep. I asked them to parcel it up and courier it, for an additional fee of course, but, no, this is a government organisation and using one's initiative is out of the question! So, we had to go to a baggage shop and buy a cheap holdall to take all the new acquired gifts and material! It was fun and the young girls seem to enjoy the contact and banter that went on. Bhopal is not yet on a tourist route and so they do not meet many foreigners; people who might visit them would be delegates to a convention or diplomatic visitors, I formed the impression that the various Eastern races like the Japanese and Koreans did not do much shopping – they always seem to be worshipping at the shrine of western designers. Shopping in India to me is a delight, and not for myself really because our home is fully furnished and adorned, but as gifts. Miniature paintings, beaded handbags for evening wear, inexpensive cotton baggy trousers for lounging around, jewellery, ornaments there is such a wealth of choice, and our friends appear to be pleased with our presents, but then I do try to choose carefully!

The Noor us Sabah allowed us to use our suite until the very last minute before leaving the hotel. This was very helpful because there is nothing more tiring than waiting around in foyers and departure lounges. I was feeling quite jumpy about the flight because, unfortunately, Indian Airlines are notorious for changing departure times and it would have been awful to lose the flight by half an hour. As it was, it seemed delayed and Bhopal airport had the benefit of our close scrutiny. We had said farewell to Gudu and were sorry to part; a long journey can bond people together and he is a nice man. We found a suitable gift for his wife and children and an appropriate financial reward for him. He said he would wait to see that our aircraft did touch down and then after that leave for the first stage of his journey back to Gwalior. I said that he should please not travel at night but of course do not know what he decided.

Airport security at this domestic airport was intense about which we felt very comfortable. The entire luggage was x-rayed and also individually inspected and we were all given a body search by male and female officers. This is pretty normal procedure anyway in India for air travel but now they are even more thorough. Just as one was about to walk out of the departure lounge on to the tarmac there was another body search and investigation of one's hand luggage. Eventually, the plane took off and, feeling quite hungry, I ate the airline food, which was tolerable. Arrival at Delhi Domestic airport was efficient and at 22.15 we were met by young Farokh from The Travel House and taken to The Maurya Hotel and Towers. This lovely hotel belongs to the Welcomgroup which is an ITC company but has a business connection with The Sheraton Group worldwide. Truly, this is one of the world's leading hotels with enormous emphasis on service and perfection. The décor and standards are amongst the best in the world and many state presidents such as Bill Clinton and Vladimir Putin stayed here on their official visits.

There had been plans to give us a full suite with our own butler but I declined as it would have been unappreciated as we had such an early start the following morning. The normal towers suite was lovely. However I asked to see the presidential suites and was shown to one. It was as if one had moved into a complete apartment, superbly appointed with its own roof garden and spa pool on the terrace. This would be a most wonderful venue for a small reception and dinner party with a good view looking out on to the elegant areas of New Delhi. We were both tired but arriving at The Maurya rejuvenated us and we decided to go and dine at The Dum Phukt.

The Dum Phukt is an elegant restaurant with a pianist tinkling the ivories and the most delicious food. Their other great restaurant The Bukhara is rated as one of the ten best restaurants in the world. The Maitre D' was helpful and friendly and nicely judged what we would like to eat at that late hour, his recommendation of a bottle of red wine from Maharashtra was good. An elegant small meal with a beautiful wine in interesting surroundings people watching was a perfect end to a busy day.

CHAPTER FOURTEEN

The Jat Regimental Reunion

T he alarm call pierced my sleep and we both threw ourselves in the shower for the start of another action-packed day. In no time at all, Brigadier Satish Kumar, our old friend would arrive and then we would set off on the fairly long drive to Bareilly. It was great to see Satish again and we piled into the Travel House car and set off. With the sun rising through the mist like a huge crimson ball, it was so interesting to watch this great city wake and its population start to go about their business. I love the early morning in the East, it is beautiful too in the West in the summer, but on a cold dark winter's morning in Scotland there is very little charm. Having grown up in the East, I immediately return to the feeling of expectation and energy that the cool dawn light brings. The smoke of wood fires, the fast food wallah calling his wares, the sweepers cleaning, men stretching and doing old-fashioned exercises and the children rubbing their eyes but looking sweet and prim and proper in their immaculate little uniforms. Look about and you will observe a devout Muslim spreading his mat towards Mecca to pray, or a gentle old Indian woman starting her Hindu devotions with some fresh marigolds with which to adorn her preferred deity. Then, there will be servants walking dogs, and the flower man setting up his stall and, inevitably, at the roadside dhabba, tired lorry drivers having a scalding cup of chai. The fly-overs in Delhi have made a big difference to the traffic and we made good progress. Now they also have a metro which will benefit everyone, though I have yet to travel in it. Kolkata has one and so does Mumbai but I am not really that fond of the Tube back home so do not need to experiment with the Indian versions; I just hope that it has helped the average person. Long hours strap-hanging on the Central

Line when working in London was one of life's less attractive memories for me. Courageously, the authorities in Delhi have said that they want to clear the roads of the cows that wander around and snarl up the traffic. This is a good thing, provided the poor beasts are taken somewhere pastoral and fed and watered; if they are just herded into some squalid compound and left to take their chances for food I would condemn the move.

The early morning drive into Uttar Pradesh was enjoyable whilst we made good progress; indeed, we could hardly believe it. Satish wanted a quick stop at a hotel for some breakfast. This proved to be quite amusing. In true military style, he ordered for us three and the bearer went off. Then the man reappeared and said that he only had two eggs, what was he to do. Satish exploded and said why was he delaying, to get on and make the omelette and divide it between us. Something about it all was so funny, but I could not laugh openly. Here was Satish, the retired efficient army officer of senior rank querulously ordering the slow shambolic waiter as time ticked by whilst we British looked on – it somehow seemed a microcosm of India: the impatience and the inertia. When Satish exploded and said in Hindi 'You fool, this is breakfast time, why do you not have enough eggs, what do people eat in the mornings? Eggs of course, hurry up we are going to be late .. What are you waiting for, get on with it?' The man replies the equivalent of 'I don't know, but we just don't, will you have toast? Does the sahib want tea?' ... all at a snail's pace! Graham and I just giggled in the end because that sort of thing can happen anywhere, the Highlands of Scotland, Italy, France, Viet Nam, wherever you are in a hurry and your mission is urgent but they are going through the dull ritual of their working lives and really are not worried as to customer satisfaction. Fortunately 'the pit stop' was clean and reasonable which is just as important, certainly for girls!

First, we had crossed the Yamuna River and then we came to the Ganges. Again, that same special feeling enveloped me: Mother Ganga, lifeblood to millions, spiritual rejuvenation, deity and wonder. Rabindranath Tagore wrote:

'I think of other ages that floated upon the stream of life and love and death and are forgotten, and I feel the freedom of passing away.'

Jawaharlal Nehru in his book '*Testament*' wrote:

'...the Ganga has been to me a symbol and a memory of the past of India, running into the present, and flowing on to the great ocean of the future.'

Both those men's writing encapsulates my feelings for this wonderful ancient holy river. I do wish my health allowed me to make a journey from its source at Gangotri in the Himalayas down to its delta where it meets the ocean, but for the early part of such a pilgrimage I would need a physical stamina which I know I no longer have.

Suddenly, we hit a problem with a 7 km tail back of huge lorries that were actually heading towards us but somehow had created a gridlock. Thank goodness for Satish, who, in true military style, got out of the car and started to use his natural authority and organise the lorry drivers and eventually we were able to drive on. It happened yet again and by this time we were very worried as we were special guests of The Jat Regiment for their annual Raising Day celebrations and reunion. Finally, we arrived at our hotel. Because of the number of guests who were attending, we civilians had been accommodated at the Uberoi Grand in the Civil Lines of Bareilly. That means in the civilian town. Well, after Madhya Pradesh's indifferent hotels, this was such a pleasant surprise with a lovely comfortable full suite with sitting and dining room and bed and bathroom and helpful staff. As we were running late we quickly changed and spruced up and drove off to the Regimental Centre where celebrations were in full swing and had been since the 18th, this being the 20th November. The parade ground was decorated and parades and events were congregated in battalion groupings around the whole area, whilst the Regimental Band and a visiting band from the Sikh Light Infantry were playing. Sadly, we had missed the wreath-laying ceremony at the Jat War Memorial which had taken place the previous morning followed by a group photo, a ladies meeting, and luncheon at Bareilly Club. Then, a band display and Beating Retreat had taken place followed by dinner at Jat House. However, here we were and the welcome was so warm and friendly.

**Welcome arch for Reception and Dinner at the Officer's
Mess, the Jat Regiment at Bareilly**

General Khanna, Colonel of the Regiment greeted us and Brigadier Shyam Lal the Commandant made us welcome (Satish Kumar had been Commandant on my previous two visits in 1997 and 1998) and we met all their ladies. People were arriving all the time and the place was swarming with generals who had all come back to demonstrate their comradeship with the Regiment. Colonel Akhe Ram arrived. He is a wonderful old man whom I just loved; he has been decorated by HM The Queen personally and is so interesting because, in his post military life, he has been hugely successful in all his endeavours and has a number of flourishing businesses. He is in his mid eighties and still wise and alert about business, yet with the depth of personality that true wisdom brings. Suddenly I felt a brush on my shoulder and it was my favourite, Gurung; it was so super to see him again. Gurung is a Nepalese and has the rank of Lance Naik or Naik by now, i.e., corporal; he made a connection with us when we were the Regiment's guests in November 1997 and again in March of 1998. Again, it was a bond that just grew and we have kept in touch over the years through stilted letters and more recently email. Gurung was going to look after me personally and, had I eaten and drunk all that he attempted to shower on me, I would have exploded!

The bands played, people chatted, retired officers met up with old comrades, shy ladies and children observed and talked quietly. The men sat in groups and, whilst the generals and colonels chatted, their ladies berated them for having yet another conference. People wanted a photograph and I took many and then they asked for me to sit with the wives and children which was fun. Brigadier

**Aline with wives and children of serving soldiers
of the Jat Regiment**

Shyam Lal asked General Khanna's wife and me to go through to lunch which is called *BaraKhana* or big meal. It is the custom on these special occasions that everyone of all ranks eat together but, in truth, that would have been a logistical nightmare so a sample of all ranks were invited and one just helped oneself and sat next to whoever. Gurung kept following me about with more plates of food but finally I tactfully convinced him that enough was enough! As soon as we had all eaten, we dispersed; it was actually quite rapid. Most of the men went off to the golf course and we were informed that there was a

Dear Gurung efficient as ever at *Bharra Khanna* (Luncheon)

full programme for Graham and me to enjoy. Subadar Major Wazir Singh of the Sikh Light Infantry Band asked if he might play something especially for me. They also had pipers amongst them so I said 'That would be wonderful, what about Road to the Isles?' It appeared as if a moment of panic entered his eyes so I swiftly said no, how thoughtless, please could it be The Skye Boat Song (having remembered just in time that The Skye Boat Song is the Slow March of The Jats, and indeed was played at my christening together with a full band programme). He grinned and the Band played and when they had finished I spoke in Hindi and told them how proud I was to be there with them and how happy they had made me. I then pointedly took some photos of the young 'jawans' or jocks in our parlance and said hello. It is always easy at these functions to concentrate on the great and the good but there would be little point to having lots of top brass if there were insufficient foot soldiers.

Again, there was this sort of timeless quality. Earlier, when I had arrived and been greeted, the camera had been left in the car, it did not seem quite right to appear at first looking like a female journalist. So when I wanted it I asked

The author with Subadar Major Wazir Singh and the band of the Sikh Light Infantry at the Jat Regimental Reunion at Bareilly

Gurung to ask our driver. Gurung strode off across the parade ground full of natural military importance but young Kishore, who was very new to us, was not going to let some stranger demand a camera and just take it. Fortunately, I saw from far away what his dilemma was and waved and shouted 'Thik Hai' – equivalent to 'it's OK'. One of the nicest things I witnessed on this occasion was the affection and respect with which Satish Kumar was greeted by the men whom he had commanded. Their faces lit up when he was spotted in our car and the greeting 'Ram Ram' was called with a salute. Westerners talk of Asians being inscrutable; well, actually, no more than we westerners. They mirror respect, warmth and admiration just as we do and when someone is welcome it is so obvious.

It was suggested that we would like to go back to our hotel for a short rest and would be collected again at 16.30 hours. This did seem a good idea as it had been another very early start. It is amazing what a quick shower and a change of shoes can do for one's energy!

At 16.30 hours, there was a tentative knock on the door of the sitting room. It was a young Jat, Santosh Lal. He had come with a JCO to give us the printed programme for the evening. When we got in the car sent by the Regiment there appeared to be no room for him and he looked forlorn and disappointed, so I said in Hindi come with us and gestured to the back seat alongside me. No, that would not have been correct but with a huge grin he squeezed next to the JCO in the front seat. What is new in India? We drove in the Jat car with its pennant flying, the two of us in the back and three big Jats in the front. They seemed very happy and so were we. Honour had been saved.

The first stop was the Regiment's Hindu Temple or *Mandir*. This was a lovely experience because, by this time, the shadows had lengthened, the Regiment was winding down and we drove through the cantonment, which is always beautifully maintained. The Temple is beautiful, colourful and so spacious. We took off our shoes as is required and walked all around. The priest came forward to greet us and put a *tilak* on the forehead and the string for the wrist was fixed on Graham's right wrist and my left wrist.

The Jat Regimental Hindu Mandir (temple), photographed here in 1947, visited by the author in 2002

Graham, I, the JCO, who was very shy but very correct, and Santosh were taken on a tour of the colourful wall paintings depicting the pantheon of Hindu Deities and the mythology surrounding them. There was a beautiful marble floor and a lofty ceiling; it was rather like being in a basilica – with no chairs. The other day in our collection of memorabilia, I came across an ancient photo of the Mandir from my late father's time. How good it is that the place is renovated and maintained to such a high standard. We gave a donation and thanked the Priest for his welcome.

Then we moved on to the Regimental Museum, which we had previously visited on both occasions. This has been superbly renovated and updated with the help of modern digital reproduction, which has eradicated the previous slightly amateur feel. We both found it very moving; I saw a photo of Daddy taken in 1945. I also explained who various people were. Colonel Sharma, the Custodian, is charming. Looking at the Siachen Glacier conditions in which the Regiment had fought against Pakistan fairly recently, it was impressive and horrifying; 19,000 feet above sea level makes it the highest battle field in the world, and no human can exist there for any length of time. We were very impressed by the upgrade and attention to duty, sacrifice and regimental history.

As we were going round, the Retreat was played outside by two buglers and it was so evocative of all the tradition and ceremony through the ages; there was a moment that I felt I almost saw my father come round the corner in his virile young days with a familiar nod of the head, truly on these occasions the past is not another country, it remains in your heart.

Our tour was to take in the Canteen and we were proudly shown the array of merchandise available: 3,500 items can be purchased from cars, jcbs, tractors, air-conditioners, radios, electrical equipment and computers to groceries, pharmaceuticals, Brasso and polish! Quite obviously, large items like cars have to be ordered, but one can easily imagine the massive buying power of the Indian Army Canteen, as it is called with an army of over one million men. It is not difficult to make the mental leap to the idea of how beneficial it must be for a contractor to be a supplier to such an institution. Graham remembered that he needed some shaving gel and it was excellent that we had a good reason to buy something.

Then we all piled into the car and returned to our hotel for a change into full evening wear. Satish joined us looking very distinguished in his dark blue woollen Nehru-style dinner jacket. Being retired, he was not in full fig any longer. This time, however, it was a positive entourage of cars. The three of us in a Jat car, the JCO and the young Jat in another and our own car; government ministers may swan around Delhi in entourages but here in Bareilly things are done in Jat style!

The Officers' Mess lawn was beautifully decorated and people were congregating for the reception. The entrances on to the lawn were elegantly adorned with flowers and there were awnings in the regimental colours and a delicate silk and floral welcoming arch and pots of bougainvillea and chrysanthemums all around. There were also rangoli drawings of welcome on the ground.

The officers looked resplendent in their Mess Dress, the ladies looked dazzling in an array of beautiful brightly coloured evening saris and they were all flashing wonderful gold jewellery, for which India is famous. The drinks were endless, mostly whisky and water for the men, I kept to coke and the eats were hot and welcome. The Regimental Band and the Sikh Light Infantry Band played from the bandstand, including a splendid rendition of *La Paloma*, which happens to be a favourite of mine. The Band Concert programme is in front of me as I write, and under each title there is a short explanation of the piece of music. Another piece was *In a Persian Market*, which I had not heard for years!

Aline and Graham with Officer's wives of the Jat Regiment

The MC very sweetly made a welcoming speech about us and then I was invited up to the front to formally present my first book *India: The Peacock's Call*, in which The Jat Regiment featured, to General Khanna. I was asked to say a few words and I chose to talk about the Memorial Gates to all those who died from the Commonwealth (which I have mentioned in Chapter 11). I explained how November was our Remembrance Season and that it is taken very seriously by all ages, not just the old who experienced the major conflicts. I told them how much the subcontinent's soldiers had been revered by Britain and that as a nation we never forget. I told them of my affection for the Regiment and wished the whole Regimental Family every good wish in the future and how privileged we felt to be able to share their Regimental Reunion with them. We then processed into dinner with a formal seating plan.

Officer's Mess, the Jat Regimental centre, Bareilly

I was seated between Lt Colonel Akhe Ram MBE and a general who was charming. Opposite me was Lt General Jasbir Singh, the Maharajah of Nabha. The food was western, which was intriguing. Everything was laid out as a Mess Night should be. When it came to clearing the tables, Gurung and his co workers bustled about; everything was done to a strict routine and timing so that all the white linen was whisked off together from every single table. We all clapped. The Toast to The President of India is always drunk in water, but with every solemnity. Then, there was the Toast to the Regiment, which could be either in wine or water, after which two pipers marched in and played some stirring Scottish tunes which were so familiar. Then, the Regimental Sergeant Major came in and was ceremoniously given what I think of as a quaich of rum. Of course, he was expected to drink it all in one go and was madly applauded. There was much drumming of the feet and General Jasbir Singh commented dryly that one day the poor fellow will fall over in all the excitement and the rum! Jasbir Singh is a keen mahseer fisherman and we talked fishing; I tempted him to come and fish the Tweed – there was a glint in his eye, so maybe he will. It was good to hear that, whether fishing for mahseer on the Cauvery or the Ramganga, the fish are put back whenever possible.

We signed the Mess Visitors' Book, for me a very special honour, as no woman has signed that book previously. Gurung, at my request, managed to extract my name card from the napiery that had been removed. It had also been nice to meet up with Colonel Vijay Singh, whom we had met previously. We said our formal farewells to as many people as we could and then drove back to the hotel. Satish was leaving very early the next day to go back to Delhi with dear Colonel Akhe Ram, so we said we would see him in a few days time when we were invited for lunch at his Delhi home.

The prospect of my bed grew very attractive and it was lovely to know that it could be a leisurely start on the following day.

It was a relaxed rise followed by an excellent tomato omelette and tea! The young Jat Santosh Lal knocked at the door and shyly insisted on helping Graham to pack our cases. He was so shy and sweet and, of course, longing to talk and find out why and what; so he and I conversed in Hindi and I explained everything. This was important, because he would be 'quizzed' in due course and would receive 'much izat', i.e. face, when he knew all the answers! The hotel said that the Regiment was hosting us and there was nothing to pay and how glad they had been to have us. Again, we departed in the regimental car with our own following. I could see that the JCO and Santosh did not know what to do with us, so I asked if we might go and sit on the veranda at the Officers' Mess and have tea and enjoy the gardens, waiting for Brigadier Shyam Lal to say farewell to all those who had come to the Reunion. That was considered a good idea. We were installed on the veranda and they retreated to a discreet distance. I assured them that all was perfect and Graham and I enjoyed ourselves. We talked to the Mess *malis* (gardeners). They were good sorts who enjoyed a 'blether' and we showed them some of our photos of our home and garden. They enquired as to who did all the gardening and I replied that Graham was the 'head mali' and I was the second mali. Well, why did we not employ proper malis he asked. Quite simple I replied, they would be paid like maharajahs. At this his eyes lit up and he briefly contemplated emigrating. But, seriously, his problem was the ravaging monkeys. They are a huge problem and, because of the sacred deity Hanuman, monkeys cannot be harmed, yet they are as big a pest as rabbits are to us. This was graphically demonstrated to us a little later when a troupe of the little monsters descended on the lawn and all the poor man could do was chase them to the road, yet again.

Finally, we drove round to Jat House and waited for Brigadier and Mrs Shyam Lal to arrive home, having said all their farewells. The Brigadier was feeling relaxed and called for some champagne. Indian champagne is extremely good and I was given a brandy glass full. Another charming colonel joined us; he had been their personal guest as they had served together before. It was lovely. The last time I had been at Jat House, we had been playing Holi, throwing coloured powder over each other in celebration of the great Hindu festival of spring. Now, there was a new incumbent in Jat House and it was ever thus. To think my mother had been hostess there long years ago for my guardian on occasions, who had been Commandant just before and up to Independence. I think we were all so relaxed that the afternoon could have flashed past but we had a journey to make so went in to eat. The lunch was delicious and Graham's love of Indian mithai had been conveyed to the cook so there were glorious *jalebis* and *gulab jamuns*. Brigadier and Mrs Lal gave us each a gift. Mine was a set of six port-size glasses, from which the Loyal Toast had been drunk the previous night with the regimental crest on each glass. I had asked if I might buy two as a memento but this made a special and practical gift. We said our farewells with regret. It had been a memorable interlude and, as we drove away, we stopped to thank the men who had acted as our escorts during our very enjoyable time with the Regiment. For me, there is always a lump in my throat because I know how happy my parents were and, though nothing in life stays the same, visiting Bareilly periodically as I have had the pleasure of doing, captures the essence of an India that was loved by so many who are not Indians. Sometimes people fail to grasp that one can have an affection for and loyalty to a place or an institution that is not actually our own – let us just say that some of us were fortunate enough to borrow it for a short time in history.

Ahead of us lay a reasonable drive but we would be leaving the plains and climbing a hugely steep pass through any amount of hair pin bends to reach Naini Tal, and the temperature was going to change dramatically the higher we climbed.

CHAPTER FIFTEEN

"Carpet Sahib's Country"

"A country's fauna is a sacred trust and I appeal to you not to betray this trust ... if we do not bestir ourselves now it will be to our discredit that the fauna of our province was exterminated in our generation, and under our very eyes, while we looked on and never raised a finger to prevent it."

Jim Corbett

Leaving Bareilly, I was, as ever, regretful but this time the anticipation of revisiting the area where I had been a toddler was filling me with energy. Nainital in the Kumaon Hills, the foothills of the Himalayas is approximately 2000 metres in altitude which is over 6000 feet. After the amalgamation of Garhwal and Kumaon along with a few other districts of Uttar Pradesh, a new state of Uttaranchal was formed on 9th November 2000.

With its tree-topped ridges, snow-covered peaks, chuckling streams, foaming torrents, famous mountain lakes and amazing valleys the Kumaon Hills had been a haven of refuge for the peoples fleeing the Central Asian plains in the first millennium BC; this continued with people arriving north from the Indo-Gangetic plains after every successive invasion and change of dynasty. With very little interference it has preserved its ancient relics and culture, as well as nurtured the religions and abstract ideals of Indian philosophy right from the times of the Vedas and the Upanishads up until the twelfth century AD.

With the Chalukyan wave of temple building in the South, just after the start of the seventh century, Kumaon became an area of energy for temple construction. Around 400 temples were built in the Almora District alone by the Katyuri kings. Almora is close to Nainital but about 400 metres lower in altitude. Most of these temples are currently still standing and, as objects of pilgrimages, they daily draw hundreds of visitors. The Pindari glacier, which is over three kilometres long and 457 metres wide, is surrounded by an alpine garden of ferns, wild flowers and rhododendrons, backed by majestic mountains that suddenly fill the horizon and leave one with a feeling of endless grandeur. Nainital is over a century old and founded by an English mountaineer who fell in love with the untamed area that surrounded the green-turning-to-blue lake. Named after the deity Nanda Devi, or Naina, the town developed into a charming hill station and idyllic hot weather destination for the Europeans escaping the great heat of the plains in the summer. Nainital Yacht Club is said to be the highest yacht club in the world and, even now, one sees the yachts out with their white sails rippling in the breeze. Nainital is a great honeymoon destination for modern India but, though I had visited it as a toddler more than once, I had no visual memory. This is the land of Jim Corbett, the famous hunter turned conservationist, who did so much to help the local people of Kumaon, yet recognised the vital importance of wildlife conservation, and in particular the plight of the tiger.

The author at Nainital

To grateful country folk who adored him he was known as 'Carpet Sahib', as they found it difficult to pronounce his name. Jim Corbett was a friend of my parents, but very much their senior and his thoughts and writings greatly influenced me as a child. From Bareilly, we had a four and a half hour drive, the last sixty kilometres of which was up a nerve-wracking mountain pass with twelve hairpin bends until we reached 6,500 feet. In daylight, this road is not worrying but, by the time we reached the foot of the mountain road, it was nearly dark and both of us were concerned as the traffic coming down seemed oblivious of the need for dipping their headlights. Our young driver was a nervous soul and the whole experience was a bit nerve-shredding! Suddenly, when the car had been brought to a virtual halt, Graham who was sitting on the right at the rear of the driver turned to me incoherent with excitement. I was alarmed and could not think what was happening. In the momentary panic, all I could think was 'Well, the car is stationary, what can be the matter?' Graham finally managed to point behind me excitedly and say 'Look, the most wonderful leopard just there!' I tried hard but missed him. Whilst the car was stationary, Graham had glanced out of the window and, in the light from our car's headlights he had looked into the eyes of a full grown leopard, which was just standing there on a concrete culvert on the side of the road. The magnificent beast then coolly walked behind our car and crossed the road, Graham continued to see him but because he could not articulate his excitement the great cat was gone before I could do anything. It was so thrilling and in fact encouraging to see that leopard is still so much part of the Kumaon hills and valleys.

I will tell you a true story but one that does not have such a nice ending. In 1948, when I was less than two years old, my mother had brought me up to stay for a few weeks to escape the summer heat. She had rented a cottage in the grounds of a property at Naukuchiatal, which is not all that far from Nainital. Naukuchiatal is named after the nine-pointed lake which forms its centre. Tal means lake and apart from Nainital there are Bhimtal and Sattal as well. Mummy had brought her beloved little miniature dachshund Jerry with her; he was her absolute shadow and devoted to me as well. The little animal appeared to be out of sorts and she had taken him out one evening for a walk thinking that would ease his discomfort. He did not appear to be any happier. Later on the little dog managed to whimper three times and mother heard a strange noise and thought there was someone at the window. She shone her torch through the glass (in those days there was no electricity) and discovered what she thought was a man with a spotted waistcoat at the window. Poor darling she must have been so frightened, but she just shone her torch and heard a strange rasping noise but then he disappeared. The next morning, Jerry was very ill and mother sought help from the owner of the property who kindly said he would take the little dog to Nainital to see the vet. This journey was accomplished on horseback, carrying Jerry. Tragically, Jerry did not respond and died whilst at the vet's. Mother's friend brought the little one back and they buried him under a favourite white fig tree in the garden. The man in the spotted waistcoat was of course a leopard, who had smelled 'dog' and come for him. The scared little animal would have known but thank goodness Mummy had not realised this at the time; the animal had probably been watching during the time that Jerry had been taken out for a walk, it could have been horrific. Graham reckons that the big cat might also have been after me. To this day when there are large numbers of leopard in a restricted space they are inclined to prey on small children on the outskirts of villages and towns, after all vulnerable little toddlers have no skills in escaping. Mummy was broken hearted by the loss of Jerry and the whole holiday must have been wretched as my father was still at his work hundreds of miles away. Seeing that leopard, or at least Graham seeing him, brought this tale to mind immediately and we 'phoned Mummy the next day and told her all about it.

We stayed one night at Claridges Naini Retreat and, having been shown to our suite, a sort of cottage, I was scrabbling around in the luggage to find my one and only sweater and pashmina. It was cold, clear and beautiful but, make no mistake, cold! I was still dressed in clothes that had been suitable for an afternoon in Bareilly. The bearer brought hot water bottles for which I was deeply grateful. You might wonder why I was so unprepared; well, the fact was that we had decided to visit Naini on the spur of the moment and, thus, had made no allowances for the altitude. Claridges was to undergo a complete renovation and I am sure will be delightful now; at the time it was a bit shabby but comfortable enough. The hotel has a superb situation with the most beautiful views of the great lake beneath it. I had gone out onto our terrace and looked at the half moon shining down on the lake and the twinkling lights on the far hillside and looked forward to seeing it at the sunrise. I was not disappointed. This whole area is wonderful but, of course, now well populated and that always has it own attendant problems. Still, it is beautiful and, for the hill walker or mountaineer, the plantsman or those who like mountain air, I recommend the Kumaon and its various destinations.

The next day was clear and sunny and warmed up quite quickly. After breakfast, we departed from the hotel and drove down and left the car in the valley car park beside the lake. We took the cable car to the summit of the ridge of hills. From there, we could look out and gaze at the snows. It was wonderful. The cable car went up another 2000 feet (approximately 700 metres) and the view was breathtaking. I have not seen the Himalayas since the 1960s when I used to fly out for holidays. In those days, the captain of the flight sometimes would elect to fly a route that allowed one to see a glimpse of Mount Everest in the sunrise. That was my experience and the only time that I have looked on the great peaks in their total magnificence. Graham was enchanted with the whole experience and I was glad that we had taken the trouble to come, however fleetingly.

People who knew Nainital in its time as a Hill Station for the British consider the place has been ruined, but look at it this way; India's population has grown amazingly since then and, with it, there are thousands who now have the income to holiday in the mountains; that puts pressure on the little town's infrastructure. I just wish they would clean up but that is going back to my previous complaints that cover the whole of India – ensure that litter and detritus is removed and come down heavily on the offenders. However, we met a stranger in a bookshop who commented that it was so nice to see Nainital had not changed in any way since his last visit 23 years ago. Ranikhet, which is another similar hill town, is still, apparently, very beautiful because it is a military cantonment and kept in ship-shape order.

Uttaranchal has a lot to offer and the Claridges Group have some very fine establishments; I have spoken of the one in Naini but we would be going on to The Claridges Corbett Hideaway near Corbett National Park, which was excellent and so attractive, plus they have the Riverside Camp at Rishikesh, which could be good for those on a spiritual trail or wanting to take part in river sports like river rafting. There is the Himalayan View Retreat at Ramgarh, the Hari Ganga Haveli at Haridwar and the Camp Harsil at Gangotri (the source of the Ganges). For trekking purposes, one can centre oneself at Nainital and have a choice of three routes or at Almora and have a choice of five routes. Then, there is Ranikhet with three other routes and Kausani with three routes, plus Chowkori with another three routes. I am told that the Pindari Glacier trek is wonderful; it requires about seven to eight days but provides beautiful views and walking. The best time to experience this is between the middle of May and the middle of June when the flowers are in full bloom and then again between September and October. Had I the energy and health I would have loved to plan a walking holiday round visiting some of the ancient pilgrimage sites and their various temples that go back about six hundred years.

We left Nainital and descended to the valley by another route because we were going to Ramnagar en route to Kaladungi, Jim Corbett's home, which is now a museum. In the midday sunshine, it was a beautiful view but I found the steepness of the road quite nerve-wracking. At Nainital, Jim and his sister had lived at Gurney Lodge, which was left to Maggie by their mother. This too is now a museum but my parents had visited them at Kaladungi and this is what I wanted to do. In fact, I had been there before, but whilst safely in my mother's womb.

Jim Corbett's life is well documented already; Geoffrey and Diane Ward's book '*Tiger Wallahs*', published in 1993 described him in quite a lot of detail. Diane agreed with me the other day that at the end of that book one is left quite depressed, as indeed she and Geoffrey were writing it, but that, a decade after, there is more real cause for optimism with regard to tiger conservation.

Kaladungi – home of Jim Corbett. Now a museum

Briefly, Edward James Corbett, known as Jim, was the son of a British couple Christopher and Mary Corbett whose family had experienced the brutality and fear of the Indian Mutiny or First War of Independence. Members of their close family had suffered cruelly before being murdered by the rebels. Christopher became the postmaster at Nainital but died when Jim was only four years old. Mary was left with Jim and eleven other children and only a meagre pension on which to survive. They did, however, own the house in Nainital and the property at Kaladungi. The Corbetts were not considered to be in the social elite and this was because India and the British Raj had imposed all sorts of cruel criteria which laid down who and what you were in life. 'Country born' was a sneering description which has never made any sense to me whatsoever. How on earth could one have avoided British children being actually born in India, given that married couples continue to procreate wherever they may be! However, the saving grace was that most children were shipped out at an early age to Britain and had to endure lonely unhappy childhoods, often punctuated with cruelty and neglect, as indeed did Kipling. So much has been written about the Raj but I am afraid that those of us in these modern times would have found the whole idea appalling and hypocritical and full of false values. I was born in India and was indeed sent back to boarding school at the age of ten, but this was accomplished with as much care and love and attention as was possible by my caring parents. Thank goodness for being born in that great land; it gave me an understanding and huge respect for a breadth of people, ancient cultures far greater than my own, a knowledge of different languages and an ability to feel at home at all levels of society, not just with those who had received a narrow protected upbringing. Believe me, Jim Corbett had all of these qualities and probably many more besides, and my father thought him the most wonderful man. The essence of the man was that he taught himself about the forest – the jungle and its denizens. He loved the local people; he worked in a humble job in the railways and, then, in the army during the Second World War where he was given the rank of colonel and asked to train men for jungle warfare. His health suffered considerably and, during his periods of ill health, he took up writing. His subjects were the tigers, leopards and other creatures of the Kumaon and, at that time, he concentrated on his *shikar* exploits (shikar is the word for hunting in Hindi). Corbett did not kill wantonly but did kill man-eaters and flagrant cattle killers. Tigers and leopards were in large numbers in those days and people did not give them the respect due as creatures sharing our planet. Anything that proved to be dangerous to people and cattle was likely to be despatched. His many books describe in detail the stories and adventures that led to the successful killing of the various tigers and leopards that terrified the humble people who lived in the Kumaon region. However, he saw for himself that the tiger was an endangered species and warned about this a long time ago in the 1930s. He was able to experience the abundant game of the East African savannah and could see for himself what population pressure and that from animal husbandry was doing to India's wildlife. He was, in fact, a pioneer in the field of wildlife with an intrinsic love of the jungle and detailed knowledge of its animal inhabitants. His imitation of bird calls and even tiger and leopard were famous and well known to my parents. My mother recalls that he told her about his pet leveret (a baby hare) which he had rescued from the forest. He felt that, after a time, it would be better put back in its natural environment but when he attempted to do this the little creature just lolloped back and sat at his feet and looked at him. So he scooped it up and brought it home to Kaladungi.

Jim Corbett's book '*Man Eaters of Kumaon*' was probably his most famous in which he wrote of his experiences tracking and killing tigers, which reflected both his courage and determination. He was the first to point out that tigers were disappearing in India and to symbolise the end of his hunting days, he buried, with the help of two trusted servants, his three rifles and two shot guns before leaving for Kenya. In his letters, he wrote to his friends that his heart remained in India. When The Queen and Prince Philip visited Kenya in late January early February 1952, it was Jim Corbett who took them to Tree Tops, the guest house incorporated into a tree from which to watch wildlife. He wrote of this account in the book of the same name. He was enchanted with his meeting with Princess Elizabeth and recalled with awe that she had been a princess on arrival but departed a queen.

At the suggestion of Jim Corbett, Sir John Hewett, a lieutenant governor of Uttar Pradesh, or Upper Province as it then was named, decided to establish a wildlife park. In 1936, the park opened under the name Hailey National Park after the governor of the UP Sir Malcolm Hailey. Later the name was changed to Ramganga National Park. Jim Corbett had in the meantime become world famous for his book '*Man Eaters of Kumaon*' and his name became a byword for anyone interested in hunting and wildlife and the preservation thereof. Corbett died in 1955 and, in 1957, it was decided to honour him by renaming Ramganga National Park, the Corbett National Park. In fact, it is quite confusing because Corbett Tiger Reserve is the title for the area encompassing Corbett National Park and the Sonanadi Wildlife Sanctuary. This is the oldest national park on the Indian subcontinent.

Thirty years ago, on 1st April 1973, Project Tiger was launched on the banks of the Ramganga River in Corbett Tiger Reserve. The launch of Project Tiger heralded the onset of scientific wildlife management in India. Thirty years on, India has not really made much progress in this regard, and indeed went through a dark phase when poaching was rife. It will never be eradicated until we have, as a world, managed to educate everyone, be it in China or anywhere else, that tiger's penises and so forth are not likely to enhance their own physical sexuality. Again I repeat, if politicians could see votes in it for their own aggrandizement, the problem would be well on its way to being solved.

Kaladungi stands at the head of a T junction. The Corbett house is a simple building, completely unpretentious and very modest in size. The garden is maintained and the various grandchildren of some of his faithful skikaris (hunters) act as custodians and guides. Corbett had invested a large part of his income and wealth in schemes for the welfare of the local people. He bought a village called 'Choti Haldwani' near Kaladungi and made it an ideal village. He divided and gifted 40 plots out of his village to the villagers and himself paid the land tax. Graham and I enjoyed talking to the descendants of his helpers, all straightforward men who had iconised Corbett for very good reason. We talked both in their broken English and my broken Hindi but thus achieved a good understanding. It is a simple, some would say dull, little museum but that is the essence of it all, not showy just telling you about a very good man of absolute integrity who did the best he could for the simple people of the area, yet at the same time recognised that the powers that be required to be galvanised into action to preserve tigers. Jim Corbett was so austere about his personal habits that he preferred to sleep outside in a tent quite often! The *palki* (rather like a canvas sedan chair) that was used by his sister Maggie when she wanted to travel to Nainital is still there. Men would have carried it on their shoulders with Maggie sitting in a sort of sling chair, all the way up the mountain side. I am glad to say my photos have been successful and therefore we have a good record of our visit. My mother was amazed to see it all after 56 years.

Gandhiji's wise comment on a sign at Kaladungi house

We drove on to Claridges Corbett Hideaway and found it quite delightful. The whole establishment is well thought out and the cottages are thoroughly charming and spacious. There is a front porch, sitting room with fireplace, spacious bedroom, dressing area, bathroom, and a back veranda to sit on in privacy in the sunshine. The gardens are well maintained and colourful. The restaurant building was good with a deck looking onto the Kosi River, thus giving the soothing sound of rushing water. This also doubles as a conference facility. The rondavel open-sided thatched restaurant was very attractive with a pool and children's pool area alongside, plus a separate thatched rondavel bar, the thatched roof of which had a sort of peacock pinnacle! There are facilities for badminton, table tennis and a friendly game of cricket with a soft ball. There was also tented accommodation each with its own facilities, presumably at a cheaper tariff than the cottages. This is a complete resort and very much reminded us of the various resorts in the Drakensberg Mountains of South Africa. A sweater or jacket was required in the winter chill and I asked them to light a fire in the sitting room of our cottage which gave a cosy atmosphere. Tea and coffee-making facilities are provided in each cottage which is so useful, though room service and laundry service was readily available. I was very grateful for the laundry service that put themselves out especially for us – I just hate carrying any amount of dirty washing in my luggage.

The food was excellent with a good variety and the chefs could be seen preparing and cooking the food in a small open-sided thatched kitchen a few feet away from the rondavel restaurant.

Claridges Hotel near Corbett National Park in Uttaranchal

The hotel has a resident naturalist called Imran Khan who was helpful to us. I did suggest that they could improve on their shop because people having a happy time invariably want to indulge in some retail therapy and, in Rajasthan, the various hotels have understood this very well. Postcards, calendars, Corbett's many books, T shirts and other memorabilia are what people want to remind themselves of a good experience. It does not have to be 'tacky', just well stocked with specific items that appeal to all ages, plus maps and reference booklets and perhaps the odd suitable 'coffee table' book showing the wildlife in all its glory.

We went out very early the next morning in a jeep wrapped up in thick blankets against the dawn chill. It is always a thrill to be up and about so early because of the possibility of seeing animals on the roadside and, indeed, our driver Kishore saw a small group of wild elephants crossing the road the night before.

The nature walk in the wide river bed of the Kosi River had been lovely in the late afternoon sunshine the previous day. We saw kingfishers, wagtails, chats and witnessed a bird catching a frog, which was a clever skilled operation. The walk took us to the ancient temple high on a sort of rock-earth stilt which is very atmospheric. The cattle and buffalo coming home at the end of the day is a familiar welcome sight, with woodcutters or wood gatherers with bundles of wood on their heads who respond to a greeting. I thought it was a wonderful spot in which to have a picnic: clear shallow water in which to paddle, beaches of white river pebbles, the riverine jungle and cliffs and, in the distance, the mountain range all bathed in the golden glow of the late afternoon sun.

Inside the park in the early morning, it was similar to Bandhavgarh and we thought it was lovely and well maintained. At Bijrani, we stopped and, mounting an old elephant called Jaisari, we set off on a delightful two to three hour trek. The pace was tranquil but with the added excitement of seeing fresh pug marks of a tiger. The various alarm calls of a chital and other deer made it plain to us that we were probably being watched and circled. Most definitely, the tiger or tigress was watching us but we could not see her! Jaisari plodded through the undergrowth, eating whenever it took her fancy, which was often. It seemed as if we were walking through an endless elephantine buffet restaurant.

When we reached the lovely wide reaches of the river she liked to stand in the water, cool her feet and drink copious amounts. It occurred to me that, had she felt playful, we could have been showered as well but she was wonderful and, with just three of us on her back and the mahawat who

Farewell after our final ride in Corbett National Park

communicated in Hindi, it was a special experience. On an elephant, one could approach really close to sambhar, chital and other animals. They did not mind the proximity because of course there was no noise, except perhaps a munching elephant. Our companion was a quiet Englishman. Another elephant came into view with an Indian trio; they too were quiet and appreciative. Interestingly, their elephant knelt down whilst in the river bed for one of the men to go off and have a pee. It is not quite so easy to jump off and climb on again without some steps, jeep or elephant mounting block. He used the rear end to scramble up again but I might have found that a real challenge with my spinal problems; the simple answer is do not drink too much early morning tea before you go out! We saw a lovely hare with his long ears which sprinted away once he saw us. There are good forest lodges or old colonial bungalows inside the park so one does not have to live outside and indeed, for the dedicated game viewer, this would be the way to do it. When we 'disembarked' from our jungle vehicle, Graham put a tip for the mahawat in Jaisari's trunk tip, and she sweetly lifted her trunk and handed it to the man but we thought he looked a little apprehensive so perhaps from time to time in the past she has gobbled it up?

Once back in the jeep, the pace hotted up and we heard a chital deer calling urgently. It was obvious that a tiger was very close but we never did get to see him. In Corbett, tigers are reputed to be more elusive but it is a lovely place, six hours drive from Delhi, so in many respects the most accessible of the big parks.

This was sadly the end of our wildlife viewing. We had been travelling constantly since our arrival three weeks ago and we needed to relax and lessen the pace. I am so glad that we had that long elephant ride at Corbett. I would have loved to go out again but that afternoon chose to relax by the pool with good food and my notebook. It was a little cool for swimming but just to sit in the winter sunshine with the clear blue sky, brown hills, green bamboos with bright yellow stems, mixed with rams horn poinsettias, Australian bottle brush trees and orange cestrum bushes, and to hear and watch the busy bird life, like the parakeets flying overhead, made for a restful experience.

The six-hour drive back to Delhi early the next morning was uneventful except that we again experienced appalling road surfaces, quite as bad as anything in Madhya Pradesh. It seems incomprehensible to us that Uttar Pradesh and Uttaranchal have not together improved the main roads to major tourist destinations. In some parts, the road whilst still in Uttaranchal has almost completely disappeared and, therefore, any modern car, other than four-wheel drive, has a heavy challenge. Our vehicle succumbed to a puncture. Fortunately, Kishore replaced the wheel but it is company policy with Travel House that the driver must immediately have the punctured tyre repaired. Mercifully, the hotel at which we had stopped with Satish Kumar was just up the road so we stopped off for the usual omelette and tea and, yes, this time the bearer had enough eggs for us both! It was a half-hour stop and Kishore reappeared with the tyre duly repaired, for which we were very grateful and relieved as we were anxious to reach our destination in Delhi in time for lunch with Satish and Saroj Kumar.

CHAPTER
SIXTEEN

Phir Milengi to Delhi,
Namaskar to Mumbai

T he pace in Delhi was fast and furious, starting with lunch at the home of the Kumars. We gave Kishore some money and told him to go and have a good meal and a rest. Saroj had put on a veritable feast and it was lovely to be with them all. Their first darling little grandson had been born at the beginning of September and Satish is a besotted grandfather. I loved watching him talk nonsense to the little baby, who already, quite obviously, had his grandad wrapped round his little finger. As a grandparent myself I know the special love one feels for these little ones a generation on from experiencing parenthood first hand. A serene child in a stable happy closely knit family, surely that would be the ideal for children the world over but, sadly, it seems to be now a precious gift not an accepted right.

After our fond farewells, we raced off to The Imperial Hotel for a little jewellery shopping. I love that hotel with its peaceful ambience of graceful marble halls, tinkling fountains and sumptuous décor. The old ballroom looks very grand and would be a place I would choose for a reception. The tall elegant palm trees that still line the drive maintain the grace of another era. Our jewellery shopping spree was very successful and Ajay Narain's shop in The Imperial is one I would recommend to anyone. Sadly, I had the misfortune to have something quite precious stolen during the trip – I still know not exactly where – but I had the good sense to talk to the jeweller and ask him to make me something precisely similar, which they have done. Obviously, it could not be completed in one day and I was leaving in 48 hours but it was sent on to me by

DHL. The Indian version is charming and, naturally, has an Indian twist to the design whereas the original had been bought in Prague.

We arrived back at Annie and Martin's home and loved our welcome back to a home from home. I had found some tiny silver bracelets for little Yashodi

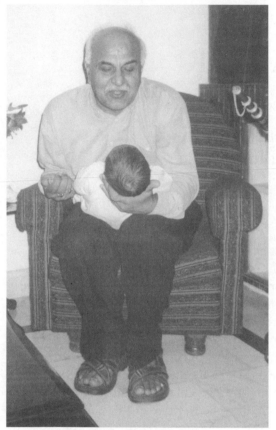

which were well received with a smothering of kisses. Wise child, she put one bracelet on but observed firmly that she would keep the other for later! She may be Nepalese but she could have been a careful Scot – it takes one to know one!

We agreed to meet back for dinner but sped off for drinks with the engaging Bhatia family. Again, one experienced that pleasurable feeling of being in the midst of a big caring family in their elegant home. The trouble with Indian hospitality is that it is so generous one would be round as a ball if one ate everything that was offered.

We had a relaxed supper with Martin and Annie and caught up on all Tikli Bottom's news and then sadly Graham had to leave for the airport after

Satish Kumar with his beloved first grandson

weeks of excellent and memorable fun. I was so sad to see him go and felt guilty being in a comfortable bed whilst he was languishing in the departure lounge of Indira Gandhi airport for a 0400 hours British Airways flight back home.

The following morning found me with a breakfast business meeting at The Maurya Sheraton, which is when I was actually shown round the presidential suites. As I said this hotel is seriously good. There were a couple of business meetings to keep in the city but I was back for lunch at The Maurya and, therefore, was able to go into Maharani of India and order up a lovely evening outfit made of different silks of my choice. The assistants took meticulous measurements and when the finished garments were sent to me courtesy of DHL for which I paid of course, they were lovely. If one has the time, it is better to have a fitting or see the completed garments in the shop but I took a risk and am satisfied with my outfits. The workmanship is excellent. I plan to wear this beautiful jacket at our younger son Stewart's wedding to Corinne in December 2004. It will be a wonderful day.

That evening I had a last supper with Annie who had invited an old and very interesting friend. The following morning, Yash came in wearing her school uniform and said goodbye to me. Annie and I watched her mount the pommel of her uncle's large motorbike with him and his girlfriend riding pillion and drive off to school. It worried me to see the little girl without a helmet and I winced inwardly at what could befall her, but this is India and people live without ifs and buts. I felt a lump in my throat because she is a bright little girl, an example of what cherished daughters can be in a land where still there is this short-sighted preference for the male. The 'Yashodis' of the new India with their multilingual skills and agile minds absorbing cross-cultures is what will give India its intangible wealth in the years to come. I will always remember the way she says goodbye. She likes to take your face in her hands and kiss you all over. I had to take a photo which has developed nicely. The little mite and her cheeky acceptance of what the world offers her as she impatiently said to her uncle 'Come on, uncle, let us vroom vroom!' and they roared off and were swallowed up by Delhi's snarling morning rush hour. However, at lunchtime when her English medium school finishes she is walked home by Anjoli and I can imagine her as I write at my keyboard; if she were here she would be bossily pushing me away and taking over the whole desk to draw a picture or perhaps write a chapter on her own.

I said my farewell to Annie who was rushing off to Tikli and had a quick meeting with someone who came and had tea with me, then it was a thank you to Anjoli for looking after us and away to the domestic airport. I felt sad; the Howard hospitality is legendary and for me will always act as a welcome haven in a bustling city. Delhi is a city in which I feel comfortable. Admittedly, it has its problems and at the time there was an outcry about the rape of a medical student. Since then, I have read of other cases of rape and car hijacking but much of this happens elsewhere in the West, let alone the East. Here, in little Scotland, with a minute population of under five million we have some awful occurrences in Greater Glasgow and the Central Belt. It might astonish outsiders but we have a real 'badlands' culture round North Lanarkshire and some of the Scottish Executive's statistics on various forms of crime are very depressing reading.

Kishore had looked after me faithfully, for which I was grateful. I gave him a good tip and said I hoped we would meet again. There are good and bad people everywhere. When I checked in I was accompanied by the baggage handlers, three of whom seemed to be competing for my business. In a trance, somehow I left my handbag and turned to go, complete idiocy on my part, and the leader of the three said 'Ma'am, what are you doing, surely this is your bag?' I thanked him profusely and gave them a good tip.

Jet Airways was my choice for the flight down to Mumbai. It was a good one. This airline is very impressive in many different ways. They had recently won an award for best domestic airline and I can see why. Efficient, courteous, running a little ahead of schedule, a well-appointed plane with delicious food beautifully presented with thoughtful touches like nimbu pani (fresh lime and water) to drink, as well as other beverages. We landed early and I rate them highly. Their security checks were throuogh and courteous but not officious.

I have been reproached gently by my friends for being critical of Mumbai so I resolved to look at it again with a more objective eye. A driver and car met me which was as ever efficiently arranged by The Travel House which has offices throughout India. As we drove in the evening light, I thought that perhaps it was looking a little better in the famous areas than on my last visit four years ago. The beach, Chowpatty Beach, actually looked as if the municipality had cleaned it and did so regularly. This is not a place from which to swim – I shudder at the very idea of the polluted water one would experience – but it is the place for people of all ages to entertain themselves in an Indian form of the 'la Passeggiàta'. In Calcutta, or Kolkata as it now is, is the *maidan* or big lawn or park, the place for taking the air, family togetherness, children playing, picnics and so forth. In Delhi, that happens around the grand imperial architecture of Lutyens's Delhi in the great swathe of lawns down from the Secretariat and Rashtrapati Bavan, the President's Palace, as far as India Gate, the War Memorial. Here, in Mumbai everything is spread out round the bay.

Early evening transforms the whole area as the lights come on and twinkle and bestow some magic. When I used regularly to fly into and out of Mumbai as a teenager, the Queen's Necklace was a lovely landmark from the plane. Over forty years on, however, this is a teeming city of over 20 million people and there is a frenetic air to the place and the feeling that it never actually sleeps. The majestic Gateway of India continues to look majestic, but it must have been awe inspiring for the young hopefuls in the time of empire when they arrived by steamer. All the young men from Britain, whether they were military officers or in the very junior ranks of the Indian Civil service, arrived here to commence their service and careers in India. So too did the famous 'fishing fleet' of young

The Gateway of India – Mumbai

ladies intent on catching a young promising husband. How totally different it was from the lives of the young of today, who are under no such matrimonial pressures in Western culture. Thank goodness, what misery scores of people must have endured through hasty marriages often of convenience to save 'face', or cement dynasties or promotional ambition.

The great historic arrivals of the various royal dukes and princes and, finally, the King Emperor and his Queen must have been wonderful spectacles. I own archival photos of the occasion and the year was significant because my mother was born in 1911 and our old cook Din, as a very young man, witnessed parts of the famous Delhi Durbar. The Gateway of India was actually built in 1924 as a monument commemorating the imperial visit. Queen Mary's account in her diaries of her visits to India, are actually quite amusing and bring such a human touch to it all. The other historic landmark near the Gateway of India is The Taj Hotel. This was built by the great Parsi gentleman J N Tata as an act of defiance because he had been cruelly snubbed and not allowed entry to the then leading hotel called Watson's. Suffice to say that the latter has long gone and I had to look up the name, whereas The Taj and the hotel group are known worldwide. This was such a symbol of empire and I considered it a bit like a mausoleum when very small, but now of course it is beautiful inside with a fusion of old and modern. Victorian Gothic architecture is seen quite generally in central Mumbai and these buildings have gradually been sympathetically renovated. This work, I am told, has not been done by a sensible municipality attempting to improve its image but by non-governmental organisations which raise the money for the face lift.

Victoria Terminus, now known as the Chhatrapati Shivaji Terminus, completed in 1888, is a marvellous eccentricity and considered to be perhaps the greatest railway station every built by the British. Now (July 2004), it has been given World Heritage status and must surely be the world's only functioning railway to receive that accolade. Its architect, Frederick William Stevens, would be delighted and astonished that his sandstone creation is now 'rubbing pillars' with the legendary Taj Mahal. Although Stevens supervised the project, two Indian engineers: Sitaram Khanderao, the PWD (Public Works Department) assistant engineer, and Madherao Janardhan, the PWD supervisor, share responsibility for this amazing building. Thus, it is an integration of Victorian Gothic, Mughal and Gujarati architecture. Indian railways now have to fulfil their commitment to restore and maintain what could become a civic and tourist icon for Mumbai and an inspiration for further conservation of other great buildings.

The Taj Hotel – Mumbai

The Prince of Wales Museum is a splendid example of Indo-Saracenic architecture but it is really now called the Chhatrapati Shivaji Maharaj Vastu Sangrahalaya – well, you can understand why it is still known as The Prince of Wales Museum! Just alongside The Prince of Wales Museum, there is the Jehangir Art Gallery which is also worth a visit as this is a showcase for contemporary art and some items are for sale. Crawford Market is another tourist destination, being one of the few remaining covered markets built in British times with its huge Norman Gothic tower serving as a landmark. I can imagine that people would find this an interesting experience with literally everything on offer from food to animals and everything in between. I prefer the New Market in Kolkata which is very similar but had to be rebuilt because of a fire a couple of decades ago. I wrote about it in my first book.

I am trying hard, my friends, but I cannot honestly say that I find Mumbai a good tourist destination. It is, however, a bustling enthusiastic city of go-getters and its night life and choice of bars and restaurants is legendary. There are a huge number of Indian millionaires resident in this metropolis and the social elite have a very sophisticated life.

Beautiful ancient bronze sculptures in the Prince of Wales Museum Gardens – Mumbai

Hospitality here is mostly warm and generous, though occasionally one finds oneself amongst people who have little depth and appear to be consumed with material competition. In the hot weather, it is just too hot to move so the Mumbai social scene whirls into action in October/November and that is also the beginning of the traditional wedding season. What I do like about Indian dinner parties is the vigour of the conversation and the wide range of topics whereas some European entertaining is so circumspect and cautious and you come away from a dinner thinking 'what was the point of that?' Here in Mumbai, wealthy informed successful people who travel widely and usually have some family members who live permanently overseas, have definite and interesting opinions and I find that invigorating. It has to be said, however, that entertaining is made a whole lot easier if one has a bevy of servants to lay it all on as is the case in the wealthy Indian homes.

Domestic households here have at least three indoor servants at the wealthy end of the social spectrum, plus a driver and dhobi who does the major laundry; plus, of course, the sweeper, who is always from the untouchable Dalit caste. To western eyes it can seem a rigid set of customs but that is India and you or I

Crawford Market – Mumbai

are not going to change it. That does not mean, however, that in one's dealings with all of these people one has to be anything less than generous in spirit. The old adage of 'treating others as one would like to be treated' works very well in India. I make a point of always greeting everyone, often to the complete surprise of a sweeper – she is doing a vital job whether in a public or private place. If I can make her day a happier one I will enrich my own. In the old fashioned flats or apartments, provision was made in the design for servant accommodation, whereas in the modern apartments penny-pinching greed has not made provision for them, yet people continue to employ staff. These people are then expected to sleep in the hallways without any sanitation provided, and then the inevitable happens – 18 storeys up, who is going to go down to the ground for a pee at night? It sounds so selfish and horrible and makes me think of the uncaring way domestic staff was treated in the West up to the Second World War over sixty years ago.

Indians are conscious of those who are disadvantaged and do give to charity but sometimes it appears to the western eye that there could be more spontaneity and more giving from the heart. The Hindu philosophy, as in my own Christian thinking, covers the credo 'give and you shall receive' but I am often irritated by the calculating way some hugely wealthy people only give if they receive public recognition. The good thing is, however, that the Indian press has no inhibitions about revealing scandal and corruption, and exposes anything and everything that could taint the country; pushy, self-publicising individuals inevitably reveal themselves to most discerning onlookers the world over.

Mani Bhavan is the Mahatma Gandhi Museum and really well maintained and interesting. This house was Gandhiji's base between 1917 and 1934 and there is also a research library. Gandhiji even wrote a letter to Hitler suggesting world peace! I liked it.

I went shopping at the Cottage Industries shop and found it worthwhile. However, having had a parcel shipped supposedly by DHL for which I had paid by Visa card, I was the victim of a 'scam'. Usually, when one pays for courier delivery, the item arrives within a week. My parcel did not arrive and as I had the email address I entered into correspondence, which, on the face of it was extremely concerned and helpful. However, when a parcel did arrive a month later it had similar items to those I had chosen but not the actual items. I thanked them, but another month later my original items arrived all sewn up in cotton in the customary old Indian way. It was delivered by the Royal Mail. I then had a demand from FedEx to pay again for the couriered parcel. This was all very vexing and thank goodness for Visa card who reimbursed me. So the lesson is that perhaps in government emporia do not go down the path of paying for courier services unless dealing with a very senior member of staff. Certainly, in the Cottage Industries shop someone was up to something and had not reckoned on my tenacity. I would personally never use anyone other than DHL as a courier as a result of that bad experience.

I went on a visit to Elephanta Island which was worthwhile, but tiring. The boat trip takes one hour and is pleasant. Once there, it is quite a long walk to the base of the steps, but there is a sort of toy train in which to ride. The path up to the summit, where the caves and statues are, is lined with the usual tourist stalls, which sell an amazing amount of goods including the most atrocious-looking ornaments whose designs obviously originated in the West. The climb on a warm day is pretty exhausting and one loses pints through perspiration! Monkeys badger one as one stands to rest. The latrine was rudimentary!

The caves, however, with their carvings, are amazing and, before they were defaced or damaged, must have been quite beautiful. Even now there is a colossal grandeur about the pillars and depictions. Originally known as Gharapuri, 'the city of Gahra priests', the island was renamed in the sixteenth century by the Portuguese, in order to commemorate the carved elephant they found at the port. The Shiva sculpture with its three-faced depiction is a very fine example of Hindu architecture. The cave is eighth century and is reached by 100 steps as I have described but the carvings were damaged by the

Portuguese. There is an annual dance and music festival at Elephanta in the winter season and this is apparently very worthwhile.

The other thing I did was to go and consult an Ayurvedic physician. This appointment was arranged for me by someone who was kind enough to accompany me and who believes implicitly in this man's advice and knowledge. It was an interesting experience because the individual in question is massive in size, obese is the word that springs to mind, and he sits amidst his pills and potions and cures derived from the herbal plants of India. I found him unattractive and a bit superficial. That does not mean that other Ayurvedic physicians would give this first impression. To me this man looked like a *banya* or merchant, not in anyway medical. Moreover, I did not think anything of the hygiene of the place but, of course, this was India. Foolishly, I took his powder in my cabin luggage and when it was put through rigorous investigation in the departure lounge at Mumbai Airport the official asked me what it was. Well, fortunately, it had a pungent smell of spice like nutmeg or cinnamon and the official dismissed it but someone trying to be officious could have made much of it and I resolved never to do something like that again. I did not follow his advice and threw away his medicine. However, I also sought the advice of a homeopath and found him meticulous and worthwhile.

I think one of my lasting impressions of Mumbai is that even the privileged live in rabbit hutches. The poverty and overcrowding of the most disadvantaged leads to the pictures of India that none of us enjoy; sadly, it is a reality for huge numbers and I marvel at their courage and determination to improve their lives given even the slightest opportunity. No, curiously, it is the immensely wealthy, who are content to live in a boxed up world of air-conditioned flats in this power house of India, that mystify me. When I was last there all the social chat was about a proposed 60-storey apartment block which had its various floor plans and apartments sold off the drawing board. I privately thought that some clever entrepreneur is trying to outdo the Petronas Towers in Kuala Lumpur for the prestige factor. Having lived in the Mandarin Oriental in Kuala Lumpur right next to the Petronas Towers and had a superb view from our suite of the cityscape on both sides, I know that regretfully nothing they do will rival that building or view. Moreover, I think someone in China is building the world's newest tallest building as I write.

After my visit to Elephanta Island, I went to the Taj and had a light meal. In actual fact, I had not been back to the building since 1951, when, as a small child, we had lived there for a few days following the extreme worry of my late father's massive coronary whilst on the train from Kolkata to Mumbai. We had been on our way to board a P&O liner bound for Britain. As it was, my father was very fortunate to survive the coronary and had to recuperate in Mumbai for months before we flew home to the UK. My memories of the old Taj building with its central well and graceful staircases go back to that time; it is possible that I do not like Mumbai for that reason, a childhood feeling of insecurity and alarm and memory of the worry and anguish of my mother and my father trying to be brave.

Mumbai is, however, a very good 'jumping off' point for lots of wonderful historic places like Ellora, Ajanta, Aurangabad, all of which are in the modern state of Maharashtra. This state was created in 1960 and is the third largest in India. The industrial might of this state accounts for a quarter of the nation's output.

Maharashtra's history is documented from the second century BC with the construction of its first Buddhist caves. Buddhism was a major influence here but, gradually, Hinduism supplanted it and, though Islam had a footing during the Moghul dominance in the North, it has made little long-term impact. Shivaji is considered Maharashtra's greatest warrior and hero. He was a Maratha chieftain who united the various local cliques and fought off potential invaders from the coast, but he also moved northwards and exploited the internecine struggles of the Moghuls. He was, however, captured in 1664 when defeated in battle at Surat, the ancient port of Gujarat. Aurangzeb imprisoned him at the Red Fort in Agra but he was able to escape and lived till 1680, by which time he had united the Marathas into a unified force and stable prosperous state. Aurangzeb actually left Delhi and came and ruled from Aurangabad (which did not yet have that name) but, though he raised the city walls and did all in his power to protect his southern lands, the Marathas persisted in their quest. When Aurangzeb died in 1707, the city was renamed in his honour and came under a new ruler – the Nizam of Hyderabad.

Modern Aurangabad is a thrusting commercial city with the added attraction of shopping malls, restaurants and bars and the old city as a tourist destination. There is a Muslim minority which has to somehow make an uneasy peace with the extreme right Hindu Shiv Sena party. Mumbai wallahs fly here for long weekends as there are so many places to see as well as good hotels in which to enjoy themselves. Daulatabad is a day trip away and has an incredible old fort that was briefly the fourteenth century Muslim capital of India. Again, this is a hilltop fort on top of a massive volcanic outcrop. Previous to its Muslim occupation, it was known as Deogiri 'Hill of the Gods'. At Khuldabad, which is a Muslim walled town, one can visit the tomb of Emperor Aurangzeb. He really was the last of the great Moghuls; after him the dynasty waned. The nicest of the five-star hotels is the Taj Residency which is not too close to the airport The Bibi-Ka-Maqbara is the mausoleum for Aurangzeb's wife but, although it is very fine, it in no way competes with the exquisite Taj Mahal. Indeed what could?

The caves overlooking the mausoleum are interesting but again are no competition for those at Ellora and Ajanta; however, in themselves they are a good example of rock art. I just feel that the potential for Buddhist tourism is yet to be reached in this whole area. One day soon, the authorities will realise how important all of this is but, as yet, there appears to be inertia about the place, rather like Gwalior, though it has to be said some of the modern development is unpleasant and diminishes the beauty of the focus of attention. Ellora is Maharashtra's most visited ancient site. There are 34 Buddhist, Hindu and Jain caves. The site's major attraction is Kailash temple, built in the eighth century, which is apparently the world's largest monolith and is quite simply spectacular. The Jain caves to the north of the main group were the result of the Digambara sect (as was the Sonagiri set of temples of which I wrote earlier). Sadly, because Ellora is not as isolated as Ajanta, Aurangzeb in a fit of religious zeal commanded that the heathen idols be defaced. In the last two years of this century, we know that the Taliban did that in Afghanistan to the massive Buddhist rock art that the experts are now trying valiantly to reconstruct sympathetically.

Ajanta is much further away and the 166 km road trip takes a few hours by car so it is wise to set out really early in the morning after a good breakfast in the hotel. These caves were discovered in 1819 by a tiger-hunting party of British officers and men. At the height of its influence, Ajanta sheltered more than two hundred monks as well as a large community of painters and sculptors and artisans. Indications are that this was started in the second century BC. Both these sites should be visited between October and March. The monsoon may also be a good time to visit as with Mandu but this area can become dangerous with swollen rivers and waterfalls, although the greenery and water enhances the beauty of the whole experience. Any visit after March until the rains would, however, be unwise as the heat and humidity is overpowering.

Both Ellora and Ajanta have been sympathetically renovated and care has been taken to ensure that there is no further degradation from flash lights and the heat of powerful lights. I think three days is required to comprehensively see Aurangabad, Ellora and Ajanta, and actually four would be better to give one a chance to relax and catch one's breath after experiencing so many quite spectacular sights.

CHAPTER SEVENTEEN

Gir National Park, Nagarahole,
Kaziranga and Pench Tiger Reserve

"The Earth like cloth consists of strands
Where worn, we ought to mend it.
For no one knows, which thread, once torn
May suddenly just end it."

Henry Gibson

There are two ways in which to visit Gir, either fly from Mumbai to Rajkot, which is 175 km away or take a train to Sasan Gir or Junagadh, again from Mumbai. There is also now an air service to Diu from Mumbai. This is probably what I will use because it allows one to have a holiday by the sea at Diu which is charming and unspoilt and the drive to Gir is not too long. Depending on the amount of time available, I think the train is better in that one sees the countryside around and absorbs the landscape and terrain. Huge car journeys are only for the dedicated as I have already written and most people want to just arrive!

Gir Forest and Sanctuary is magnificent with rugged hilly terrain particularly in the northern and western areas with the Gir Hills reaching a height of 530 metres or approximately 2000 feet. This famous lion sanctuary lies at the bottom of the Saurashtra peninsular in Gujarat.

Gir is home to the Asiatic Lion of which I will speak, but is also home to the largest leopard population of any park in India. There are now approximately 300 lions in the park and Gir has proved to be one of the great success stories because at the turn of the twentieth century it was reckoned that only 20 lions remained.

Lions are thought to have entered the Indian subcontinent around 6000 BC and, during the Indus Valley Civilization, lions were present in many parts of the country. They were also found in what is now Pakistan, Syria, Iraq, as we now know it, and Iran. From 275 BC through to 188 AD, lions were found in great numbers all over the Indian subcontinent except in the south.

The great Mauryan emperor Ashoka used the lion as his icon and symbol in the famous rock pillars and, as I said earlier, urged the first message of conservation on his people. Tragically, once firearms became available, lions were exterminated from most parts of the country. In 1870, the last lion surviving outside Gir was shot at Dessa. Mercifully, Lord Curzon, the great Viceroy (who is often vilified these days, but had foresight for his time) declined the invitation to shoot lions at Gir, but asked the then Nawab of Junagadh to consider protecting and conserving the last remaining handful of lions. By 1913, the population of the Asiatic Lion plummeted to about 20. Then, in 1944, a British cavalry officer is reported to have shot 80 lions during a three-year stay in the region.

Whenever I read of these appalling deeds, I am covered in shame for the shallow thinking and futile ambitions of some of my race who have 'enjoyed' themselves in India. I know that hunting lions in ancient times was a royal privilege and a symbol of manliness. The motif of a king stabbing a lion was the royal seal of the kings of Assyria and the Mesopotamian Kings decorated the walls of their palaces with hunting scenes. Man pitting himself against nature has been a universal theme since the beginning of pictorial history but, truly, in the time of the British rule and the zenith of the maharajahs' glory, hunting and killing appeared to reach extremes that today we would find difficult to comprehend, let alone condone. Reading royal diaries and accounts of King George V's shooting parties I found it repugnant that he took so much pleasure in killing thousands of pheasants and partridge at Sandringham. In the medieval days, when kings went hunting, admittedly for sport, the stag or the hind was brought back for the feast. By having royal deer forests at least the animals were protected from extermination by the ordinary man. No-one ate lions or tigers or leopards and trophy killing is just man's vanity and desire to boost his own ego.

Albert Einstein wrote "Any society which does not insist upon respect for all life must necessarily decay."

How right he was and in fact today the societies which glorified themselves through wanton shooting and needless trophyism are in decay and being replaced by much more thoughtful appreciative people who see themselves as custodians of the land.

The lion population may have increased in Gir from 177 in 1976 to 327 in 2001 but, until their numbers reach 500, the species will continue to be listed as highly endangered. The worry now is that Gir may have reached its capacity for a lion population. Worryingly, 54 lions have died in the past two years, and lions are beginning to be seen outside the park as far away as Porbandar. Inevitably, if they are viewed as a threat to humans the whole conservation topic becomes political.

Lions, unlike tigers and leopards, live in social groups called prides. Each pride comprises five to seven lions, which need at least 40 sq. km of territory in which to move around. The lions of the Gir sanctuary ideally require 2,500 sq. km of land, but Gir's total area is only 1,412 sq. km including a 257 sq. km national park at its core. Ideally, they require an extra 1000 sq. km and if you consider that they share this area with over 300 leopards (panthers as they are often called in India) and a huge population of around 46,000 antelope plus 10,000 cattle herders and approximately 30,000 cattle, it is obvious that the park is under strain.

Interestingly, the migration of lions southwards to places like Kodinar and Una has been welcomed by people there. Ram Kumar, the deputy conservator of forest at Gir Sanctuary has an explanation. Lions do not attack people like tigers or panthers do, and their presence keeps away the nilgai and wild boar which destroy crops. The lions in turn subsist on the villagers' cattle. Villagers do not protest because they are compensated by the Forest Department. This is a symbiotic relationship with human beings, but at no time should one forget that lions are carnivores.

In 1999, the Kruger Park in South Africa which is immense and truly wonderful and where I saw my first lions in 1970, lost half of its 2000 lions to illness in a few months; that brings up the debate as to whether it is wise to concentrate the Asiatic Lion in only one place. There have been ideas of translocation to places like the Kuno Palpur Sanctuary in Madhya Pradesh. This was a good and practical idea but, when the Gujarat and Madhya Pradesh governments locked horns over the sharing of the Narmada River's waters, the sharing of lions became linked. Moreover, a chief minister of Gujarat discarded the idea of translocation on purely parochial grounds declaring them the pride of

Gujarat, which indeed they are but surely politicians can see a little beyond their noses?

The following is an account by Annie Hayes-Watkins's of the beautiful experience she and her friend Julie had on a visit to Gir. They are both devoted to wildlife and their impressions mirror my own. Fortunately, Julie's fall from the jeep at Ranthambhore was not a long-term injury and they had a superb time at Gir.

"The Gir sanctuary lies to the south west of Gujarat state, covering an area of approximately 1540 square miles. At least 65% of the forest is covered with teak trees and the rest with ber, Flame of the Forest and acacia, sprinkled with the occasional banyan tree. On our visit, most of the leaves were falling from the trees but it still made visibility into the forest very difficult.

There are occasions when the lions come onto the tracks, but they are now few and far between as there are still a lot of cattle herders called Maldharis, who live within the forest, and in turn they and their cattle drive the lions deeper into the forest. The cattle form a very substantial part of the lion's food, which makes sightings of sambhar, chital and nilgai more difficult as the herdsmen's cattle push the lions' wild prey further in as well.

The bird life is abundant, and we were lucky to see fish-owl, black vulture, Bonelli's eagle and stork, to name but a few, all in beautiful settings especially around the Kamaleshwar dam, which is a very peaceful place to see the birds and huge crocodiles that bask in the sun on the banks.

Julie and I were fortunate enough to see five leopards in our time there. One was just sitting about ten feet from the road relaxing in the morning sunshine. This particular leopard we were able to photograph really well and in close up but the others were some distance away though very visible through binoculars.

Lion sightings were more elusive. There are approximately 327 lions in the sanctuary but it is very difficult to see them. After three safaris, we were just about to admit defeat, when our driver/guide met up with some forest rangers, who were his good friends. They all had quite a discussion and the upshot of that was that having pooled their knowledge they were able to get us within twenty feet of a huge male lion relaxing in the afternoon sunshine. We even went back later in the afternoon to see him and, by that time, he had been joined by another male lion that was sitting behind a bush about 15 to 18 feet away from us; it was a fantastic moment. The following day, we were able to see two lionesses which had just made a kill and we were only about 18 feet away. This was truly marvellous.

On the third day, they took us again to see the same two lionesses, but they had moved into a dip on the side of a hill, we were actually only 15 feet away when they popped their heads up to look at us; it was a heart-stopping moment. It was really marvellous to be so close to those magnificent animals, they are far prettier than the African lions, but with shorter and darker manes. The rangers are not permitted to carry guns, all they have are large sticks, but they go into the forest every day to keep an eye on the lions. If a lion kills one of the Maldharis' cattle the owners are compensated.

I would imagine that a lot of visitors would be very disappointed as 'lion sightings' are very few and far between. The forest itself is a beautiful and tranquil place and it is indeed lovely just driving around, even when one is not lucky enough to see many animals. Unfortunately, both our cameras and my video recorder could not take the dust and heat, so we do not have any particularly good photographs, but we do have a wealth of memories of our stay, and we would definitely like to return some day."

Leopard, as Annie said is quite easily seen in Gir and, though I talked of the animal briefly earlier on, I feel it is only right to return to it here. I do not now necessarily agree with the various titles given to animals in their kingdom! For me, the tiger is King of the Jungle, but Lions are considered the ultimate ruler of the animal kingdom too by a great many. Surely then, the Leopard is the Prince of Cats? The leopard is recognised to be cleverer than either the tiger or the lion and my father always said they have cunning. They are also one of the most beautiful and graceful animals in the jungle but really dangerous to man.

Like human fingerprints, no two leopard skins are precisely similar in their markings; Colouration varies from the normal buff- or straw-coloured sleek yellow coat with black rosettes to a rich yellow-orange. Leopard is powerful and capable of dragging its prey with an equal weight to itself for 9 metres or up a tree so as not to be harassed by lions, jackals or hyenas. Leopards are spread over much of Gujarat and, in Gir, they have the ideal habitat. Whereas the tiger kills with its great powerful jaws, the leopard principally kills with its claws. It is said that it was the leopard that inspired the camouflage material used for jungle warfare uniforms in the Second World War. Generally, they are smaller than the tiger or the lion but they are a deadly predator and observe all that is happening around them in the forest whilst seldom being seen themselves. Jim Corbett's book, '*The Man-Eating Leopard of Rudraprayag*' illustrates the skills of the animal. For eight years, the population around Rudraprayag in the

Garwhal region not far from Nainital and Corbett National Park, were in fear of this wily beast until Jim Corbett was able to kill it. This is a book I highly recommend to anyone interested in wildlife who has not yet come across it. It is still published in India.

There is no reason, however, to fear them in Gir while visiting the park. The park authorities are very alert to any abnormal behaviour and as long as you abide by the park's rules no harm will come to you. Leopards do prey on dogs and small children as I have already indicated when they experience a loss of their natural habitat but, even when something untoward occurs, Indian villagers try their best to relocate an animal by luring it to a big trap, often baited with a dog. Then, when successfully trapped, the animal is sedated and transported to the most convenient wildlife park.

As well as lions, leopards and all the other wonderful creatures, Gir is also known for its snake population. However, had it not been designated a lion sanctuary, it could easily have been declared a bird sanctuary. Over 300 species of birds have been identified in Gir over the years and it could easily rival Bharatpur in this respect. The sheer wealth of bird-life and the noise, sometimes loud and chattering but often gentle and individual makes a morning out in Gir memorable and, although it will perhaps not compensate you for not seeing a lion, the beauty of the birdsong is special

India has so many wonderful trees and I did mention a few of my favourites in the first book but it is worth mentioning them again. The red silk-cotton tree, *Bombax ceiba*, is one of the most beautiful trees of India and it grows up to 40 metres in height. The flowers are brilliant crimson and hold so much nectar that birds and insects converge on it throughout the day in large numbers. As a small child, I clearly remember the silky cotton that the fruit produces, in which the seeds are embedded. I used to decorate my dolls' beds with this silky cotton stuff. The peepal tree, *Ficus religiosa*, is considered to be sacred; I love the shape of its leaves which are often used to paint miniature Indian scenes – it dries most beautifully and the skeleton of the leaf is exquisite; a form of fig, it is constantly in demand from birds and monkeys. The banyan, *Ficus benghalensis*, is a stunning tree with its aerial roots which descend from branches to enter the ground, and then they thicken like a trunk and it is as if one if walking under an arboreal ceiling with arches. Flame of the forest, *Butea monosperma*, has a slight Scottish connection in that the botanist John Stuart, otherwise the Marquis of Bute, named this tree. It derives its name from the fact that in the spring time the flame-coloured flowers look as if the forest is on fire. All these trees are seen at their most beautiful in springtime which is February to March. There are so many from which to choose but another personal favourite is the neem, *Azadirachta indica*. This is truly an incredible tree and can be called nature's pharmacy. Every part of it seems to have medicinal value and neem oil is an antiseptic. The ripe fruit and the oil are remedies for skin diseases. Leaves may be ground into a paste and used to heal wounds. The bark serves as a tonic and the smoke of the leaves acts as an insecticide. If one puts dried leaves in cupboards it helps to ward off insects. In days gone by, the twigs were used as nature's own toothbrush (but though it was normal to see people using it in my childhood probably now most are converted to a conventional toothbrush). As a child of nine, I was driven nearly mad with the rash and itching of chicken pox but a water made from boiling up the leaves soothed the irritated skin. These days I only have to go to my local pharmacist to buy neem products that are produced here in Scotland. I think it is rivalling Tea Tree Oil. Neem trees are especially suited to dry areas as it consumes very little water but is an excellent shade tree and owing to its large leaf area gives out more oxygen than most other trees. The other botanical name for neem is margosa, or certainly the products are sold under that name in Sri Lanka, where Ayurvedic medicine is widely used and respected with good reason.

The Maldharis are the peaceful livestock owners that have coexisted with the lions for over a century. They are a tribal people, who used to be nomadic but are now pastoralists, with a great concern for their environment and they are strictly vegetarian. Their cattle are milked for the fresh product, which being perishable has to be marketed quickly. Ghee, the product of milk, is not apparently as lucrative a product as fresh milk. They are in fact no threat to the lions and the wildlife but their huge herds of cattle and buffalo are, as they are non-selective eaters and just decimate the vegetation unlike the various herbivores in the park.

An ecosystem can only support a limited number of wildlife and humans. I do not know what the future holds for Gir with the increasing cattle population of the Maldharis, who for obvious reasons want more modern facilities for themselves, which would soon impinge on the park. If a solution could somehow be found to resettle the Maldharis amicably and free their land in order to incorporate it in within the sanctuary, this would be a real step forward.

As a supporter of The Vanishing Herds Foundation here in the United Kingdom, I can explain that the Foundation's aim is to create a major international education and research foundation. This centre will provide ongoing training for world-class conservation experts within India and will support eco-tourism; thereby, bringing local people and their cultures fully into the ecological and wildlife management equation.

The international centre and educational programme will introduce the issues of Indian wildlife and species in danger to a wide public both at home and abroad. In turn, this will not only facilitate correct management of India's wildlife to ensure a future with a balanced ecology, but will also heighten public awareness of ecological issues – something that is fundamental to persuading government at all levels to take conservation issues into the realm of urgent action and support.

VHF has already purchased the first 12 acres of land not far from the Forest of Gir and is hoping to purchase a further 30 acres in the near future. The centre will provide both undergraduate and post-graduate programmes in wildlife conservation, ecology and related disciplines affiliated to premier national and international universities.

Education and respect for natural resources are the key to sustaining wildlife; neglect of the environment through non-action or over-exploitation of natural resources leads to depletion of natural resources and degradation of biodiversity, which, in turn, leads to perpetuation of poverty. The two together spiral into an exhaustion of natural resources that ultimately leads to extinction of life. If, however, more information and knowledge is acquired by us all about the earth's natural resources and biodiversity with a broadening knowledge supported by education, research, and dissemination of information, then a wider awareness about nature and the acknowledgement and respect of nature's resources in sustenance of life leads to a judicious use of those natural resources in pursuing economic activities.

Nagarahole National Park in Karnataka is a park to which Graham and I very much want to go and so we shall on our next visit to India but, in the meantime, I am including an account of the wild elephants of that beautiful region, written by Suniti Bhushan Datta. Suniti is the resident naturalist of Bagh Van Lodge, at Pench, the newest tiger reserve. Asian Elephants are the most wonderful beasts as I have described elsewhere, but to see them in large numbers in the wild one should go to southern India or Sri Lanka, and a book on India's great wildlife parks would be inadequate without an account of them in their natural habitat.

Elephants in their Natural Habitat. By Suniti Bhushan Datta.

The early morning mist rising off the Kabini Reservoir gives the land a surreal look. The sun has not risen yet and the grassy banks of the reservoir are calm. A dark shape looms out of the Bamboo on the fringes of the forest; the mist swirls around as it slowly walks to the water's edge. The elephant has spent the night grazing on the juicy grasses that are abundant at this time of year and needs a drink of water before retreating into the forest. The rising sun soon burns away the last tendrils of mist, beginning another hot day at the Nagarahole National Park in Karnataka, South India.

In a country with a population exceeding a billion people, there is scant place for animals as large as an elephant to survive. From a distribution which spanned most of the Indian subcontinent, elephant habitats have shrunk to a few scattered forests in Northern, Eastern and Southern India. The healthiest population, by far, exists in the diverse forests of South India. Ranging from dry teak to tropical evergreen, these habitats are home to about 15% of the world's wild Asiatic Elephant population.

Elephant society is typically headed by the eldest and most experienced female in a herd, known as the matriarch. The matriarchs know, through experience, which areas will have a certain variety of food in a certain season, the location of water in the dry season and areas where they will be safe. Over the centuries, herds have followed rigid migration routes that take them through areas of optimum food and water during the course of the year. These routes are ingrained in the matriarch's memories. However, in modern times, these routes are being fragmented by man-made obstructions, such as coffee plantations, farms and human settlements. As a result, elephants are increasingly coming into direct conflict with man. The fallout is human casualties by elephants desperate for food and water and elephant deaths due to poisoning and electrocution. In a land dominated by a large and hungry human population, elephants are seen as pests and have little local support.

Despite a bleak prospect, there is hope for these gentle giants. In South India, the elephant still has a fighting chance at survival. That chance lies in the Nagarahole National Park, on the border between northern Kerala and Karnataka. This Park is a part of what is perhaps the largest area of unbroken elephant habitat in India, known as the Nilgiri Biosphere Reserve. This stretch of forest covering in excess of two thousand square kilometres comprises the larger protected areas of Nagarahole National Park and Bandipur Tiger Reserve in the state of Karnataka, Mudumalai Sanctuary in Tamil Nadu and the Wynaad Sanctuary in Kerala, along with several smaller sanctuaries and protected forests.

For the Nagarahole elephants, the migration routes go through either Kerala in the South, or through the Brahmagiri Hills in the west and north. These migration corridors which are still reasonably intact, allow the elephants a relatively safe passage between the lush monsoon forests in the hills and the grassy banks and abundant water of the Kabini Reservoir in the summer. This reservoir which forms the southern boundary of the Park provides sustenance to a whole host of animals, elephants inclusive, during the hot, dry summer months.

Every year, around November, the waters of the Kabini Reservoir are gradually drained to provide irrigation to the farmers in the catchment areas around the city of Mysore. The resultant mudflats are rich in silt washed down from the Western Ghats and, by the time the forest dries up in April, there is an abundance of fresh grass to sustain the elephants. It is perhaps a unique phenomenon, where a reservoir which has drowned some twenty-five square kilometres of forest, has actually benefited the ecology of that forest. Indeed, the seasonal movements of the Nagarahole herds are intrinsically dependent on the annual drainage cycle of the reservoir.

By the beginning of March, the now lush banks of the reservoir start to fill up with elephants. As summer advances, more and more herds descend from the hills to partake of this annual feast of grass. This is also a social aggregation for the elephants as matriarchs meet each other and the meadows echo with the rumblings, squeals and trumpets of elephant vocalizations. Calves that were born the previous year are now old enough to eat the soft nutritious grass and they too get a rare chance to play, tugging at each other's trunks and tails and butting each other. Younger calves stick close to their mothers or gambol playfully with their elder siblings. Adult elephants are remarkably tolerant of their young. The big bull elephants, that are normally solitary, mingle with the herds, getting a chance to mate and pass on their genes. Conflicts occasionally occur as is wont to happen in any society, but these are soon resolved by the matriarchs and peace returns to the vast sea of grazing elephants.

Towards the end of May, the grass has worn away, leaving behind short, dry stubs. These too are kicked up by the elephants, leaving bare, dusty patches of soil. Soon the rains will come and the reservoir will once again fill up and it will be time for the matriarchs to lead their herds back up into the cool green heights of the Brahmagiri hills. The lone bulls remain behind, feeding on the bamboo and fresh leaves of the teak forest. The great elephant congregation dwindles to just a few individuals.

While the Nagarahole National Park is a safe haven for the elephants, many other reserves are not. Killed for their ivory and continually persecuted by man in a land where they are revered as a God and were once allowed to roam free, these animals are now regarded as pests and have little respite. Elephants arriving on the banks of the Kabini frequently carry the scars of shotgun pellets, fired at them by the irate owners of coffee plantations whose land the animals

934

have trampled through. Many are blinded by the pellets or maimed by crude electric fences connected to high-tension cables. In this Park at least, they are well protected and are allowed to live in peace.

However, even as Nagarahole is a refuge for these animals, their traditional migration corridors are being disturbed and the herds are becoming increasingly isolated populations leading to inbreeding, making them vulnerable to disease and bringing them into repeated conflicts with man. Protected areas such as Nagarahole are not sufficient to conserve elephants. There is an urgent need for more such areas that can be connected by viable, undisturbed corridors. A sustained and dedicated effort is required to prevent these beautiful, innocent giants from disappearing into the murky, grey mists of extinction.

Kaziranga National Park

Kaziranga is a wonderful wildlife park. It is the largest undisturbed representative area of the Brahmaputra river, its flood plain, grassland and forest. People speak of it as being a mini Africa in the Indian sub-continent. The Park has 70% of the world's one-horned rhino population, 70% of the world population of the Eastern Swamp Deer and 75% of the world's wild Asiatic Water Buffalo. It also has a significant population of the Asian Elephant. The Park has more than 450 species of birds, 18 of them are globally threatened species. Because of the varied habitat types that the park comprises, and because of the strict protection accorded to them, birding in Kaziranga is very special. The Eastern Range is good for water birds such as falcated teal, white-eyed pochard and spotbilled pelican (a colony of 200 pairs is located in this range). For grassland birds, the Western Range is ideal. The Bengal florican can be seen during elephant rides in the Central Range. The nearby Panbari Reserved Forest is good for spotting woodland birds such as yellow-vented warbler, great hornbill, and redheaded trogon. There is a wealth of interesting birdlife. Kaziranga is quite remote and one has to travel from Kolkata to Guwahati by plane and then make a long car journey. For those dedicated travellers who want to experience a really wild place, I recommend a visit to this region, for, although accommodation is of a modest nature, the intrepid wildlife enthusiast is rewarded by wonderful experiences. Moreover, the region has some outstanding historic sites and the hills in this region have hundreds of megalithic monuments, and apparently North-East India is the one place in the world where megalithic customs survive to this day. Harshad Patel made a journey to Kaziranga in March 2004 to photograph wildlife and enjoyed himself enormously.

Pench Tiger Reserve

The team members of Indian Explorations are also very committed to the conservation of India's wildlife, and like me they are passionate about the vital importance of tiger and big cat conservation. They have very kindly contributed the following account of Pench to my book as I have not yet had the pleasure of going there. Reading their account has made Graham and me want to make a visit this coming season if at all possible.

> *There is a pleasure in the pathless woods,*
> *There is a rapture on the lonely shore,*
> *There is a society where none intrudes,*
> *By the deep sea, and music in its roar:*
> *I love not man the less, but nature more*

> **Lord Byron**

If you ask any seasoned traveller to India the question, "Where should I go to see tigers?" you would probably receive the following answers: "Kanha", "Bandhavgarh", "Nagarahole", or "Ranthambhore". Very few would answer, "Pench". A select few know about this little slice of paradise, so exclusive that it is not yet mentioned in any Lonely Planet or Bradt Travel guides, yet the montage of meadow and forest that characterizes the landscape of Pench Tiger Reserve is classic tiger country.

Pench Tiger Reserve is one of the latest in the string of Project Tiger Reserves designed to protect key areas of India's tiger habitat. Project Tiger, India's largest Tiger protection project, was launched in 1973. Initially, just nine reserves were earmarked, but this has since increased to twenty-seven reserves. The Project's aims are twofold: firstly, to increase public knowledge and awareness of the tiger and its fragile existence, secondly, to work with parks staff on a grassroots level to protect the tigers within their parks. The Project now encompasses reserves covering 37,761 sq. km, with approximately 1,650 tigers in these reserves. A recent success has been involving Indian children in the campaign – and the project now has just over one million "Tiger Kids" members.

The inclusion of Pench Tiger Reserve in the Project Tiger system in 1991 heralded a change in the management of the reserve. Efforts have been concentrated on the relocation of the two villages that remained within the reserve, followed by the initiation of management and protection measures to improve the habitat of the reserve. It is clear that these measures have met with significant success, borne out by the fact that the populations of predators and prey have increased considerably.

Pench is now being developed for wildlife tourism, with the emphasis being on an eco-friendly and non-invasive approach. Lessons, learned from other tiger reserves in the state, are being applied to moderate the traffic that enters the park. As in other reserves in Madhya Pradesh elephants are being used to track tigers and improve the chances of seeing these highly elusive cats.

Located in the rolling terrain of the Satpura Hills and straddling the states of Madhya Pradesh and Maharashtra, Pench Tiger Reserve supports a rich and varied array of wildlife. The forested hills, mainly teak and flame of the forest, are punctuated with the eerie pure white ghost trees, and were once known as the Seoni forests. It was here that Kipling chose to locate his story of the wolf boy Mowgli, adopted son of the Seoni wolf pack. The area of the reserve is 758 sq. km with a core area of 293 sq. km. The park has populations of chital, sambhar, gaur, nilgai, four-horned antelope, wild dog (Dhole), wolf, leopard and the tiger, and nearly three hundred species of birds. The reserve is drained by the Pench River, which has been dammed - the resulting reservoir in the centre of the park adding to the wealth of habitats of the reserve. Perennially full, the reservoir provides a much-needed source of water for the animals and birds of the reserve during India's very dry months.

One of Pench's greatest advantages is that it is low profile, thus retaining that sense of uncharted wilderness that has been lost by so many of the more famous parks. The reserve is easy to reach both from Delhi and Mumbai. A flight of a little over an hour, followed by a two-hour drive on excellent roads and there you are in the middle of some of India's most beautiful bush. Pench is perfectly situated on the "Tiger Trail", five hours from Kanha and seven hours from Bandhavgarh. There are few lodges to choose from and this is a great advantage – fewer lodges mean fewer jeeps in the park, thus guaranteeing peaceful and uninterrupted game viewing. There is no queuing to enter the park and the guides have free rein to drive where they wish. The park employs over seventy forest guards, and a guard accompanies every excursion into the park. They are knowledgeable and talkative, often jumping up out of their seats to point out this animal or that bird. Their enjoyment of the park is very obvious.

The tigers in the park are elusive, still slightly wary of vehicles, but are being spotted with ever increasing regularity. The last estimate is that there are fifty-one tigers, but since that census, two females are known to have given birth to cubs. The Bodha Nallah male, the largest tiger in the park, is a wonderful sight to behold, comparable to the male tiger Charger, from Kanha. He frequents a nallah in the centre of the park, and often his calls can be heard echoing up into the forests. His presence is often shown by scratch marks on the trees, the highest of which started at just over seven feet! A tiger spends most of his day resting, and hunts at night. Tiger sightings in Pench have slowly been increasing as the mahouts have been getting a feel for the local tigers, where they like to rest up during the day, where they come to drink, where they like to hunt. There is nothing like the experience of moving slowly through the forest, your giant taxi stopping here and there to pull a branch off a tree for a snack, then suddenly stopping, your mahout points, you peer and suddenly the white, black and orange stripes appear, blending in seamlessly with the foliage – he raises his head, and you look directly into the large round eyes of a fully grown tiger.

Another attraction of the park is the Elephant camp, Alikatta, situated some fifteen kilometres into the park. The park currently uses four elephants, which, in the middle of the night, set out with their mahouts to track tigers. Mohan Bahadur and Jeng Bahadur are the males, enormous imposing creatures with massive ivories and a sense of immobile power – but they like nothing more than having their trunk scratched and being fed "elephant chapattis" which they take delicately with the tip of their trunks and then post into their bubblegum pink mouths, while eyeing the next snack appreciatively. The ladies of the group are Chanchal Kali, Saraswati and Damini. Chanchal Kali is presently not working, as she has a year old calf, Pench Bahadur, born on May 10th, 2003 – a very cheeky chap! Visitors, thinking he is approaching them to greet them get a shock as he suddenly puts on a spurt of speed, sometimes chasing them right up the steps of the mounting block! A highlight of visiting Pench must be a trip to the Elephant camp, where, if the timing is right, you will see the elephants being bathed and fed.

Of the four lodges in the area, Bagh Van (which, literally translated, means "Tiger Jungle") Lodge has recently been built to the highest standards to provide the perfect base from which to explore the reserve with trained naturalist guides on staff. The lodge, consisting of twelve rooms, is set amongst Saja and Mahuwa trees on the edge of a nallah, a small streambed which becomes a roaring torrent during the monsoon. The décor in the rooms is warm and rustic, using earthy colours which blend in beautifully and add just the right touch of elegance and comfort. Leopard are often heard calling in the nallah, and sometimes even tiger. Ask to see the flying squirrels – a Bagh Van speciality!

Throughout this chapter, the reader has had the opportunity to read the accounts of four people, other than me; each of them bringing the same passionate enthusiasm to their wildlife watching and their respect and admiration for those who assisted them to see these various beautiful animals in their natural habitat. I can think of nothing better than to be with all of them and young Chris Brunskill, (whose book '*Tiger Forest*' is a beautiful pictorial record of the Tigers of Ranthambhore) over a period of time in perhaps January or over Christmas watching and 'drinking in', as it were, the sheer beauty of the wild experience. Certainly, Graham and I will go to those places we have not yet experienced and if circumstances allow, return to those we already love.

The Earth has enough for everyone's need, but not for anyone's greed.

Mahatma Gandhi

CHAPTER EIGHTEEN

My Personal Reflections
on Departure

I was driven to Mumbai International Airport in very good time to catch my flight back to the UK. The stringent security at this airport is to be commended. It seems to far outweigh anything I have experienced in European airports. The meticulous way the officials go through one's hand luggage is very good. Oh yes! It proves profoundly embarrassing for some because the man unpacks the luggage in full view of the other passengers waiting in the secure departure lounge. I saw many people feeling so awkward and agitated that they left their vital documents or mobile phones behind on the counter. My advice would be not to have any dirty laundry or 'eccentric' items in the hand luggage, they are frequently held up for everyone to observe and, believe me, everyone is so bored and tired their eyes lock onto this activity! As I already mentioned, I had a small polythene bag of herbal medicine which was questioned, fortunately its pungent aromatic smell made it quite clear what this was. The BA cabin crew were put through equally stringent inspections just before boarding the aircraft to receive us passengers.

In August of 2003, Mumbai again experienced two evil bombings that left a young family orphaned. The second bomb was detonated right next to the Gateway of India and was obviously planned to create a symbolic tourist outrage, never mind who else tragically was affected. India will understandably tighten up its security and I know it feels under siege from these evil forces, that are possibly operating from a neighbouring country which sadly has been subsumed by terror and elements of sectarian extremism. In no worthwhile belief or philosophy is there a directive to hate, torture, rape, terrorise, subjugate or kill one's fellow human beings. How many times fanatics in every belief have twisted doctrines to achieve cruel ends but that is all man-made and self-serving, as we are witnessing elsewhere in the world.

Being on my own, I had plenty of time in which to indulge in reflection and there are some quite comfortable lounger chairs in one part of the departure area which mean that one can virtually stretch out, while keeping a watchful eye on the hand luggage at the same time. I went into a kind of reverie whereby my mind was reflecting on all that I had enjoyed and also on all that troubled me about India.

Wisdom makes light the darkness of ignorance.

Six simple words that encapsulates all one's thoughts, uttered by the Buddha thousands of years ago. They are as effective today as when they were first written. India is entitled to have a pride in the nation's Hindu heritage, but constructive pride leads to benevolent behaviour whereas destructive fervour and hate leads to a downward spiral. India and its great worldwide diaspora must ensure that the country does not implode with hatred and destruction with regard to the Hindu and Muslim conflict of belief. The birth of Independent India was accompanied by tragedy and we do not need to see any of it re-enacted for the horrified eyes of our grandchildren.

This does however require people to be civic minded and not feel that they can continue to enrich their personal lives but leave the welfare of the nation to someone else. Inevitably, the resulting moral vacuum will be filled by someone who has a greed for power and self-aggrandisement, usually with psychopathic tendencies as a characteristic. The twentieth century was full of leaders like that both in the West and the East. Africa as a continent continues to display some of the worst features of humanity when people accrue total power and dispense with democracy.

India should be a permanent member of the Security Council of the United Nations, and I know that there is currently a huge lobby seeking to achieve this with which I agree but, were there to be further sectarian violence and killing, that would become an empty achievement.

India, however, is justifiably proud in being the world's largest democracy, now embarking confidently on its 21st century journey as a prosperous global power. It seems to me to have shed its mantle of saintly third world developing country. Indians, in their energy and enthusiasm, are, whenever possible, embracing the modern world and I think India is going to be the giant of this century; indeed

Indian expertise in so many scientific fields is immense and most particularly in the IT industry. The call centre industry is already huge with perhaps some negative aspects but McKinsey predict that by 2008 IT services and back-office work will swell fivefold to a £57 billion annual export industry employing four million people and accounting for seven per cent of India's GDP.

China is perhaps India's biggest foreign threat. Their economic growth has made theirs the fastest growing economy in the world and in two decades it will overtake not only Britain and France but Germany and Japan to join the United States at the top of the international wealth rankings. There are, however, global repercussions in the emergence of China and the US has discovered that there is a trade deficit of $100 billion a year with China and is considering a bill to impose a 28 per cent tariff on Chinese imports. China has a standing army of 2.3 million and a longstanding sense of grievance that for two centuries it has not been accorded the world respect it deserves. Underneath the perceived westernisation and integration into the world, an aggressive streak still lurks. India suffered from this form of imperialism in 1962, and I was in Calcutta (Kolkata) at the time and experienced the humiliation of India who had allowed herself to be totally unprepared with vain leaders who did not see the vital importance of a well-equipped efficient army and naively thought that having turned a blind eye to the invasion of Tibet they had no reason to fear China. That has, however, been rectified in the intervening years with India's army now up to strength and very well-equipped, and by having become a nuclear power. China seeks international respect in the world and that quest for greatness can be potentially a breeding ground for ultra nationalism.

The official view in both Britain and America is that as China becomes more prosperous it becomes more relaxed and therefore less of a threat. However, the recent meetings of the South East Asian Nations and Asia Pacific Economic Co-operation gave people a reason to think again. They have an ambitious proposal to create a free-trade zone to cover more than half the world's population from India eastwards. At the APEC meeting in Thailand, it was obvious that everyone was behaving in a sycophantic way towards the next economic giant. However, its economy is overheating, its banks are heavily indebted, yet any correction would unleash a revolutionary wave of discontent. Tens of millions of workers are being laid off from state-owned firms. A banking crisis coupled with an economic downturn could put a halt to China's renaissance and challenge the rule of the Communist Party. Either way, China is a challenge, because if the country succeeds economically and becomes the supreme global giant then the country will seek to shape the world in ways that benefit China. If, however, China fails then she might embark on military imperialism once again. Either way, she is a significant threat to India.

India, I am convinced, could be the real global economic giant of this century for a variety of reasons. Firstly, being the world's largest democracy, that immediately appeals to other countries and earns their respect. Secondly, India has in the last three years reformed its whole economic strategy. These reforms have created companies that are capable and willing to compete in global markets. However, the competition for foreign investment is easily won by China, whose government wisely put in a good modern infrastructure with which to attract foreign investment. India mistakenly seemed to want foreign investment in her infrastructure which naturally did not have the same appeal to the outsider.

Investment analysts point out that India could increase its growth rate to China's level easily – with lesser investment than China – if it really decided to open the economy to foreign investors. The saying is that if one wants to get things off to a flying start go to China, but if you want to make money go to India. Today, India is at the same stage that China was a decade ago but, because now the Chinese are experiencing the resultant problems of their phenomenal growth, India could surge ahead. However, she must have the commitment to improving her infrastructure not just expediently but for the future, which means building to excess (not something of which the United Kingdom can ever be accused sadly). Indian industry can duplicate the success of China if it gets the flexibility that Chinese firms enjoy. "We are confident of competing with the best in the world. This is a new India", those words were spoken by the President of the Confederation of Indian Industry. I do believe him and have confidence in the country. Unlike China, India's software success rests on its human capital. It has the second largest pool of English-speaking technical power in the world and, as Bill Gates predicted, India is likely to be the next software superpower. Moreover, very recently a small Scottish company has been rewarded for its commitment to finding oil in India and significant quantities of oil have been found in Rajasthan, this can only be a good thing for Rajasthan, a relatively poor state and for the country as a whole. I like the connection with Scotland!

The image of India in the eyes of the world has also changed. It is known for its brainpower, its millions of talented engineering, business and medical graduates. Goldman Sachs predicted recently that India will become the world's third largest economy by 2050. 'Offshoring' is the new ugly term used to describe the age-old phenomenon in which economic activity moves to where the skills and cost mix is most attractive to employers. Thus, has India become the call centre of the world. There is quite strong feeling here in Britain about this with the perceived subsequent loss of call centre jobs in this country, but this is what 'globalisation' is all about. Manufacturing jobs followed by service jobs were the front runners of this move and when one considers that wage costs are less than a fifth of levels here, with the Indian staff having a commitment to work and a good understanding of English, one understands the business motivation. America is also being affected by this trend and their politicians are beginning to bring this subject emotively into their rhetoric for the coming US election. However, as all of us know, protectionism of any kind usually leads to recession, and our countries should continue to generate and develop new jobs within our own countries with the money saved. Free trade is essential to prosperity in both the West and the Third World.

There are however so many Indias. The India of the twenty-first century surging ahead with its expertise in information technology plus the recognised advances in medicine, engineering, management consultancy, pharmaceuticals, textiles and tourism. What about that other India, the one that haunts and worries me, the India that still persists in her ambivalent attitude to women?

The ugly aspect of increasing dowry deaths across the social spectrum is a sinister medieval shadow that obscures India's light and potential to be a global giant in this century. The whole dowry idea was officially outlawed forty years ago but it appears that everyone disregards that fact, and the authorities turn a blind eye. I am ashamed of this aspect of Indian life and can have no defence for the country when people who know I love and am loyal to the land of my birth, accuse it of this horrifying relic of ancient custom and practice. What does it say about some of India's young men, who collude with their materially greedy parents or worse, calculatingly carry out these various murderous acts? Within seven years of a woman's death, her family can file a case of dowry death but very little is achieved and usually the man is free to marry again and receive yet another dowry. Officially, there are 6,500 dowry deaths annually, but unofficially the figure could be 25,000. Because of the apparent ineptitude and corruption of the various police forces and the reluctance of the system to investigate and prosecute these crimes, in which the victim is usually burnt, supposedly in a kitchen accident, India is socially continuing to sanction the devaluation of women and this occurs across the broad spectrum of social caste and class, not just within the illiterate village communities.

Female foeticide is reaching alarming proportions. Those of us in the West who have been shown in documentaries the ruthless and heartless female infanticide of China have often said of the latter 'we won't go there until that country behaves in a civilised manner...' ethical travelling does exist, but China has become aware of her bad image – I would not know if what is being done has actually reduced or just become camouflaged from western eyes. In India, where thank goodness there is a courageous and outspoken press the female foeticide nightmare is being exposed.

North India is where dowries are the biggest and dowry deaths most common. In Bihar, marrying off a daughter can reduce parents to penury. It is estimated that in Bihar 163,200 female infants are killed annually. The state is ruled by a woman! In Haryana, mobile clinics brought sex determination to the patients' doorsteps with doctors carrying a generator and an ultrasound scanner to carry out the devious ritual. Apparently sex determination is done at one clinic and the abortion at another, making it difficult to accuse patients of female foeticide and often all this barbarism is carried out in makeshift operation theatres using equipment that has not been sterilised adequately. This adds to the risk for the young women and is the biggest cause of death of young women in India.

The social fault line runs deep and the alarming drop in the number of girl children can have serious social consequences. The decline in the gender ratio will play havoc with India's population stabilisation programme, which requires a balanced gender ratio and a limit on the number of children born every year. Even those who do not believe in female foeticide but still want sons will need to examine their motives; otherwise, it might lead to an alarming reversal in the trend towards a declining population growth.

Female foeticide will disempower Indian women and as sociologists stress, it is only empowered women who raise similar children and nurture strong families. Fewer girls will also mean that their childhood, their marriage and their future will come under a variety of social and physical threats, where only those who have power, wealth, and influence and are male will dictate their choices in life.

To end this sad subject on a positive note a positive campaign to promote the girl child is being started and, in 2004, the Health Ministry plans as its Republic Day theme to promote daughters. They do, however, need the support of religious opinion makers to eradicate the belief that only a son ensures a passage to heaven.

The final appalling fact is the rising number of girl children sold into slavery either for the marriage/servant market or as prostitutes. India has become one of the biggest slave bazaars for minor girls. Other than as sex workers, they are also exploited as labourers, drug peddlers and for their organs.

In the Murshidabad district of West Bengal, there was an unsavoury trade in minor boys who were supplied as camel jockeys for the Middle East. Now, it is the biggest supplier of minor girls for prostitution rackets involving Haj tourists. The Bedia community of Uttar Pradesh, which traditionally sold daughters to brothels, now gives them away to rich clients from abroad. There is a village in West Bengal called Jamtala Daspara in South 24 Parganas that has no teenage girls. Trafficking is the word to describe the slave trade in girls and the UN has said it is the fastest growing criminal enterprise in the world. Mumbai, Delhi and Kolkata serve as business hubs. Mumbai is the import–export point and the undisputed capital of this foul trade.

These are the ugly sides of India. Every country has its unattractive aspects, be it bigotry of religion, criminal underworld, racism or some other human evil. Exploitation of its females is a blot on modern day India's record as the beacon of democracy and religious pluralism. India has the ability to overcome and totally subdue these practices. It just has to have the will and courage to implement sufficient legislation that cannot be misconstrued or sidelined to ensure that females are given their rightful place in society. There must then be a determination to use that legislation to eradicate all evil forms of gender exploitation. Naturally, all that goes hand in hand with a national commitment to reducing bureaucratic venality; were it to do all of these things, I think the country would power ahead as an economic force strong in principle and morally sound. India would become a country that we would all be able to admire and respect and, for people like me, continue to love, but it does require Indians both at home and abroad to stand up and be counted.

From time to time I become thoroughly cast down about the various awful injustices in the world, such as those of which I have just written. I have told you about them because they prey on my mind as an ordinary individual who wants to help and try and contribute to making the world a safer and a better place. The Esther Benjamins Trust is trying to do just that. This determined little charity was born out of one man's personal deep grief at the loss of his first wife, Esther. Philip Holmes formed the trust in memory of Esther who took her own life in January of 1999 because of her childlessness. At the time of her death Esther was a Judge whose admirable qualities combined a sense of justice for the neglected and oppressed with a deep love for children. It is these values that now Philip and his co-workers are perpetuating through the work of the Trust that bears her name.

They work exclusively in Nepal, India's very poor little neighbour state, on projects that help those children and young people most marginalised and discriminated against by society. The Trust has formed their own partner organisation in Nepal to run projects on the ground, The Nepal Child Welfare Foundation (NCWF) run by a core staff of former Gurkha officers. The close relationship between the two organisations and between the founding directors Philip Holmes and Khem Thapa lies at the heart of their increasing success. Jail children, i.e. those whose parents are jailed and with whom until recently they had to live though themselves innocent are stigmatised and disowned by ashamed relatives; Street children too are held in contempt in Nepal as they are looked upon as being 'khate', the Nepalese word for thieves. Disabled children too are victimised as the religious belief in Nepal is that disabled people are serving a sentence for misdeeds committed in a previous life and Circus children are the victims of illegal trafficking of children into India who are then enslaved into circus life. Recently reports show that there are also a high percentage of ethnic Nepalese children within India in the northern areas of West Bengal that fall victims to exploitation and cruelty.

Esther Benjamins Trust is achieving so much so rapidly and it is down to Philip Holmes and his new wife Beverley's personal commitments that this is happening. Now they intend to go and live in Nepal for a two year period to help and encourage the ideas and implementation of the Trust's aspirations to give Nepal's underprivileged children a childhood.

For you who have read this book I just ask you to think of adorable Yashodi Gurung, of whom I have written; imagine her, the loveable little character that I have described to you, frightened, homeless, vulnerable, repeatedly raped, beaten, and enslaved; think too of the youngsters I described at Butterflies. Perhaps you know also of Future Hope the wonderful charity that does so much work in Kolkata for the street children, of whom I spoke in my first book.

When I was growing up in India the charity that made the most impact on me was Dr Graham's Homes, in Kalimpong, which is in the foothills of the Himalayas. In the days of British rule Kalimpong was a hill station destination throughout the searing heat and humidity of the Bengal summer. My parents did their best to support the charity's work and bought a lot of goods from the charity shop in Calcutta of the 1950s era. The Reverend Doctor John Graham laid the foundation of his dream – a Home and School for orphaned and abandoned Anglo Indian children in 1900. Today Dr Graham's Homes proudly safe-guarding the name of its founder and his ideals, still remains the only school that caters to nearly four hundred supported Anglo Indian children. In a world where traditions have given way to modernisation and globalisation, this small island of hope and love survives against all odds, balancing with great skill the traditional with the modern but never quite relinquishing the invisible threads tying it to the great dream that was started more than a hundred years ago.

How can we ignore their collective plight? If ever Gandhiji's words had resonance it is with all these little ones: if we each do a little we shall achieve a lot. My respect and gratitude goes to all the founders and workers in these children's charities for what they achieve against appalling challenges. Let us please try to help them. Both the Non-Resident Indians or NRIs and Overseas-Born Indians or OBIs can play a part in supporting the land of their ancestry. They have become a force to be reckoned with and respected in their adopted countries like the United States and Britain.

When one concentrates on negative issues it is only fair to talk also about the positive achievements. The child immunisation drive, launched in 1978, has saved the lives of close to 20 million children in the past 25 years. Satellite television has created a whole new industry and completely changed the way Indians are entertained and informed. In a country where owning a phone was more difficult than owning a house, the mid 1990s heralded the era of private service providers and introduced the concept of customer service. Millions of people across India's cities and villages own cell phones. At the beginning of 2004, there will be over 19 million mobile phone users. Communication is always a tool for education.

For many in the countryside, prosperity has created a new rural middle class but others remain hopelessly poor, untouched by the changes that have swept through the cities. There is, however, a new attitude towards India's immemorial poverty. The feeling is growing that its gigantic one-billion strong population can be a fantastic resource rather than a burden and that poverty is not immutable. India's economic boom is being driven by the software and IT industry and people are really beginning to think of it as being able to deliver the country from poverty. Indeed, I do hope so.

Project Tiger became the role model for preserving the country's ecosystems and also resulted in a range of legislation to protect wildlife. The number of tigers in 1972 before the inception of Project Tiger was 1,827. By 2002, the number was 3,642 but this commitment continues to face severe challenges as was shown to be the case in the 1980s and early 1990s.

Concluding on a cheerful and encouraging note it is so good to see the successful projects that various groups and charities have been able to fulfil.

Global Tiger Patrol, the charity that is achieving so much in many different ways with regard to tiger conservation throughout India is now in its 15th year. There is much that it has helped to achieve of which its Trustees and Volunteers can be proud. In its 2004 Report emphasis is laid on how dismal the prospect for

Ranthambhore Tiger Reserve was in the Spring of 2003 when people thought the park was unlikely to survive under the climatic stress it was experiencing with such a prolonged drought. That indeed was how I saw it in November 2002 and about which Graham and I were so sad. However, thankfully the park is now looking as good as when it was in its heyday 20 years ago before the disaster years of the 1990s.

In preparation for the last dry months before the onset of the 2003 monsoon, the Forest Department sank 13 tube wells in the park and 6 in the outlying villages. Stocks of fodder for the ungulates were provided and used. Thankfully as a result of this support very few ungulates perished. When the park was originally created, 16 villages were moved out leaving behind many traditional wells. Two of the traditional step wells have been resurrected. Thirteen of the old village wells have been reactivated; the water holes have been deepened and additional tube well sunk. With the low capacity wells water is dragged out by hand, whilst seven others have been equipped with diesel generators. Every day more than 200 water holes around the park were monitored, with water from the tube wells being transported by the two park tankers, one of which was donated by Global Tiger Patrol.

The ongoing drought situation had resulted in the local people outside the park having to sell 60% of their cattle and buffalo, which has reduced the grazing pressures. It is calculated that the numbers will not reach the previous level for another five years.

The Food for Work programme, initiated by the Indian Government in response to the drought resulted in a 6ft tall, thick wall, 15 kilometres in length being built by local people. This has provided a very successful barrier between the park's buffer zone and some of the villages – village cattle are prevented from moving into the forest for grazing and animals from the forest are less likely to stray out and cause crop damage.

Amanda Bright, the Chair of Trustees of Global Tiger Patrol says "It is hoped that the drought has not caused any long-term harm and may have resulted in further measures being put in place to stand the park in good stead for years to come. Another golden period for the park perhaps? We wish it well." I sincerely echo those sentiments and salute all who sought to help and maintain Ranthambhore through its drought-ridden years.

Within the last two months in 2004 The Prakratik Society, which was established in 1994, when it took over projects from The Ranthambhore Foundation, was awarded a sum of money in recognition of its success by The

Ashden Awards. Dr Rathore, the son of Fateh Singh Rathore, the courageous former field director of the Tiger Reserve says "I could see that the park versus people conflict would ultimately result in the destruction of both the tiger and Ranthambhore. I knew the long-term solution lay in finding a way in which both the people and the park could live in harmony. This meant creating sustainable alternatives that could both improve the life of the local people and allow them to have a symbiotic relationship with the park and the tigers".

The answer was found in the form of biogas digesters that provide gas for cooking to villagers around the park and so ease the pressure on the dwindling forest resources. So far Prakratik, under the tireless leadership of Dr Rathore, have installed 225 biogas plants using cow dung as the raw material. Over 1,350 villagers are currently benefiting from this technology that not only produces gas for cooking but also provides organic fertilizer in the form of slurry which is proving to be a better and cheaper alternative to commercial fertilizer. This is benefiting villagers in numerous ways including improving the health of women and children by reducing indoor air pollution, saving time and energy otherwise spent in collecting fuel wood, reducing dependence on chemical fertilizer which saves much needed rupees. Employment is also created through the use of skilled masons as well as unskilled labour in the construction and maintenance of the biogas energy plants.

Award money will be used to expand the energy programme to all of the villages around the park by constructing a further 150 biogas units and developing a wood for wood programme where people are encouraged to plant trees to meet their fuel needs instead of relying on forest resources.

It is so heartening to have this report and I have such admiration for the Rathores, father and son for all that they have accomplished in and around Ranthambhore.

"If we wish to maintain democracy, we must hold fast to constitutional methods of achieving our objectives."

These were the words of Babasaheb Ambedkar, one of the architects of the Indian Constitution; they are as true today as they were in 1950 and India has much of which to be proud. Beloved Bharat, land of my birth your 'tryst with destiny' was and is to show the world that tolerance and respect for your diverse peoples and their beliefs is your great strength. The polyphony of culture, caste and language can exist hand in hand with unity and pride in nation.

At the end of a long journey, however enjoyable it has been, there is a powerful longing for home. After weeks in India, the idea of my own bedroom suite, lovely home cooked food, Raju my little cat, my family and friends, with the prospect of Christmas round the corner was a powerful attraction. Now, writing a year later, I look forward to another trip to India but, this time, we will be arriving by ship at Mumbai from Dubai and Oman and exploring the West Coast of India and then on to Sri Lanka. The journey by ship will have started in Dubai. It will be exciting and I have no doubt immensely enjoyable. The prospect of Christmas in Goa will be lovely. I have heard that Christmas Eve in Goa is really a very special event. The prospect of visiting Sri Lanka fills me with excitement.

My abiding memory of these most recent Indian travels will be the wonderful wildlife parks and their animal inhabitants. Cold misty mornings, travelling by jeep in the sunrise, the anticipation, the thrill, and the sheer beauty of seeing tigers and other beautiful creatures will live in my memory for ever. These are some of the gems in India's crown and she must protect and conserve them for ever. I am prepared to do whatever I can to help with others to achieve this.

At Bandhavgarh there is a notice that one sees as one leaves the park:
"Do not be disappointed if at the end of your visit you have not seen me!
Believe me I have seen you!"

At the side of the notice there is the painting of a tiger's head with a benevolent expression, almost wistful in my opinion.

Oh! King of the Jungle, Icon of India, I saw you many times and delighted in your beauty and strength. I looked into your golden eyes and was grateful to know that you did not feel threatened by my own presence or by those around me. Those ten sightings will live in my heart for ever, and truly I can say I have heard 'The Tiger's Roar'.

Notice at Bandhavgarh National Park

EPILOGUE

This book could not be published without some comment on the astonishing outcome of the Indian General Election 2004. Briefly, it should be explained that Atal Behari Vajpayee, the personally respected Prime Minister and head of the B J P – the Bharatya Janata Party decided to call an early election because the government was riding high on India's perceived commercial and economic successes of the last two years. Their slogan 'India Shining' appeared to have in the first instance bedazzled a large number of the electorate. In truth however the bulk of the Indian electorate have not benefited from an economic bright light, and when Sonia Gandhi took to the hustings and travelled the country with her slogan 'Gareebe hatao' – which in translation means eradicate poverty, those two words resonated with tens of millions of the rural poor who have very little, and certainly no running water or domestic electricity. Sonia Gandhi and her children used all their charisma, determination and family name and harnessed all the unpalatable facts that affected the majority of the electorate.

In fact a voter does not need an education to realise that their living standards are so appalling that no-one actually wants to know about them and their poverty stricken life. By voting, just by making a cross, the rural voters of India showed how to have pride even if one owns nothing. These rural masses used their voting power with dignity. Truly, the world's largest democracy showed the world how to use that vital democratic strength, and at a time when the rest of the world was reeling from some hugely repugnant truths that were being revealed about a dominant nation as an occupying power. I feel so proud of India that whilst the world focussed on mayhem in the Middle East her massive general election resulted in a completely unforeseen result and the country has completed the transition of power peacefully.

The new Congress led government under the premiership of Manmohan Singh has severe challenges ahead. He however is universally regarded as a man of integrity and quiet stature. In 1991 he was P.V. Narasimha Rao's finance minister and he initiated the economic reforms with which the world has largely credited the recent BJP government. He had however also been economic advisor to Rajiv Gandhi, Chandra Shekhar and before that Indira Gandhi. As well as having presented five budgets he had served as a governor of the Reserve Bank of India. Now he faces a daunting task. When he stepped down as finance minister in 1996 he commented sadly 'So much more could have been done…' Now it would seem 'Cometh the hour, Cometh the man'. In his Independence Day speech on August 15th he said '…I have no promises to make, but I have promises to keep.'

Sonia Gandhi has with wisdom and strength of character shown India that she is very worthy of the country's respect. Astutely she had declined the premiership and handed the job to a most loyal ally, who we know will do his best to serve India well.

As a team and a government the Congress led new government must deliver some of the aspirations of the great rural masses. She is the Leader with supreme control as she remains the President of India's oldest party, and her moral authority may well overshadow the Prime Minister himself. Sonia Gandhi could indeed become the embodiment of Mother India, but it would seem that there is a good dynamic between Mrs Gandhi and the Prime Minister of India. If each respects the other for what they can achieve together for India, the synergy will continue to be positive.

For me personally this outcome is a good one, as above all the things I wish for India it is that as an ancient land of amazing diversity, beauty and spirituality she retains her position of secular democracy and religious pluralism. Hopefully, then a light will, in time, shine on the lives of all of her peoples as they strive for their rightful places in the sun.

October 2004

www.thepeacockscall.co.uk

BIBLIOGRAPHY

Ali, Salim, *The Book of Indian Birds*, 1941.

Allen, Hugh, *The Lonely Tiger*, 1960.

Bainbridge, Fletcher T., *Birds of an Indian Garden*, 1936.

Brunskill, Chris, *Tiger Forest, A Visual Study of Ranthambhore National Park*, 2003.

Devee, Sunity (Maharani of Cooch Behar) and Rose, Aline, *Bengal Dacoits & Tigers*, 1916.

Corbett, Jim, *Man Eaters of Kumaon*, 1944.

Corbett, Jim, *The Man Eating Leopard of Rudraprayag*, 1948.

Corbett, Jim, *My India*, 1952.

Corbett, Jim, *Jungle Lore*, 1953.

Corbett, Jim, *Temple Tiger*, 1954.

Corbett, Jim, *Tree Tops*, 1955.

Divyabhanusinh, *The End of a Trail, The Cheetah in India*, 1999.

Gee, E. P., *The Wildlife of India*, 1964.

Ions, Veronica, *Indian Mythology*, 1967–1992.

Kipling, Rudyard, *The Jungle Book*, 1894.

Lydekker, R., *The Game Animals of India, Burma, Malaya & Tibet*, 1907.

Matthiessen, Peter, *Tigers in the Snow*, 2000.

McCann, Charles, *100 Beautiful Trees of India*, 1959.

Mountfort, Guy, *On the Brink*, 1974.

Mountfort, Guy, *Back from the Brink: Successes in Wildlife Conservation*, 1977.

Sen, Mala, *India's Bandit Queen: The True Story of Phoolan Devi*, 1991.

Sen, Mala, *Death by Fire*, 2001.

'Silver Hackle', *Man-Eaters and Other Denizens of the Indian Jungle*, 1928.

Singh, Arjan, *Tiger Haven*, 1973.

Stewart, A. E., *Tiger and Other Game*, 1927.

Stockley, C. H., *Big Game Shooting in the Indian Empire*, 1928.

Thapar, Valmik, *Land of The Tiger: A Natural History of the Indian Subcontinent*, 1998, University of California Press (book of the BBC/PBS television series).

Ward, Geoffrey C. and Raines, Diane, *Tiger-Wallahs: Saving the Greatest of the Great Cats*, 2000.

CONTACTS AND DETAILS OF INTEREST FOR THOSE VISITING INDIA

1.   **Tikli Bottom** (the gracious guest house close to Delhi)
Martin and Annie Howard
Email: honiwala@vsnl.com
Website: www.tiklibottom.com

2.   **Butterflies Programme for Street & Working Children in Delhi**
U-4 Second Floor, Green Park Extension
New Delhi 110 016 India
Email: butterflies@vsnl.com
Website: www.butterfliesindia.org

3.   **Future Hope UK** (registered charity no. 1001769) Helping Kolkata's Street Children
6 Queensdale Place
London W11 4SQ UK
Email: info@futurehope.co.uk
Website: www.futurehope.co.uk

        Future Hope India
1/8 Rowland Road
Kolkata 700020, West Bengal   India
Website: www.futurehope.co.uk

4.   **Esther Benjamins Trust** (UK registered No 1078187)
Refuges for street, jail and circus children in Nepal
Tel: +44(0)20 8877 2519
Wandsworth Business Village, 3-9 Broomhill Rd, London SW18 4JQ
Email: ebtrust@hotmail.com
Website: www.ebtrust.org.uk

5.   **Dr Graham's Homes**, Kalimpong, India (charity registered in Scotland SCO16341)
Kintail, The Causer, Nethy Bridge PH25 3DS Scotland
Tel: +44(0)1479 821222
Email: dghukctsec@vcassie@fsnet.co.uk
Website: www.drgrahamshomes.co.uk

6.   **LifeForce Charitable Trust** (wildlife charity registered in UK)
Email: lifeforcelink@hotmail.com
Website: www.lifeforceindia.com

7.   **Global Tiger Patrol** (registered charity no. 328126 The Ranthambhore Society)
87 Newland St, Witham, Essex CM8 1AD   UK
Tel: +44(0)1376 520320
Email: globaltiger@compuserve.com
Website: www.globaltigerpatrol.co.uk

8.   **Chris Brunskill's Tiger Watching Trips and Wildlife Photography**
Chris Brunskill
Website: www.ranthambhore.info

9.   **Save China's Tigers**
       Tel: +44 (0)207 451 1296
       Email: kate.reynolds@mailbox.co.uk
       Website: www.savechinastigers.org

10.   Websites of particular interest: www.worldwildlife.org
                                            www.projecttiger.nic.in
                                            www.sanctuaryasia.com

11.   **The Vanishing Herds Foundation** (registered charity no. 1098958)
       102 Higher Road, Purley Surrey CR8 2HL
       Tel: +44(0)20 8668 2048
       Email: vanishingherds@hotmail.com
       Website: www.vanishingherdsfoundation.org

12.   **Discovery Initiatives Ltd**
       51 Castle Street, Cirencester GL7 1QD UK
       Tel: +44 (0) 1285 643 333 Email: enquiries@discoveryinitiatives.com
       Travel Operators for Tigers – Responsible Tiger Tourism set up in 2003
       Website: www.toftiger.org Tel: +44(0) 1285 643 333

13.   **Responsible Travel**
       Email: info@responsibletravel.com
       Website: www.responsibletravel.com

14.   **Indian Explorations Ltd**
       Afex House, Holwell, Burford, OX18 4JS UK
       Tel: +44(0) 1993 822443
       Email: safaris@globalnet.co.uk
       Website: www.explorationcompany.com

15.   **Alastair Sawday's**
       Special Places to Stay, INDIA
       www.specialplacestostay.com

16.   **Trans Indus Limited**
       Northumberland House, 11 The Pavement, Pope's Lane, Ealing
       London W5 4NG
       Tel: +44(0)20 8566 2729
       Email: enquiries@transindus.co.uk
       Website: www.transindus.co.uk

16.   **The India Tourist Office**
       7 Cork Street, London W1S 3LH
       Tel: General Enquiries +44(0)207 437 3677
       Tel: Brochure request: 08700 102183
       Email: info@indiatouristoffice.org
       Website: www.incredibleindia.org

17   **The Ashden Awards for sustainable energy**: www.ashdenawards.org

18   **Aline Dobbie's own website: www.thepeacockscall.co.uk**

FOR THOSE INTERESTED IN VISITING THE BEAUTIFUL SCOTTISH BORDERS

19.   **The Royal Burgh of Peebles**   website: www.peebles.info
        The Scottish Borders   website: www.scot-borders.co.uk